Hoddlesden & its

Satellite Villages

To Barbara my wife; Kathryn, Paul, Mark and Judith my children

The illustration shows the village of Hoddlesden viewed from Pickup Bank Height (Great Hill). The village now comprises nineteenth century working-class housing and late twentieth century residential housing. In the background can be seen Darwen Tower built in 1898 to commemorate Queen Victoria's Diamond Jubilee.

Hoddlesden & its Satellite Villages

by Roy Parker

Contents

The photograph was taken from Sett End above Hoddlesden. It portrays the scattered configuration of dwellings and farm houses in Yate Bank. However, the ribbon development at Belthorn can be seen in the top right hand portion of the landscape.

Acknowledgements

The preparation of this book has materialised over several years and has resulted in a stimulating journey for the writer. The writing experience has been challenging and the many dialogues with people showing interest have been most enjoyable.

It is impossible to record personal thanks to all those who have contributed relevant information in both large and small measure. Nevertheless, without these contributions our knowledge of this corner of east Lancashire would be much poorer. In general, thanks must go to the many staff dealing with archival resources, particularly those working in the National Archives at Kew, London; the County Record Office at Bow Lane, Preston; Blackburn Library Local History Department; Darwen Library History Section and Lancaster University Library. I am also indebted to Martin Simpson for his contributions to many of the illustrations. Thanks and appreciation is offered to Dr Michael Winstanley of the History Department at Lancaster University for encouraging me to research and compile a thesis entitled *Forgotten Lancashire? Rural Settlements in the east Lancashire Textile District*, c.*1800–1914*, in partial fulfilment of a Doctoral Degree and from which this local research has emerged. Furthermore, I am indebted to him for his continual guidance, suggestions and patience during researching and preparation for the thesis. A large debt of gratitude is owed to my wife Barbara for accompanying me on field visits, unceasing support and understanding whilst compiling this book and not once complaining about my permanent distractions. My children have also shown both interest and support. Others too numerous to mention have been ever willing to assist in so many ways. Finally, my thanks fo to the staff at Caraneige Publishing who have been most cooperative, helpful with their suggestions and extremely professional, particularly Anna, Alistair, Catherine and Penny.

Abbreviations

APR	Abstract of Parish Returns of Acreage, Crops and Live Stock.
BA	*Burnley Advertiser*
BL	Blackburn Library
BM	*Blackburn Mail*
BS	*Blackburn Standard*
BT	*Blackburn Times*
CEB	Census Enumerator's Book
ChetSoc	*Chetham Society*
CSR	Census Statistical Return
DA	*Darwen Advertiser*
DL	Darwen Library
DN	*Darwen News*
EconHR	*Economic History Review*
Lancs, CRO	Lancashire County Record Office
LDC	*Latter Day Saints Companion*
LDS-RF	*Latter Day Saints Resource File*
LVO	Local Valuation Officer
O.S.	Ordnance Survey maps
PP	Parliamentary Papers
RGR	Registrar General's Records
RSSJ	*Royal Statistical Society Journal*
TLCAS	*Transactions of the Lancashire and Cheshire Antiquarian Society*
THSLC	*Transactions of the Historical Society of Lancashire and Cheshire*
TNA	The National Archives, Kew, London.
VCH	*Victoria History of the County of Lancaster,*
VB	Valuation Book: The Finance (1909–1910) Act.

This view of Pickup Bank was taken from Sett End above Hoddlesden. It illustrates the rural nature of the area with the escarpment from the moors in the background and 'Old Rosins' Public House in the centre of the landscape.

Introduction

WHILST RESEARCHING FOR THIS local history I had the pleasure of speaking to many pleasant and enthusiastic people with a strong interest in the area both for their own curiosity and an insight into the lives of their ancestors. Many have enquired as to when this work would be available and I suspect they have become either tired of waiting or believed the project was a figment of my imagination. Nonetheless, at last here it is, a story of a district close to my own heart and those of many others.

Many other east Lancashire rural townships were similar in some respects but different in others to *Hoddlesden and its Satellite Villages*. During the middle ages much of east Lancashire was comprised of hunting grounds in which wild animals roamed and human habitation was minimal. Nevertheless the industrial revolution formed a watershed and changed the direction of many of these rural villages.

The narrative following is a brief account of the early history of the area that then concentrates on the way in which ordinary people earned a living, encompassing the early stages of domestic cottage industry and early industrialisation through to the late nineteenth century. The work is both detailed and related to developments in nearby industrial towns.

Settlements such as Blacksnape, Eccleshill, Hoddlesden and Yate and Pickup Bank were originally sparsely populated and dependent on the dual occupations of small-scale farming and domestic textiles. By the late eighteenth century, mechanised carding and spinning was producing larger quantities of yarn, effectively expanding hand weaver numbers and diminishing dependency on farming. These villages made an important contribution to the industrial revolution; initially in local domestic textile manufacturing, early mechanised spinning, later supplying labour to the power loom sector and farm produce to the nearby burgeoning urban cotton towns. Growth of population in these communities continued until around the second quarter of the nineteenth century. However, the introduction of power looms from about 1820 caused a demise in handloom weaving along with large-scale out-migration and population decline from these townships.

The valley represents the boundary
between Yate Bank and Pickup Bank.
Within this valley Blackburn Waterworks
created a reservoir during the
mid-nineteenth century.

Using census enumeration schedules to analyse demographic trends, the preponderance of short-distance multi-directional movements are identified. Analysis has demonstrated the movements were dominated by rural to urban flows but that also significant numbers of migrants returned to their place of birth.

The extent to which these townships exhibited domination by small farms is investigated. Analysis has been based on data extracted from agricultural parish returns, census enumeration and documentation produced by the Finance (1909–1910) Act. From these data, a portrait has been obtained of farm buildings, size of holdings, family contributions to farm work and sources of farm household income.

The impact of the emergence of factory industry and other means of earning a living during the second half of the nineteenth century is explored. This includes an investigation into the nature of the workforce, which is contextualised to both that earlier in the century and in nearby towns. Moreover, characteristics of both early and mill housing in the case study townships are compared with other factory villages and 'cotton towns'; differences have then been identified between the families living in mill and non-mill households.

This micro-study has both challenged some of the conclusions offered by past historians and amended the sparse attention paid to rural communities after the introduction of power loom weaving around the second quarter of the nineteenth century.

Finally the author hopes that readers will gain both useful knowledge from reading the book and enjoy a pleasurable experience whilst doing so.

YOR
Wiersdale Forest
Wiersdale
Slatborn
Baterby
Esington
Gisborn
Ribble R.
Calder R.
Bowland Forest
Edmarsh Chap.
The Laund
Newfton
Grinleton
Sawley
Braswell
Bardford
Chatburn
Rimington
Waddington
Downham
Worston
Chipping
Longridg Hill
Clethero
Pendleton
Pendle Hill
Stony hurst
Wiswall
Gawthrop
Barton
Longridg Chap
Whaley
Paddingham
Ribble R.
Read
Boxton
Langho
Salesbury
G. Harwood
Habergham
Broughton
Osbaldeston
Martholm
Altham
Shutleworth
Ribbleton Hall
Rishton
Dunkinhall
Huncot
Plumpton
Samsbury Hall
Little Harwood
Church
Preston
BLACK BURN HUN.
Accrington
Keuerdale
Haudley
Blackburn
Rossendale
Law
Penwortham
Darwen R.
Houghton Tower
Hastingden
Walton Hall
Brindall
Darwen
Tockholes
Laland
Clayton Hall
Aytenfeld
Mannor of
Entwisel
Hawcolm
Brotherton
Werden
Longworth
Turton
Newhall
Bankhall
Exton
Chorley
Tottingt
Brandlesham
Croston
Asley
Walmesley Chap.
Eccleston
Hill
Egberden Hill
Bradshaw
Ashworth
The Pele
Burgh
Smethels
Hall of the Wood
Cockley Chap.
Bury
LAYLAND HUN.
Raventon
Harwich Chap
Bispham
Adlington
SAL FORD
Little Bolton
Harrock Hall
Andtonford
Dean
Bolton
Amsworth
Little Lever
Blak Rode
Lastok
Great Lever
Parbold
Worthington
Ratlif
Brinsap
Highfield
Farnworth

The Early Years

U NTIL THE BEGINNING OF the industrial revolution rural areas in east Lancashire were fairly stagnant: they had very little industry, commerce, major agriculture or large-scale business enterprises. Communities were of a scattered nature, generally poor and relied on smallholdings for food products and the domestic manufacture of cloth for income. As the industrial revolution gained impetus from around the third quarter of the eighteenth century the rural communities of east Lancashire became populous, but this was later followed by decline in population. Blacksnape, Eccleshill and Yate and Pickup Bank followed this trend but Hoddlesden was different, as we shall see later.

This first chapter is a brief history of the district before the industrial revolution. It provides a very brief overview of the administration and structure of the Forest or Chase of Rossendale of which Blacksnape, Eccleshill Hoddlesden and Yate and Pickup Bank lay on the far western fringe. For those wishing to undertake an in-depth study of the district there are several specialist works dealing with the History of the Forest.[1] The chapters that follow provide evidence of social and economic features in the later history of the townships that started around the time of the industrial revolution.

Pre-disafforestation

During the Roman occupation of Britain the areas being described provided important terrain for a road built by the order of Julius Agricola in AD 97. This formed a highway between the Roman Forts of Ribchester and Manchester, passing through both Blacksnape and Eccleshill. Later the Saxons who entered Britain *circa* AD 400 to 600, made an early contribution to a communication route in the area by creating 'Limmers gate', a pack horse route from west Lancashire to the east of the country; but there have also been claims that it may have existed during the pre-Roman era.[2] This route was for transporting

Robert Morden (c.1650–1703) was a renowned mapmaker. His map of Lancashire was published around 1695 and subsequently reissued. This section shows Blackburn Hundred.

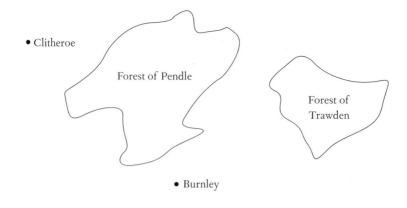

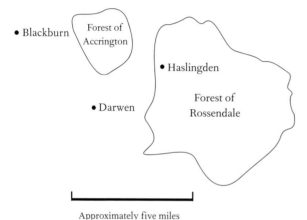

Approximately five miles

The map shows
the locations of
the four Forests
in Blackburn
Hundred. Forests
were only
deemed to be
so when in Royal
ownership, they
were otherwise
technically
known as
Chases.

lime, starting at Preston, traversing Tockholes, Printshot on the south side of
Darwen and entering the area of study via Pole Lane, proceeding along Heys
Lane, Slacks, Langshaw Head and leaving the area at the top of Lang Hey Lane,
Pickup Bank to continue through Haslingden Grane.[3]

Before 1066 the Forest of Rossendale along with the Forests of Accrington,
Pendle and Trawden were embraced in the Blackburn Hundred. The term Forest
was reserved for Royal ownership alone, since for other ownerships the term
used was Chase. Both Forests and Chases were generally uncultivated areas
used as hunting grounds for the King's or private owner's pleasure and usually
inhabited by both large wild beasts and smaller wild life, although these areas
were not necessarily thickly wooded areas as maybe first thought.[4] In Rossendale
the high bleak altitudes, physical configurations and the thin coverings of soil
were not attractive to early settlers. The owner of the land was the Fifth Duke
of Buccleugh and a Mr Atherton West was the principal landowner. The land
was entirely copyhold of the Honor of Clitheroe.[5]

In the twelfth century, Eccleshill, Hoddlesden and Yate and Pickup Bank
formed the most westerly part of the Forest or Chase of Rossendale, which
extended westwards to Hoddlesden Brook, although the parameters are not

precisely defined.[6] However, during this period there were variants of these present day names,[7] examples of which were 'Hoddendene', meaning Hod's valley,[8] Pecopp, Pickopp, Picoppe, and Yatebanke.[9] Later the Lords of Clitheroe at a later date created a vill in Haslingden and hence broke up the wastes and severed these townships from the Forest.[10]

During the latter part of the thirteenth century Henry de Lacy, Baron of Blackburnshire, vigorously developed the estates of the Forests: land was enclosed, farms cultivated, large herds of cattle raised, mines and quarries worked and this suggests some increase in the numbers of inhabitants. From this regime, Rossendale began to grow. Cattle were raised on permanently established farms on the lower ground where water was available; these were called vaccaries, cow pastures or booths. In 1296, there were 28 vaccaries or stock-raising farms in Blackburnshire with around 70 to 100 cows each. These were under the jurisdiction of the Earl of Lincoln who was also Lord of Clitheroe.[11] Rossendale's share of the total vaccaries was a significant eleven.

The vaccary at Hoddlesden in 1296 was unusual in that it acted as a collecting area only, whereas by 1323 it had become an ordinary vaccary where the dispersion of the 75 to 80 cattle in the charge of a cow keeper was about half cows, one bull, steers and heifers about seven per cent each, yearlings 15 per cent and calves 20 per cent; in addition to which there were pigs. The vaccary covered a large acreage within and close to Hoddlesden village. To the north of the village just beyond the site of Vale Rock Mill and to Slacks in the south was winter pasture. Further south almost parallel to the Roman Road stretching to Rushton's Height was an area called New hey and to the east of this was the summer pasture bordering on the site of Lark Hill Farm.

Records of payments indicate further evidence of early activity in Hoddlesden. These include mowing grass and transporting hay from 72 acres of meadow, cleaning ditches and providing fencing. Within the hamlet was a smelting furnace and evidence of habitation occurs since there were payments for repairs to a dwelling house and a new house was being thatched. In 1342 Queen Isabella owned a stock of breeding cattle at Hoddlesden.[12]

Following the death of Henry de Lacy in 1311, baronial interest in cattle abated. Vaccaries were let; for example, the herbage of the 'Chase of Hoddlesden' including lodge and meadows was let to Robert de Holden in 1322 at a yearly rent of twenty-four shillings.[13] Later cessation of herbage and agistment fees was replaced by an increase in income to the Honor from rent paying tenants who farmed the land.[14] The change of policy was indicative of a gradual withdrawal from forest administration to transference to a private agricultural economy since the Forest was receding as a hunting ground. This resulted in a growing occupation of wasteland by an increasing number of small farmers.[15]

The extent of the population that lived in the Forest is somewhat difficult to determine. Newbigging has pointed out that it is unlikely that many more than twenty families lived in the Forest of Rossendale before the sixteenth century. Tupling noted the earliest reference to a church in the Forest was at Whalley in 1296 and soon after seven others were erected, one of which was at Haslingden. The presence of places of worship indicates evidence of communities, so there is doubt as to whether the numbers of people living in the Forest were as small as indicated by Newbigging.[16] Nevertheless, the Poll Tax for 1379 shows 21 inhabitants, each paying four pence in tax, and the marginal notes states they were 'Shepherds of the Lord Duke of Lancaster'. From this we may assume that the total population was around one hundred.[17] However, it is known there were evasions and Professor Postan has claimed these could account for 40 to 50 per cent.[18] Even with these additions the total population of the Forest was probably very small and the people very poor as indicated by the minimum tax rate levied.

Post-disafforestation

In 1507 the status of the Forest of Rossendale was radically changed from a hunting ground to a revenue-raising district, a term known as 'disafforestation'. Commissioners authorised sub-division of the eleven vaccaries in Rossendale and increased the number to twenty. The reason for sub-division was a consequence of demands from both the King and Honor of Clitheroe to fund both wars and their greed.[19] This process included separating Hoddlesden from Yate and Pickup Bank, but retaining a 'vacherye' at Hoddlesden. Both townships became designated ex-parochial.[20] Subsequently income from the land at Hoddlesden was increased by fifty per cent, and this became the sixth highest of all the booths in Rossendale.

Following disafforestation Manorial Courts approved the allocations of land and farms to tenants, although the Honor of Clitheroe Court Rolls also demonstrates evidence of illegal encroachments and misuse of commons. Following the 1507 reorganisation, administration of holdings governed by the new regulations was simplified since all tenants became copyholders of a Halmote Court.[21] Jurors were instructed to inquire 'whereupon any encroachments have been made within the said Forest either by digging of Cole mynes, inclosure or erecing of cottages, and particularly concerning a parcel of Common Land called the Yate bancke or nere adjoining thereunto containing about 160 acres with two or more tenements or edifices thereon'.[22] Illegal encroachments mainly involved individuals carving out fields from the wastes and sometimes building a cottage, but the courts normally accepted the practice providing a modest fine was paid. This process produced scattered habitations and very small farms, which are still to be observed, especially at Yate and Pickup Bank, which bears the pattern of this early period.

In Rossendale an officer called the 'Greave of the Forest 'or' 'Master of the Forest' undertook governance of the Forest. He was nominated by the main landowner and had to serve personally or provide a deputy or deputies. Greaves were appointed from the various booths on a rotational basis. The person appointed for Hoddlesden also represented Yate and Pickup Bank.[23] The Greave held multi-responsibilities; he was a Taxing Officer, Detective, Social Worker (relieving the poor), Auditor of men in the Forest capable of serving the King in war. No task appears to have been too great or small. Constables and bailiffs were responsible to the Greave, but in addition, the Greave in conjunction with the Halmot Court appointed Butcher, Market-Looker, Fence-Keeper, Bellman and Ale-Taster. The latter was probably kept very busy since there were 150 beer houses in Rossendale.[24]

At the time of 'disafforestation' the countryside of Rossendale had been uncultivated open space but this was gradually enclosed during the sixteenth and seventeenth centuries. Nevertheless, it was unlike the present-day landscape, which bears the archaeological remains of an industrial revolution beyond which lies hilly slopes dissected by walls built in stone. Both the Tudors and Stewarts during the sixteenth and seventeenth centuries saw the wastes of the Forest in Rossendale and elsewhere as an opportunity to increase Crown revenue, and encouraged yeomen to acquire smallholdings of land so they may obtain increased rents.[25] Vaccaries were re-let in the process and generally divided into two or more lots occupied by different tenants. There were 72 new holdings let to 68 different tenants and these were considerably in excess of the previous number of holdings. This reorganisation increased revenue from £105 11s. 4d. to £170 6s. 6d. or over 60 per cent. Moreover, these arrangements were very attractive for would be settlers who could erect a dwelling and cultivate the necessities for a mere existence.[26]

The change from payments of fees to lettings of parcels of land continued throughout the sixteenth and seventeenth centuries. The Halmote Court attended by local copyholders laid down local laws and enforced them when disputes occurred between tenants. Examples of disputes were grazing rights and intensity of stocks on the common land, obstructions to rights of way, drainage, care of land and so forth.[27] Sub-division of land was progressive; the number of copyholds in the Forest rose to 110 by 1539, 200 by 1608 and 314 by 1662. At Hoddlesden, the escalation was also dramatic. In 1507 there had been only one copyholder, two in 1539, seventeen in 1608 and twenty five in 1662.[28] An approximation of the population change would be around nine in 1539 increasing to about 112 by 1662. At Yate and Pickup Bank the booth had been separated into two parts by 1630. Records indicate that there were seven tenants in 'Piccoppbank in Hoddlesden' and nineteen tenants in 'Yatebanke in Hodlesden'.[29] During the reign of James I there were 14 inhabitants in Yate and Pickup Bank between 1605 and 1625 and the same number during the reign of Charles I between 1626 and

1642.[30] This area was therefore clearly very sparsely populated.

Despite an extensive number of copyholds issued in the sixteenth and seventeenth centuries, there remained enormous areas of unlet land, known as 'common land'. This was probably owing to the geological and climatic conditions in Rossendale, which were unsuited to arable agriculture; so only pasture farming could be economically adopted as a means of generating income. Since the copyhold acreages were small the privilege of using common land acted as an extension to a letting.[31] Initially, unrestricted numbers of animals were allowed to graze the common, but this led to overgrazing and the need for regulation. The result was that each tenant was apportioned a fixed number of one or more types of animals that were allowed to graze in proportion to rental or in proportion to the number of beasts which a tenant's parcel of land could support during winter months.[32] The Halmote Court undertook control of the common land, and this was different to the custom in most other parts of Britain where it was usually under the jurisdiction of the lord of the manor.

Apart from the use of common land for pasturing animals, there were other rights such as taking from the commons anything necessary for maintaining a homestead or farmstead. Hence, a copyholder could cut timber for repairing or rebuilding a house, mending hedges, gates, ploughs and carts. Fallen branches of trees could be collected and peat dug for fuel.[33]

The apparently harmonious nature of tenancies referred to above all changed during the reign of James I, in the early seventeenth century, who disputed the legal validity of the estates in Rossendale. This challenge had not been unknown in other parts of England where the engrossing of small holdings had occurred, resulting in an inherent diminution of their numbers in order to establish large sheep grounds. However, in Rossendale the dispute was for a different reason. The Crown here questioned tenures for the prime purpose of raising larger

Manor House, Eccleshill in 2012. It should be noted that the present appearance has changed from the original *Listed Building*

amounts of money.[34] Initially the dispute did not call into question tenures granted prior to disafforestation, which were deemed to be unsafe copyholds.[35] The result was that large sums of monies had to be paid collectively by apparent copyholders to the Crown in order to have their tenures legalised.[36] Later the Crown also challenged pre-1507 tenures and extracted further, albeit smaller sums of monies.[37] This process of copyhold tenancies was the forerunner of twentieth century copyholds in Yate and Pickup Bank rather than a system of leaseholds and freeholds that existed elsewhere.

Although tenants in the 'Forest' and later copyholders were expected to pay rents, there were also tithes to be paid to the parish incumbent. In 1650, the Parliamentary commissioners stated that they deemed Pickup Bank and Yate Bank to be in the Forest of Rossendale as a parcel of land in the rectory of Blackburn, the tithes for which amounted to £5 per annum.[38] Eccleshill and Mellor were in the same parish and paid a joint tithe, nevertheless, the former had its own Manor House. By the nineteenth century both Eccleshill and Yate and Pickup Bank were ex-parochial and had parish council status. However, at Hoddlesden almost fifty residents fought for a similar status but it was refused and so Hoddlesden was incorporated into Darwen.[39]

The smallness of the farms in Rossendale, that still remain to the present time, was caused by land division as a result of partible inheritance by copyholders to their off spring, albeit not necessarily in equal proportions. Alternatively, estates were separated between sons during a father's lifetime in order to provide homesteads on marriage but the father retained copyhold. These modes of division were contrary to primogeniture inheritance practised by the aristocracy and which also took precedence locally in circumstances of intestacy.[40]

Growth of population in the Rossendale district occurred rapidly from around

Date stone in manor house garden

Date stone in manor house porch

1,000 during the mid-sixteenth century to 3000 during the mid-seventeenth century. Thereafter there was a slow increase of about 300 by 1715 but then a rapid escalation occurred to between 10,000 and 11,000 by the late 1770s.[41] King has claimed that the main core areas of Rossendale had a population of approximately 11,500 in 1780 and by 1801 it was more than 14,000, which was an increase of around 22 per cent.[42] This rise he claims was due to natural increase rather than migration, although there was some in-migration from Yorkshire into east Lancashire, but some north to south out-migration was also probable. In addition there was a great deal of short distance mobility within Rossendale.[43]

The 1666 Hearth Tax returns reveal the approximate population numbers in the townships of study. They show the number of properties in Yate and Pickup Bank with hearths to be 51 small dwellings since only two had more than two hearths each. At Eccleshill there were 36 properties with hearths, this suggests an estimated 230 inhabitants at Yate and Pickup Bank and around 160 in Eccleshill.[44] Therefore, both townships were comparatively sparsely populated. However, as we shall see below increases occurred as industry was developed in both of the townships. Blacksnape and Hoddlesden were combined with Darwen in the returns and an interpretation into an assessment of the number of hearths would be dubious.

Turning to the industrial economy of the uplands of Rossendale, Tupling has suggested there were 'unmistakable signs' that domestic manufacture based on wool was being undertaken in the early sixteenth century, and this may have been the reason for keeping sheep.[45] Moorlands were good for grazing sheep, but the manor court records indicate abuse by over-grazing and that many sheep were starving. Nevertheless, wool from sheep farming was being sold for manufacturing, and this income was a partial solution to the reduction in average farm sizes. During the seventeenth century, the woollen industry grew; involving local domestic carding, spinning, weaving and other textile activities. Whole families were engaged in the manufacturing process, women and children spun yarn and men usually undertook the weaving activities, and even those designated husbandmen were also often engaged in weaving.[46] In towns such as Rochdale, where there was a close relationship with Rossendale, there were merchants, chapmen and wool staplers involved in the manufacturing and marketing of cloth. Weavers were concentrated in the hilly countryside of the district during this period rather than in towns as they were from the mid-nineteenth century onwards.

Nonetheless, the intertwining of farming and textiles aided survival since the copyholders' husbandary consisted of no more than the odd cow, a few sheep and hens. Therefore, farming was undemanding on time and allowed families to concentrate on working with wool. Inhabitants dividing their time between farming and textiles were referred to as yeomen.[47]

Further escalation in woollen manufacturing occurred during the eighteenth century and weaving became progressively more specialised. References to occupations listed in parish registers, albeit entries were both sparse and spasmodic, demonstrate the growing importance of textile manufacture. For the early eighteenth century the local registers extant show that weavers had become at least as numerous as agricultural workers and this does not take account of women and children engaged in carding and spinning and those engaged in both farm work and weaving.[48]

Transportation of raw and finished textile goods was executed by trains of packhorses travelling mostly over boggy moor land tracks from rural communities to both centres of industry and commerce.[49] Before the eighteenth century horse drawn wagons and carriages were little used but later this mode of transport escalated, although the roads were crude and accidents frequent. However, the introduction of turnpike roads from the mid-1720s improved conditions. 'Roads were widened, bends were eased, new surfaces laid and drainage ditches and milestones were provided'.[50] A turnpike road from Blackburn to Haslingden bypassed Yate and Pickup Bank at Belthorn. Otherwise, roads in the townships were rough cart tracts and packhorse routes.

Even by the late eighteenth century Blacksnape, Eccleshill, Hoddlesden and Yate and Pickup Bank were sparsely populated and the dwelling were in a scattered configuration. This scenario can be viewed on the Yates Map of Lancashire dated 1786. It is from this period onwards that the following chapters trace the evolution of these townships.

In summary Rossendale had changed very little before the sixteenth century. After 1507 settlers were attracted to the Forest and from this emerged population growth. They set up small farms, which became even smaller between the sixteenth and seventeenth century because of partitioning and partible inheritance. This reduction in size must have made earning a living progressively difficult and created a need for supplementary earnings. Turning to arable cultivation was not a viable option because of the poor soil and unkindly climate. Nevertheless, there were large tracts of common, which allowed expansion of farm stock, although this land was more suited to sheep grazing than cattle pasture. There is evidence in the Clitheroe Court Rolls of sheep becoming an important part of the economy, since these documents provide details of tithes in the form of lambs and wool being received by the Abbott of Whalley.[51] The down side of this was overstocking of the commons, as stated in fines imposed by the Halmote Court. As we shall see below, our townships were transformed from sparsely populated and barely cultivated Forest terrain into firstly thriving domestic and then industrial centres.

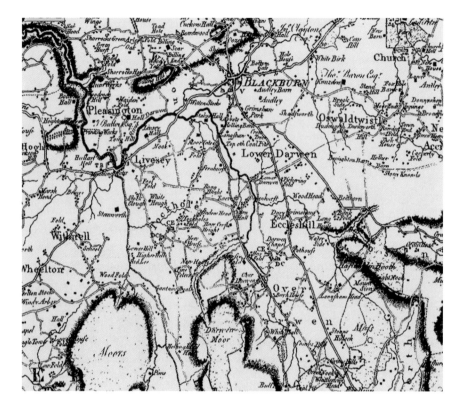

Yates Map of 1786, probably surveyed ten years earlier, demonstrates the scattered and sparse nature of building in and around the Hoddlesden district.

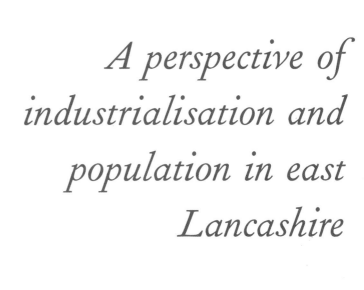

CHAPTER TWO

A perspective of industrialisation and population in east Lancashire

T HIS CHAPTER SEEKS TO provide an overview of both textile manufacturing and population changes, between the mid-eighteenth and
mid-nineteenth centuries. Both of these features were highly influential on
fashioning east Lancashire, during the period, of which Blacksnape, Eccleshill,
Hoddlesden and Yate and Pickup Bank were part. The end of this period was
a watershed for once thriving rural industrial settlements, which resulted in a
transition from rural to urban centred industry. The first section examines what
these rural settlements were like prior to this transition, and considers the impact
on them from the growth of industrialisation and urbanisation, which points to
the extent of survival in rural communities and the options open to them in the
latter part of the nineteenth century.

The chapter structure is broadly divided into two parts dealing respectively
with the growth and decline of rural textile manufacture and then the growth
and decline of rural population in east Lancashire. Together, they encompass the
nature and impact of changes in textile manufacturing, particularly the transition
from spinning and weaving as domestic industries to mechanised and urbanised
production, which were instrumental in causing a shift of population from rural
communities into urban centres.

John Aikin's Description of the Country from Thirty to Forty Miles Around Manchester
was a general survey of the landscape, economy and history of that area, derived from
the contributions of numerous local gentlemen and antiquarians, of variable reliability.
As part of the volume was prepared a detailed and fairly accurate map of the area was
covered in the book. The roads, canals and features are all clearly marked.

Growth in the manufacturing of textiles

Morris and Rodger have highlighted sustained increases in population and urbanisation as components of industrial urban development.[1] Changes occurring in Lancashire from the late eighteenth century reflected these components and also sustained growth in the textile industry, which created thriving industrial textile towns throughout the valleys of east Lancashire, but which also led to the erosion of domestic industry in upland parts of the region. Berg has noted that, 'Industrial transformation in the eighteenth and early nineteenth centuries meant not only the rise of new industries and the reorganisation of the old. It also entailed the decline of old industries and erasure of old methods of production.' This was abundantly evident in textile manufacturing.[2] As we shall see, much early proto-industrialisation in textiles was concentrated in upland pastoral districts of east Lancashire where there was a cheap and plentiful workforce,[3] but the changes in textile manufacture from the late eighteenth century had a fundamental impact on both the economy and population in these areas. The aim in this section is to describe this economic expansion and the structural changes associated with it up to the second quarter of the nineteenth century, the purpose of which provides background for the villages on which this study is based.

Until the early eighteenth century textile manufacture in England had been based on wool and linen, dispersed countrywide, although most densely located in the South West, East Anglia and Lancashire.[4] However, by the end of the century manufacture of British cotton and cotton-mix fabrics had mainly gravitated towards Lancashire (Figure 2.1). The total extent of textile manufacture in the county was

Figure 2.1 *Raw cotton consumption in Great Britain*

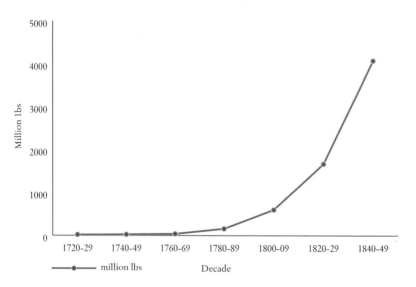

The graph illustrates the rapid escalation in raw cotton consumption from the end of the eighteenth century onwards and particularly from the first quarter of the nineteenth century. The implications were that there was a higher demand on manpower for hand weaving and later power weaving, along with British and Overseas consumption.

Spinning wheel

PHOTOGRAPH TAKEN AT
HALL ITH WOOD MUSEUM

Below: Spinning wheel photgraphed in the museum at Moscow Mill, Oswaldtwistle now called Oswaldtwistle Mill. The photograph illustrates a typical cottage room where domestic textile manufacture was undertaken. Note that spinning and weaving were being carried out the latter on the heavy wooden loom seen in the background. Early spinning wheels were only able to spin a single thread. They were used in cottages and frequently varied in design, the wooden frame being turned and shaped to individual styles. The one shown here is less crude than many that were used in the domestic process.

PERMISSION TO PHOTOGRAPH AND PUBLISH HAS BEEN KINDLY GIVEN
BY THE MANAGEMENT OF OSWLDTWISTLE MILL

Spinning Mule. This machine is a replica of the invention created by Samual Crompton. It is to be found at Hall ith Wood Museum, Bolton where it was photographed.

Spinning Jenny. The jenny in this illustration has about 30 spindles whereas James Hargreaves prototype had only six spindles and was small enough for use in a domestic cottage. The machine in this illustration was photographed in the museum at Moscow Mill, Oswaldtwistle now call Oswaldtwistle Mill.

The scene is an artist view depicting Samual Cromton in his living room playing a violin. This room was also used as a workshop where he constructed the mule that is indicated partly completed. .Crompton was an ordinary man without entreperneural ambitions. He never copyrighted his mule and allowed others to profit from his skills
COPYRIGHT BOLTON COUNCIL.

Each spinning machine innovation became larger than its predecessor along with a capacity to produce more strands of yarn and at a more rapid rate.

undoubtedly greater than raw cotton import figures portrayed, since, as noted by Walton, it often encompassed a 'cotton-mix', an example being fustian (cotton weft and linen warp).[5] Exceptions to cotton production occurred near the Yorkshire border and in Rossendale, where woollens continued until at least the end of the eighteenth century, but even in Rossendale, they eventually gave way to cottons.[6] Textile production until at least the late eighteenth century was largely a family operation, based in scattered countryside settlements, where the head of the family could engage in other part-time occupations such as farming or an extractive industry.[7] However, the expansion of employment opportunities in textile manufacture by the late eighteenth century meant that more people in east and central Lancashire became primarily dependent on earnings from the domestic production of cotton cloth.[8]

Increasing demand for cotton-based goods created steady growth in both the spinning and weaving sectors during the middle decades of the eighteenth century. Inventions such as Kay's 'flying shuttle' produced momentum in weaving but irritated a bottleneck in spinning. However, by the 1770s further inventions such as Hargreaves's 'spinning jenny' were being introduced to super-

A PERSPECTIVE OF INDUSTRIALISATION AND POPULATION IN EAST LANCASHIRE   21

cede the spinning wheel in an attempt to release the bottleneck. These machines were able to spin multiple threads consecutively compared to the single thread of the spinning wheel and produced increasing supplies of yarn and of better quality. The Jenny was initially small enough to be used in cottages but as size increased, it was located in workshops,[9] but it was also amongst the first of a succession of spinning inventions such as the waterframe and spinning mule that increased yarn output, resulting in expansion of the weaving workforce to keep abreast of yarn output.

Increasing demand for more weavers broke the strong nexus with agriculture, resulting in the emergence of a landless society who specialised in commercial weaving, motivated by the possibility of achieving higher wages. Handloom weavers' wages nearly doubled between 1770 and 1790 and continued to rise until the end of the century. These wages were probably double those of agricultural labourers; handlooms cost only a few pounds, so the business could be established with very little capital (Table 2.1).

Table 2.1 *Estimates of handloom weavers weekly wages*

Year	Wood	Hopwood	Bythell
1770		8s	
1780		10s	
1790		15s	
1800	25s	25s	
1810	19s 6d	19s	
1815			11s 6d
1820	9s	9s	9s
1830	5s 6d	5s	6s

Sources: G. H. Wood, The History of Wages in the Cotton Trade during the Past Hundred Years (Sherratt, Manchester, 1910), pp. 107–9.
E. A. Hopwood, A History of the Lancashire Cotton Industry and the Amalgamated Weavers Association (1969), pp 6–7.
D. Bythell, The Handloom Weavers (Manchester University Press, 1969), p. 115.

As demand on the weaving workforce increased; wages also increased but from the beginning of the nineteenth century wages began to decline. By the end of the first quarter of the century weavers became very poor.

Timmins has pointed out that 'specialising in the weaving trade would have enabled rural workers to earn much more than they could have earned by combining farming and weaving and with a good deal less effort'.[10] Weavers became increasingly prosperous in the late eighteenth century and rural east Lancashire was dominated by what were essentially handloom weaving settlements.[11] The result was a thickening of population across much of the region, rather than concentrated growth in a few towns.

As spinning machines were developed to produce more yarn they became larger and needed greater power, causing a shift from a domestic to a water-powered industry, but much of this remained in rural surroundings, widely dispersed across the region.[12] East Lancashire had the characteristics required for this change with high rainfall that drained from the high slopes to supply power via streams to the lower grounds. In the last quarter of the eighteenth century, entrepreneurs took advantage of these conditions[13] by building small mills on the banks of streams. Despite some streams drying up in summer months, freezing in winter and becoming raging torrents following heavy rainstorms,[14] water provided a cheap supply of energy once the initial infrastructure was in place.

From the 1790s steam engines with higher capacity output began to replace water wheels as a means of power.[15] This removed the need to build mills near to watercourses and allowed relocation to the valley floors where there was convenient access to coalfields.[16] In terms of east Lancashire generally, this development was further assisted by the development of good canal and road communications, which enabled coal in particular to be transported cheaply.[17] When deep mining became sufficiently developed around the middle of the nineteenth century, the restricted supply from the east Lancashire coalfield was supplemented by superior fuel from the Wigan area collieries, aided by rail access.[18]

Despite available facilities, transition from water to steam power was still relatively gradual. As pointed out by Southgate, the choice facing entrepreneurs was not straightforward. Water power was cheap and renewable but steam power was more reliable and more easily controlled.[19] Hill summed up the eventual transition, 'Steam power immeasurably extended the range of man's economic activities, freeing him from dependence on water power',[20] but waterpower was not completely displaced until late in the nineteenth century.[21] However, as spinning turned to steam power, this branch of the industry gradually became more urbanised, particularly in south-east Lancashire, but weaving continued to dominate the economy further north and remained a hand powered and essentially rural industry until well into the first half of the nineteenth century.

Indeed, the expansion of urban steam powered spinning mills increased yarn production immeasurably and actually resulted in a significant increase in the rural weaving workforce. By the 1820s, handloom weavers formed the largest group of workers in Lancashire. According to Timmins and Wood, they were then at their peak, and in east Lancashire largely involved in cotton production, as this branch of textiles rapidly ousted linen, fustians and wool. Estimates of the numbers of weavers in Britain suggest that there was as many as 240,000 by the 1820s, the majority of whom worked in Lancashire[22] (Table 2.2). This trade had the advantage of being neither age nor gender specific and as Timmins noted

Handloom
weaver numbers
were at a peak
in the 1820s but
then severely
declined towards
mid-century
because the
power loom was
overtaking the
weaving process.

Table 2.2 *Handloom weavers in Britain and Lancashire*

Year	Handloom Weavers in Britain (Wood)	Handloom Weavers in Lancashire (Timmins)	Factory Power looms in Britain Baines & Wood	Cotton Powerlooms in Lancashire (Timmins)
1806	184000		A few	
1813	212000		2400	
1820	240000		14150	
1821	240000	168000		
1829	240000		55000	
1835	188000		108189	61176
1844	72000		150000	
1850	43000		249627	176947
1862	3000			
1895				539,000

Sources: G. H. Wood, The history of wages in the cotton trade during the past hundred years (Sherratt, Manchester, 1910), pp. 125 & 127.
G. Timmins, The last shift (Manchester University Press, 1993), p. 19, 20 & 37.
E. Baines, History of the cotton manufacture in Great Britain (1966 reprint of 1835 Edition), p. 234.

it 'must often have provided far greater employment opportunities for country people than would any other occupation'. The gradual introduction of power looms in the early nineteenth century and the integration of industrial spinning and weaving under one roof, particularly in south-east Lancashire, spelt the death knell for the handloom weaver. According to Baines only 2,400 power looms had been installed in the whole of Britain by 1813; but then 14,150 by 1820; and 55,000 by 1829. By 1835 there were about 50,000 British power loom weavers of cotton and 60 per cent of these worked in Lancashire,[23] although estimates of numbers vary. Timmins quotes figures of 61,176 power looms in Lancashire by 1835 and 176,947 at mid-century, a three-fold increase in just 15 years.[24] Nevertheless, he questions these figures pointing to the fact that factory inspectors' returns were incomplete,[25] and Taylor has suggested there were 50 per cent more looms in 1835 than indicated in the inspectors' figures.[26] What is undeniable is that large-scale investment in power looms was undertaken during the major economic upturn of the mid-1840s.[27]

In the Calder Valley of north-east Lancashire, however, power looms were more slowly introduced than in the south-east corner of the county. Taylor's research shows most looms were operating in south Lancashire and his revised estimates of the 1835 factory inspectors' report claim that only 12,000 (13.3%) were operational in the east of the county. According to Wallwork, in 1835 only 14 per cent of power looms (8565) of the Lancashire total were in the Darwen/

Calder Valley area.[28] If these estimates are accurate then the district, including towns such as Blackburn, Burnley and Colne, appear to have been very slow in adopting power loom weaving.[29] However, as Timmins notes the location of the new weaving mills was very different to the early spinning mills. They were largely built in urban areas. In 1835, the Blackburn parish had 4000 power looms but only one of the mills was located in a village.[30] Therefore, although power looms were only introduced slowly in east Lancashire, very few of these were installed in rural areas, and increasing competition from large integrated mills further south faced the district as a whole. Nevertheless, by the mid-century almost three-quarters of British looms were in use in Lancashire and east Lancashire was specialising in weaving in preference to spinning, the latter gravitating to south Lancashire.[31] The relocation of workers from the country-side to towns and the shift of power from water in rural areas to steam in towns became in the words of Farnie, 'the great separation of the past'.[32]

Collapse of the domestic economy

The following section reviews the effects of proto-industrialisation decline and considers the impact of factory manufacture on the rural populations of east Lancashire. Rapid growth of both population and textile manufacturing that occurred in some towns of east Lancashire before the mid-nineteenth century was not widespread throughout the district. Nevertheless, the importance of handloom weaving in 1821 is demonstrated by the fact that one in six Lancastrians was engaged in the trade and probably one in four of those occupied.[33] However, most of the upland rural communities experienced de-industrialisation, some decline in population and reductions in the numbers of handloom weavers from the second quarter of the century.[34] By the third quarter of the century hand-loom weaving had become virtually extinct. What is less certain is the process in terms of geographical locations and rate at which decline occurred. Was the rate of decline similar everywhere? Was it linear, abrupt or linked to economic cycles? It is to these questions that we now turn.

Farnie, has pointed to difficulties in estimating hand weaver numbers but suggested that decline was most evident during and after depressions. He observed 'their numbers stabilised in the 1820s and did not begin to decline until after the commercial crisis of 1825 and the riots of 1826 and 1829'.[35] Bythell, too, maintained that handloom weaving 'fell continuously after 1826 … but that decline was irregular'. Within thirty years, he claimed it had become a 'pictur-esque anachronism encountered only in small numbers and in odd localities'.[36] Timmins in the 1990s put the beginning of the decline a decade later, arguing that 'no substantial diminution in overall hand weaver numbers occurred prior to the late 1830s'.[37] This assertion, however, depends on the definition of 'substantial' since he acknowledges that numbers had already fallen.

Contemporary opinions provide contradictory perceptions of decline in handloom weaving. References to Blackburn in Parliamentary Select Committee reports,[38] and a report of a vicar's comments in a local newspaper,[39] state that handloom weaving was at an end in 1826 and the people were very poor. Economic depressions undoubtedly caused widespread poverty in the handloom-weaving district, and no doubt prevented people from continuing with the employment but such dramatic comments appear to be exaggerated since it is clear varying degrees of revival followed decline. A select committee in 1838 reported large numbers of cotton handloom weavers in various parts of Lancashire being employed, which suggests a semblance of survival.[40] Other reports show that they actually peaked in Rossendale in 1842.[41] The upturns in textile production in the mid-1830s needed large numbers of hand weavers to produce the output required.[42] During this period mill owners had installed only sufficient power looms for average trade and used the handloom sector as a reservoir. Although this imposed a fluctuating lifestyle on the weavers and caused distress in times of low demand or over production it maintained a lifeline.[43] Yet contemporary evidence also highlights the undoubted longer-term decline. Handlooms were no longer being made in Lancashire after the mid 1820s.[44] In the east of the county in 1837 widespread distress of hand weavers was reported[45] in the far east of the county and in 1838 the *Blackburn Standard* stated that 'the number [of handloom weavers] was decreasing daily'.[46] Timmins estimates weaver numbers in the Blackburn parish to be 14,570 in 1821, reducing to 5,411 by 1851, whilst in the town of Blackburn there were only 1000 handloom weavers in 1841.[47] Whatever the speed of decline, the existence of widespread distress is undeniable. Handloom weavers were essentially becoming a poorly paid reserve army of labour, used to supplement power loom weaving during periods of rapid growth, but they were the first to suffer during years of depression. Handloom weavers could no longer compete with mechanisation and, according to Wood, the domestic workforce in 1845 had fallen to one-quarter of that in the early 1830s.[48]

By the 1830s, handloom weaving had become a difficult occupation in which to earn a living. In the late eighteenth century, wage levels had been rising, probably because of improved productivity from the increased supply of weft, but by the 1830s, they had fallen to 20 per cent of rates at the turn of the century. Although rates varied according to the economic climate, type of cloth, locality of production and capacity of output from individual weavers, the more important issue was the higher remuneration available to the more productive power-loom weavers. Rates for basic cloth woven by power loom in Manchester were approximately double hand rates, and it is probably safe to assume that similar ratios existed in east Lancashire, making the power side of weaving considerably more lucrative. Bythell also pointed to employers' criticisms that hand weavers were undisciplined, found factory work irksome, and weavers often remained unemployed and relied upon other family members to provide the household income rather than work in a mill.[49] Whatever the reasons for the handloom weavers experiencing hardship, the once prosperous rural communities were moving into an uncertain future.

The rate and length of survival was not the same in all parts of east Lancashire and decline was not complete at mid-century. Although Bythell argued for an early decline of handloom weaving he also concluded decline was slower in rural areas than in towns and found that it persisted most in the uplands of Rossendale and around Pendle Hill.[50] In the 'cotton towns' of Accrington, Blackburn, Darwen and Haslingden, for example, the percentage of handloom weavers was between 2 and 9 per cent of the total population in 1851.[51] But in fifteen rural townships in the Blackburn parish mean handloom weaver numbers represented 27 per cent of the total population. Timmins argued that 'In many country districts, meanwhile, dependency on hand weaving remained remarkably high, the power loom making very limited impact. It was only gradually during the mid-Victorian years that rural hand weavers were displaced'.[52]

Timmins has suggested that a contribution to the survival of handloom weavers came from diversification. Power looms were less efficient than hand processing for manufacturing delicate fabrics, fancy patterned cloths and small consignments.[53] Whilst using this argument Timmins makes the point that in rural east Lancashire 'numerous handloom weavers were willing to adapt to changing circumstances, including moving into fine and fancy cotton, or into non-cottons…', and suggested that this was the 'key reason for their survival'.[54] The *Blackburn Standard* in 1838 also reported survival was achieved by diversification since weavers were working fancy cloth such as jaconnets and cambrias rather than calico.[55] By the mid-nineteenth century, of the non-cotton weavers, Timmins observed, 'silk weavers comprised the majority', and survived into the third quarter of the century.[56] 'The higher grade cloths succumbed only gradually to the power loom and … continued to provide considerable employment opportunities for hand weavers beyond mid-century'.[57] In order to illustrate this point Timmins extracted the proportions of hand weavers by fabric type from the 1851 to 1871 census schedules.[58] In 1851, handloom weavers engaging in 'cotton', 'silk' and unspecified weaving were in almost equal proportions. By 1861, cotton hand-weavers accounted for a half, silk two-fifths and 'unspecified' hardly existed. By 1871, cotton hand weavers had declined to two-fifths and silk increased to 55 per cent of the total identified weavers. However, these were proportions of an unspecified magnitude of hand weavers and there is no indication as to whether each category was constant in decline or fluctuating. Nevertheless, it appears that finer cottons and silks assisted in the survival of handloom weavers,[59] but protracted decline left many rural townships without their main source of employment, and population decline occurred in many of the rural settlements of east Lancashire.

Population change

Significant growth and restructuring of the textile industry in Lancashire during the eighteenth and early nineteenth centuries was accompanied by unprecedented demographic change. The first part of this section provides a brief overview placing the population changes in Lancashire within a national context. The changing demography in the east of the county is then contextualised from analysis of census data and references to births, deaths and migration. The second part of the section discusses population changes in the rural uplands of east Lancashire during the first half of the nineteenth century.

Deane and Cole have pointed to the strong influence of industrialisation on population growth. They calculated that the percentage population of the four most industrialised counties, West Riding, Staffordshire, Warwickshire and above all Lancashire increased from 17 per cent of the total national population in 1781 to 26 per cent by 1861.[60] Tranter supports this notion in asserting that the greatest nineteenth century population increases of the country occurred in the industrial areas of the North West, Yorkshire, Midlands, and later in the century in the South East.[61] Furthermore, Redford and others have shown that growth of textile manufacturing in Lancashire during the late eighteenth and nineteenth centuries had a strong influence on demographic trends within the county.[62]

Pre-industrial Lancashire was a thinly populated area and there is evidence that the case study townships were typical, but Smith has demonstrated that during the eighteenth century population increased in Lancashire much more rapidly than countrywide.[63] Additionally, Lawton noted that between 1700 and 1750 population in Lancashire rose more rapidly than in England and Wales, and this continued in the second half of the century.[64] Schwarz suggested that the growing rural textile industry in Lancashire provided choice between financial rewards entirely from textiles or retaining an agricultural lifestyle with dependence on subsistence level earnings.[65] Large numbers chose the former and the higher incomes available from textiles made earlier marriage possible and hence led to population growth.[66] Because of this, the population of east Lancashire increased at a faster rate than the rest of the county from the eighteenth century onwards.[67] As Arthur Young observed at the end of the eighteenth century, 'It is employment that creates population'.[68] The largely unmechanised weaving sector provided a substantial proportion of this employment and this was reflected in geographical and temporal variations in growth.[69] Population growth continued in the nineteenth century; in east Lancashire where more people worked in textiles than in any other occupation, there was a two and a half times increase during the first half of the nineteenth century (Table 2.3).

During the
first half of the
nineteenth
century the
population
of England
and Wales
approximately
doubled whilst
that of east
Lancashire
increased by
around two and
a half times,
due mainly to
an increase
in textile
manufacturing.

Table 2.3 *Comparison of 19th century population trends*

	Absolute numbers		
Census year	Total England & Wales	Total Lancashire	East Lancashire
1801	8892536	673731	94730
1811	10164256	828499	117832
1821	12000236	1052948	156280
1831	13896797	1336854	183148
1841	15914148	1667054	208242
1851	17927609	2031236	242447

Source: CSRs.

Significant increases in population occurred in the majority of townships in east Lancashire between 1801 and 1831. The intensities of these increases are illustrated on Map 2.1. Decline occurred in only six of the townships, while six grew by more than 150 per cent, one of which was Yate and Pickup Bank. The group of townships showing the largest increases were situated mainly in the uplands of east Lancashire where handloom weaving was still expanding rapidly, and not in the Calder and Darwen valleys, where expansion of industrial weaving occurred at a later date. However, after the third decade of the nineteenth century textile manufacturing grew rapidly in pockets of intense activity situated along the valleys of the cotton district, which was to the north and west of Rossendale where population growth was also most intense. Here cotton operatives and their families lived in colonies arranged around the new mills, which Marshall described as 'a mass of growing industrial communities surrounded by countryside'.[70] This process was accompanied by population decline in most rural communities, which are examined below and in later chapters.

Reasons for population growth

Historians have advocated various reasons whilst attempting to account for population growth: increases in birth and fertility rates; declines in mortality rates; and immigration to an area. Most now argue that the first of these was the most important. At the end of the seventeenth century, Gregory King estimated 4.1 births per marriage but by the 1860s; the Registrar General's statistics revealed it had risen to 6.3 births per marriage.[71] Although some, such as Drake, Crafts and Ireland, have argued that lower age of marriage had a limited effect on fertility rates, Habakkuk, and Wrigley and Schofield have concluded that the lower age of marriage along with a shortening of birth intervals resulted in a higher incidence of children per

MAP 2.1 *Population changes in east Lancashire between 1801 and 1831*

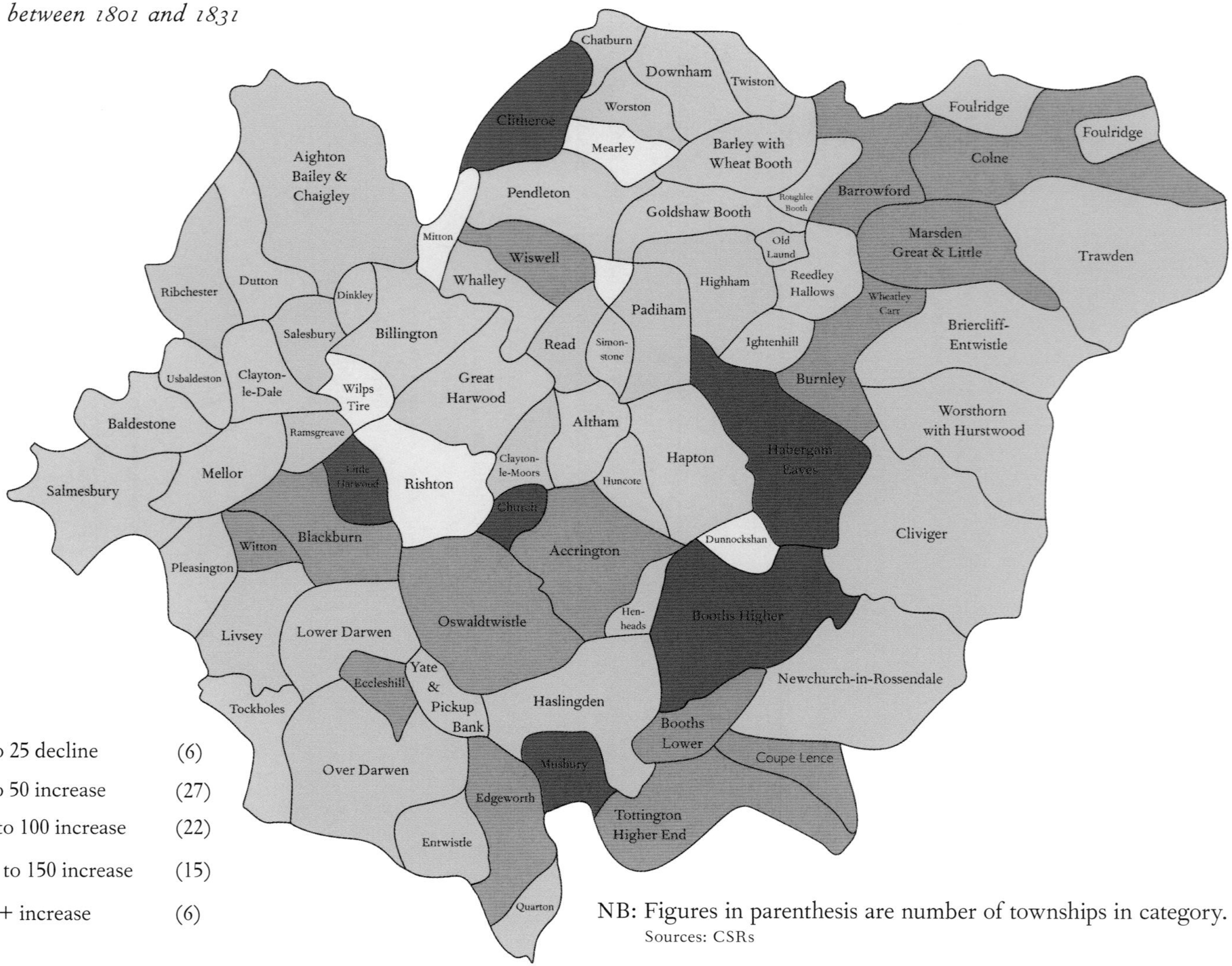

NB: Figures in parenthesis are number of townships in category.
Sources: CSRs

Key %

Yellow	0 to 25 decline	(6)
Medium Blue	0 to 50 increase	(27)
Green	51 to 100 increase	(22)
Pink	101 to 150 increase	(15)
Dark Blue	151+ increase	(6)

family.[72] Hudson observed that the age of marriage tended to decrease where proto-industrialisation and the available independent income early in life occurred.[73] The rural areas of east Lancashire were proto-industrialised, involving large numbers of textile workers and if the thesis of Hudson is accepted then these conditions would have promoted earlier marriages and a rising birth rate.

Both birth rate and population increase were higher in Lancashire than the national average from the eighteenth century until the 1820s.[74] This accords with Hudson's thesis, which is also supported by other historians. Marshall deduced that the early rise in fertility occurred mostly in townships with large proportions of weavers.[75] Both Walton and King imply that a lowering in age of marriage and a reduction in intervals between births occurred in Rossendale early in the eighteenth century,[76] and Lawton and Pooley concluded that higher wages were favourable to early marriages and larger families. When specialisation in textiles occurred during the late eighteenth century, wages rose, and Schwarz argues that this encouraged earlier marriages.[77] Fleischmann concluded that, 'Lancashire had higher birth, death and marriage rates, shorter life expectancy and a younger population than any other county in the nation' during the first half of the nineteenth century and that this was largely the product of the sustained increase in the birth rate.[78] Therefore, evidence suggests that lower age of marriage intertwined with textile manufacturing occurred over a prolonged period of time. J. D. Marshall has provided for us a succinct summary and highlighted the importance of industrialisation and income towards population growth.

> lower ages at marriage, extending the child-bearing period for women (resulting in high fertility-rates); more and more young incoming married couples who raised children in the county; the survival of more infants in face of killer diseases like smallpox; greater longevity; all such influences, effective as they may have been, are less certain than the overriding fact that without extensive economic development, this great and growing population could not have sustained at all. The jobs and food were plainly there.[79]

In emphasising a link between population growth and textiles Walton pointed out that 80 per cent of the bridegrooms at Newchurch-in-Pendle in the 1810s and 1820s were handloom weavers.[80] However, Timmins has provided a wider picture comprising 54 Lancashire parishes between 1818 and 1822. He found 82 per cent of bridegrooms at Newchurch-in-Pendle were weavers, but this was exceptional and the average for parishes in east Lancashire was 40 per cent, although large variations existed.[81] The Bishop's Transcripts for St Mary's, Blackburn (Cathedral) in 1821 revealed that 63 per cent of bridegrooms in solemnised marriages for the town and surrounding district were weavers.[82]

The early stages of industrial growth in east Lancashire, therefore, involved significant population increases apart from six townships, such as Mittan, Mearly and Wilpshire. From the 1820s and 1830s, this began to change. Birth and fertility rates peaked in the 1810s and 1820s, at precisely the point wages in the domestic textile industry started to fall.[83] Large parts of east Lancashire, which had once been populous rural industrial settlements experienced population decline from the second quarter of the nineteenth century onwards. Just under one quarter of the townships in east Lancashire experienced continuous growth of population between 1801 and 1851, examples of which were Blackburn, Darwen and Oswaldtwistle (Map 2.2). The remainder declined, the majority of which was first indicated in the 1831 and 1841 census, such as Tockholes, Rishton and Altham in 1831 and Edgworth, Mellor and Great Harwood in 1841. The 1820s then appears to be a pivotal decade in this growing contrast. By 1851, populations in many townships were often significantly lower than they had been a quarter of a century earlier. While the towns showed continuous growth the majority of 'rural' townships experienced decline. The rates of decline for each township from when population peaked in the first half of the nineteenth century to 1851 is illustrated in 10 per cent bands (Map 2.3). The rates of decline varied; for example, Eccleshill and Yate and Pickup Bank declined between 11 and 20 per cent; Wilpshire 21 and 30 per cent, Pleasington 31 and 40 per cent and Worston 41 and 50 per cent.

From the second quarter of the nineteenth century, therefore, there was a clear divergence evident in east Lancashire between a minority of expanding industrial towns and a larger number of declining or stagnant ex-industrial rural townships. Seventy per cent of townships experienced some decline during this period. What is not clear from analysis is the actual year when decline started to occur since census tables only provide an approximation of the date for depopulation, but the timing for the majority of townships can be narrowed to between the years 1821 and 1841. It is clearly no coincidence that this is approximately parallel to when handloom weaving went into serious decline. An explanation for population losses in rural areas following peaking is given in the notes to the census in 1841, 'the removal of labourers to large towns', and 'want of employment for hand-loom weavers'.[84] The contrast widened over the rest of the century. At mid-century, only six towns had populations exceeding 10,000, but, as the century progressed more towns came within this category, but most communities continued to experience decline and populations remained small.

In summary it has now been demonstrated that the development of east Lancashire is not just a simple tale of increasing industrialisation and urbanisation. Initially industry led to population rise in a large number of townships, and it was only from the second quarter of the nineteenth century that it was reversed. Large parts of the area therefore, experienced population stagnation or

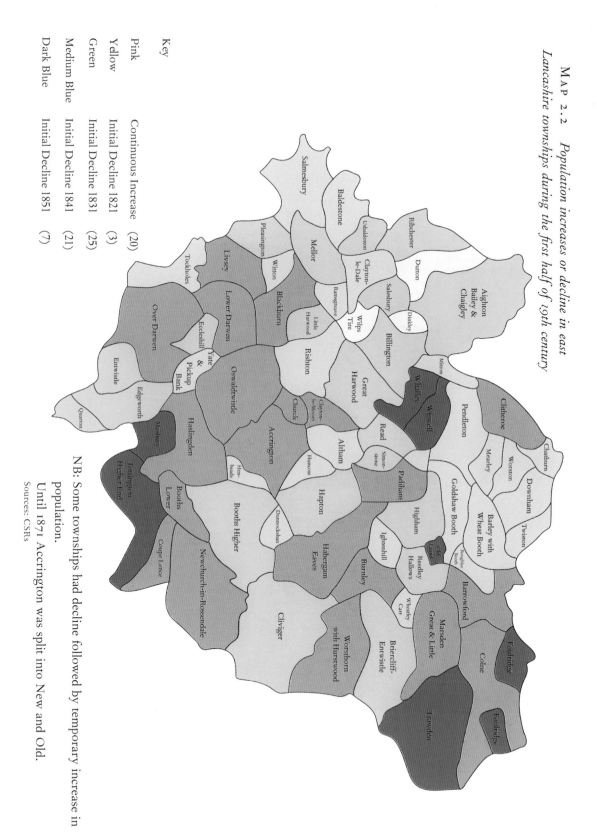

MAP 2.2 *Population increases or decline in east Lancashire townships during the first half of 19th century*

Key

Pink	Continuous Increase	(20)
Yellow	Initial Decline 1821	(3)
Green	Initial Decline 1831	(25)
Medium Blue	Initial Decline 1841	(21)
Dark Blue	Initial Decline 1851	(7)

NB: Some townships had decline followed by temporary increase in population.

Until 1871 Accrington was split into New and Old.

Sources: CSRs

MAP 2.3. *Percentage population declines between decennial peak in first half 19th century and 1851.*

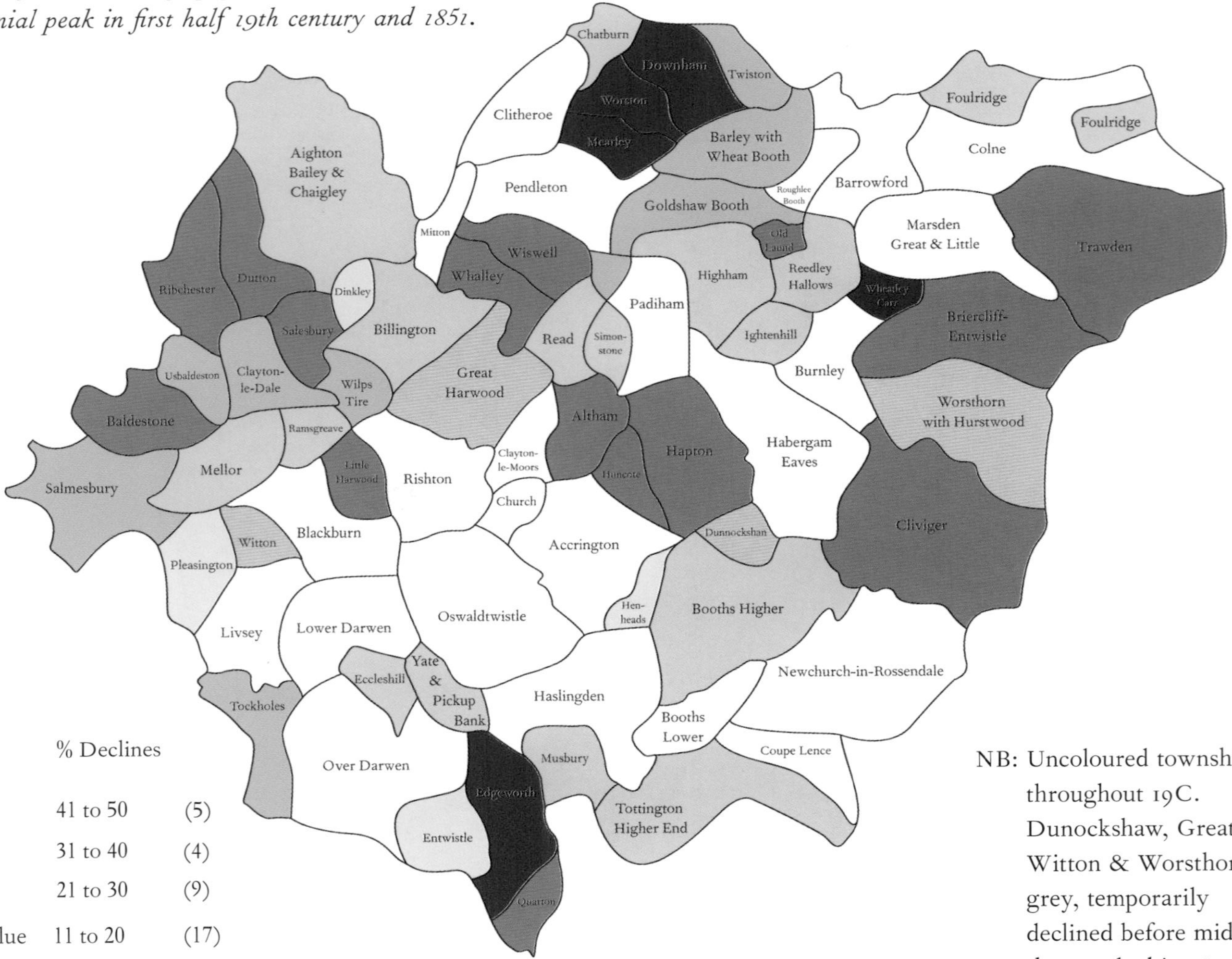

NB: Uncoloured townships increased throughout 19C. Dunockshaw, Great Harwood, Witton & Worsthorn shaded grey, temporarily declined before mid-century but then peaked in 1851.

Key	% Declines	
Red	41 to 50	(5)
Yellow	31 to 40	(4)
Green	21 to 30	(9)
Medium Blue	11 to 20	(17)
Dark Blue	1 to 10	(15)

decline. These have been largely ignored in the histories of the district.

Rural townships, therefore, developed very different characteristics to their more rapidly growing urbanised neighbours. The next few chapters will explore just what these characteristics were and what the relationships between urban and rural areas were in the second half of the century. It will focus on some of the experiences of these rural townships, which did not always conform to the picture of a buoyant expanding industrial economy or to the expectations of what 'rural' society was like.

This chapter is only a very brief account of the general history that fashioned life in Blacksnape, Eccleshill, Hoddlesden and Yate and Pickup Bank. Nonetheless, it hopefully contextualises the micro-histories dealt with in the following chapters.

CHAPTER THREE

Demographic characteristics of the townships

Blacksnape, Eccleshill and Yate and Pickup Bank followed the declining population trends of many rural communities in east Lancashire during the second half of the nineteenth century.

THIS CHAPTER REVIEWS THE demographic structures of the townships during most of the nineteenth century, following the demise of a cottage textile industry. The purpose is to explore whether each of the communities developed similar patterns and how these patterns compared with those in nearby towns, which grew at a greater rate than could be expected from natural population change.

Demographic profiles in our rural villages varied both from each other and those in the adjacent urban towns. Figure 3.1 illustrates the undulating nature of population magnitudes in the villages and Figure 3.2 charts the population changes in the nearby towns, noting particularly the contrasting rapid expansion

Figure 3.1
Population trends in the villages 1841-1901

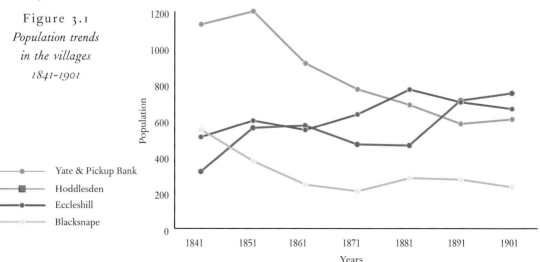

of populations. Yate and Pickup Bank was typical of one-third of the total townships in east Lancashire, which experienced population decline throughout the second half of the nineteenth century. Eccleshill was unusual in that the township was one of only half a dozen experiencing population increase between 1851 and 1881 but then decline (Table 3.1 & Map 3.1).By the end of the century the population of Yate and Pickup Bank had fallen to 58 per cent of the total population in 1801, but in Eccleshill it had doubled. Population figures for Blacksnape and Hoddlesden cannot be compared in the same way since they are unavailable for the earlier part of the century because they were an integral part of Darwen in terms of census statistics.

Figure 3.2. Urban centres in east Lancashire demonstrated rapid population growth during the second half of the nineteenth century.

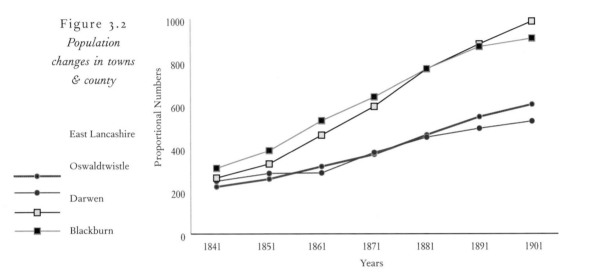

Figure 3.2
Population changes in towns & county

East Lancashire

Oswaldtwistle

Darwen

Blackburn

Table 3.1 *Population changes in east Lancashire rural townships during 2nd half of 19C.*

To be read in conjunction with Map 3.1

Key to Map 3.1	Total Townships	Number declining 1851-1871	1871-1901	Number increasing 1851-1871	1871-1901	Average % change/ decade 1851-1871	1871-1901
Pink	19	19	19			13.5	7.7
Blue	18			18	18	24.2	15.7
Green	19	19			19	11.9	31.1
Brown	6		6	6		22	3.6
Yellow	Towns > 10,000 population in 1901 with continuous increase between 1851 and 1901						

Sources: CSRs.

Map 3.1. *Population changes in east Lancashire rural townships during 2nd half of 19C.*

Key: See table 3.1

In the villages of this study, population changes in the second half of the nine-teenth century were very different to the large population increases occurring in the weaving towns of east Lancashire during the same period. The reasons for popula-tion losses occurring were stated in the marginal notes to the 1851 census statistical report referring to many of the east Lancashire rural townships including the case study townships. These read 'the township of [name given, e.g. Yate and Pickup Bank] has decreased in population in consequence of the migration of families to the neighbourhood of the cotton mills'.[1] Furthermore, notes in the 1871 census stated that population movements from rural areas were due to lack of employment oppor-tunities but that employment was available in the nearby cotton towns.[2]

In summary, it is clear that patterns of population changes in most rural communities of east Lancashire during the nineteenth century were very different from those occurring in the towns. All this leads to an assumption of population movement away from rural communities where expansion from natural popula-tion growth should have occurred had there been no migration. If out-migration from these rural communities was for the purpose of seeking employment in the nearby cotton towns as the census suggests, then migration was of a short-distance nature. However, this possibility is addressed below.

Occupational profiles for the townships derived from the CEBs revealed that in 1871 and 1881 between a half and three fifths of inhabitants were employed. The majority was engaged in textile manufacture, a smaller number in agri-culture and the remainder was scattered over various occupations such as coal mining, shop keeping, paper manufacturing, general labouring and service (Table 3.2).

Table 3.2. *Occupational Proportions of Total Population 1871 to 1881.*

| | \multicolumn{8}{c}{Population occupied in:} | | | | | | | |
| | Agriculture | | Textiles | | Other | | Total employed | |
	1871%	1881%	1871%	1881%	1871%	1881%	1871%	1881%
Blacksnape	5.4	5.4	26.8	27	26.8	27	59	59.3
Eccleshill	5.6	8.2	34.6	29.1	14.2	16.3	54.4	53.6
Hoddlesden	6.3	5	32.3	30	18.3	21.4	56.9	56.5
Yate & Pickup Bank	9.5	11.4	40.8	32.3	10.8	10.3	61.1	54

Textiles were the most important single occupations towards earning a living in these communities.

Sources: CEBs

NB: Latter-Day Saints Resource File (LDS-RF) shows that 27 % of the total population in Blackburn were engaged in textile manufacture in 1881.

Therefore, textiles employment was of paramount importance to these communities.

Migration

That population shifts were commonplace in search of work following the demise of handloom weaving after the third decade of the nineteenth century has been well documented. However, population movements were frequently enforced before this period. In the century before the Poor Law Act of 1834 local support for the poor was well established but under strict rules, this meant that individuals not of native birth or self-supporting were removed from their temporary residence back to their 'settlement villages' (birthplace village). An earlier Act of 1572 had introduced compulsory local poor law tax. Two overseers were elected each Easter to carry out the administration of the tax and they were responsible for setting, collection and distribution to the poor. To receive poor relief the recipient had to satisfy certain criteria such as being born in the parish, renting property worth £10 per annum or more, having served an apprenticeship of seven years, have been in employment for given periods, although this varied overtime. Females changed their legal settlement to that of their husband at marriage. When a person or family became reliant on parish relief and was not entitled to legal settlement status, a removal order was sought from the local Justices of the Peace for them to be returned to their legal parish. The poor in a parish and those returned were often required to work for the parish surveyor in repairing roads, walls and cleaning ditches. Details of such orders are to be found in abundance in County Record Offices.

Prior to 1834 the specific numbers of poor law orders related to Eccleshill were difficult to assess because of the township being integrated with Mellor. Nonetheless, an approximate estimate revealed that no less than 19 orders were made for 120 inhabitants to leave the township and 25 orders for 125 people to return to the township between 1713 and 1834. From Yate and Pickup Bank at least 40 orders were implemented to remove 168 individuals and 31 orders for returning 134 people back to the township. Removal orders were not found for Blacksnape and Hoddlesden, but in any event they were combined with Darwen and probably referenced as such, nevertheless, during this period these villages were very sparsely populated, so it is likely that very little movement occurred.

Turning to nineteenth-century population movements, the censuses only provide an indication of migration, and as stated by Lawton 'are of little value' for assessing migrational flows.[3] What is more important is an assessment of total movements into and out of townships. Pooley and Turnbull have also stressed the importance of basing migration studies on gross movement figures, since as they pointed out these provide a more significant insight into social, economic and cultural aspects of areas gaining and losing inhabitants.[4]

The earliest study of population distribution in Lancashire and Cheshire is that by Danson and Welton. Using published census tables, they argued that very little outward movement of population had taken place from Lancashire during the first half of the nineteenth century. They wrote:

> ... The county of Lancaster has retained among its permanent inhabitants a larger proportion of those born within its bounds than any other county; and has also drawn very largely from the adjacent counties, and from Ireland and Scotland. It is also apparent that from those parts of England lying at a distance it has received comparatively small contributions to its population.[5]

Therefore, they established that more people moved into Lancashire from elsewhere than those leaving. However, they did not concern themselves with short distance movements within Lancashire, which were crucial, particularly in rural communities.

The strong influence on rural and urban population trends in east Lancashire, following the demise of handloom weaving and growth of urbanised and industrialised textile manufacture, appears to be occupational opportunities. This raises many questions the most important of which is perhaps whether migrants did indeed move relatively short distances into towns where work was plentiful.

The remainder of this chapter will question if migration was mostly of a short distance nature as a rural to urban flow towards industrial centres, or whether there were counter-currents or return migration and whether it was related to occupation. The investigation includes multi-directional aspects of migration, entailing rural to urban, urban to rural and rural to rural movements that took place in the second half of the nineteenth century, particularly between 1871 and 1881 since when this research was executed there were more detailed sources available for this decade than any other part of the period.

Inhabitants leaving the townships

As noted from census data, population changes occurring within the townships between 1871 and 1881 varied from an increase in Blacksnape and Eccleshill to decreases in Hoddlesden and Yate and Pickup Bank. The assumption is that at least some of these net changes were influenced by migration. However, as affirmed by Pooley and Turnbull and others, such figures mask the fact that gross movements occurred well in excess of net movements,[6] and it is likely that the townships used in this study were no exception. By 1881, between 70 and 81 percent of the 1871 populations were no longer present in the townships, however, these include those dying and females having changed name at marriage, for which identification is impossible from census material. Even if these unknown moves could be excluded, it would still leave substantial numbers of individuals and families living elsewhere by 1881 that accounted for the majority of losses,

Large numbers of the population were leaving many rural townships in just a single decade during the latter part of the nineteenth century owing to decline in handloom weaving.

Figure 3.3. *Percentage of total 1871 inhabitants departing between 1871 & 1881*

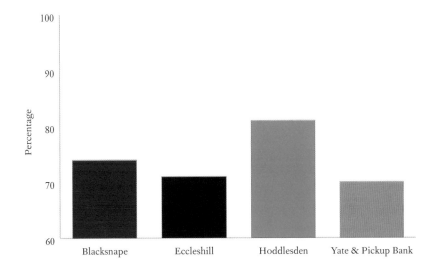

many of which are identified below at their destination. Nevertheless, as we shall also see below significant numbers had arrived during the same period.

The shift of population away from the townships raises questions as to whether population movements were of an occupationally specific nature as broadly indicated (Table 3.3).

Table 3.3. *Occupational Proportion of Migrants 19871 to 1881*

Most people leaving the rural communities were moving into nearby towns in order to work in the textile industry.

Township	Agriculture	Textiles	Other	Total employed
	Departure cohort			
Blacksnape	5.9	25	15.8	46.7
Eccleshill	4.9	34.1	15.7	54.7
Hoddlesden	6.4	31.1	17	54.5
Yate & Pickup Bank	6.7	44.1	11.8	62.6

Sources: CEBs.

The census revealed that at least half of the inhabitants in the townships, except for Blacksnape, which was marginally less, were in some kind of employment in 1871, the remainder being mostly children, 'scholars' and wives. Between 1871 and 1881 absolute numbers of those employed fell in Yate and Pickup Bank and marginally so in Hoddlesden, but increased in both Blacksnape and Eccleshill.

Although, over half of the inhabitants in the case study townships generally were in employment between 1871 and 1881, substantial numbers were recorded in the census with no occupational designation. Between two thirds and three quarters of those unoccupied in 1871 were no longer present in the townships in 1881.[7] The reduction in the number of employment opportunities was particularly pronounced in the textile trades and this may have accounted for a drift in population, possibly to a nearby 'cotton town' where employment was available.

Farming communities in the 'villages' comprised farmers who were largely male, a few widows, farmers' families and agricultural labourers. The numbers of these workers in all four townships were fairly constant in both 1871 and 1881.[8] Nevertheless, between half and four fifths of the farmers in the four townships present in 1871 could not be identified in the 1881 census from which it has been presumed they had either moved elsewhere or died; this pattern was also noted for farmers' family members. Only a small proportion of farmers was traced to a destination in 1881 using the *Latter Day Saints – Resource File (LDS–RF)*, but this was not entirely surprising since the average age of farmers not present in 1881 was 40 to 50 years in 1871 and absences may have been compounded by omissions in census enumeration. Of the ones identified, very few were farming elsewhere in 1881 and it is possible that others considered themselves of an age that was not conducive to setting up a fresh farm. Only five of the total farmers identified for all townships had continued in farming and these were mainly located in nearby Darwen. A mere 14 per cent of farming family members and agricultural labourers combined, in the four townships, continued in farming after leaving and a further nine per cent moved into other occupations such as general labouring and a few females found employment in textiles. This discontinuation in farming was different to the findings of Pooley and Turnbull, who noted that farmers continued to work in agriculture in their new abode. Furthermore, 'farmers wife' and 'farmers daughter' continued to be described as such even when the ex-farmer was designated as being without occupation in 1881 and this casts some doubt regarding the census descriptions of occupations.

Those working in the extractive industries comprised men mostly working as colliers and a few as quarrymen. A large turnover of these workers occurred, ranging from 75 to 90 per cent between 1871 and 1881. Between 38 and 46 per cent of extraction workers leaving were still engaged in the same occupation elsewhere in 1881. A few others were working in service and textiles but those not traced may have died owing to the advanced ages of some workers and the high fatality rates in mining. In contrast to farmers, the average age of these workers ranged from 25 to 32 years of age in 1871. So it is likely that members of this all male industry where between one-third and a half were married had family needs that encouraged continuation with work. However, very few of those living in the townships in both 1871 and 1881 were still in extraction by the end of the decade.

In 1871, general labourers were entirely male with average ages ranging from 33 to 46 years; numbers marginally increased during the following decade. Large proportions left the townships during the period except in Eccleshill, but they could not be traced in 1881, so their destinations and possible occupations were unavailable. Very few of those living in the townships in both 1871 and 1881 were general labourers at the end of the period and this suggested a possible change in enumeration practice rather than real change.

The service sector was multi-occupational and comprised both males and females. Occupations ranged from vicars to chemists and grocers to domestic servants with an average age of 40 years, their combined numbers being slightly larger than those employed in agricultural activities. Turnover for service workers was very high and only one-quarter of those leaving the townships could be traced; most had moved longer distances than in other occupations. Those traced were in scattered destinations and the majority were no longer in their 1871 occupation. The total numbers engaged in service for each township were maintained between 1871 and 1881 except in Yate and Pickup Bank where numbers fell to half.

The smallest occupational groups leaving were those employed at a paper mill and an iron works, mainly living in Eccleshill and Yate and Pickup Bank. The ironworkers were totally male dominated, as were three-quarters of those working in the paper mill. In 1871, only a few workers in either of these occupations were natives and by 1881, the majority was no longer in residence and had been replaced by workers born elsewhere. Around half of the ironworkers were engaged in the same occupation at their destination. At the paper mill there had been a quadrupling of workers by 1881 but this is focused upon in the section dealing with arrivals. The average ages in these industries were between 29 and 31 years respectively.

By far the largest occupational group leaving the four communities was that of those working in textiles. This industry alone provided income for between a half and two-thirds of the working populations in Eccleshill, Hoddlesden and Yate and Pickup Bank between 1871 and 1881, although there was some decline during the period in all three townships, suggesting a decline in occupational opportunities and possibly providing motivation for out-migration. However, the textile industry was less important to the local economy at Blacksnape since only 34 per cent of those engaged in employment in 1871 worked in textiles, although this rose to 45 per cent by 1881. Nevertheless, the textile industry was still relatively more important to these communities than it was to the cotton towns of east Lancashire, where approximately one-third of the working population was engaged in textile manufacture.

Between one-third and two-thirds of those engaged in textiles in 1871 could no longer be identified as living in the townships in 1881. Change of name for females at marriage was no doubt a significant contributory factor for the apparent absence, since it was in the main working age group of textile workers that marriage was most common. Nevertheless, many cotton operatives leaving the townships between 1871 and 1881 have been traced to their destinations and their occupations identified in 1881. Substantial numbers of those leaving the four townships were still working in textiles elsewhere in 1881, the majority of which were 'cotton weavers'.

The age profiles in 1871 for the total population of the townships, and the profiles of the cohorts leaving each township between 1871 and 1881 were almost mirror images. Those leaving the townships comprised between two-thirds and three-quarters of persons less than 35 years of age. The average ages of both sexes leaving were similar and these were virtually the same as those in 1881 for the nearby towns of Blackburn, Darwen and Oswaldtwistle, this suggests that these rural communities were not dominated by specific age groups. Therefore, it was mainly a cross-section of the communities' age structures that was relocating.

Historians have raised opposing views as to whether out-migrants moved in family groups or as single people. The big question is, what is a 'family', and therefore, how can a family movement be measured? Where a nuclear house-hold moved as a combined unit, the process was straightforward but when the household movements were divided, the process of establishing movement configuration becomes problematic and arbitrary decisions become necessary. Examples encountered were when one parent relocated and the other remained in the family home, and this sometimes included a split of the children. Occasionally, both parents moved and left some children with older siblings or even grandparents, in other instances family members moved to different destinations. There were an enormous number of combinations, and this necessitated a simplified strategy in order to assess approximate trends.

The following methodology was used in this study. Where a husband and wife apparently moved together and there were no children they have been classified as a family. Where only one person was living in a dwelling, this was classified as single person movement as were non-nuclear relatives along with lodgers and boarders. In households, where there were split movements the majority leaving or remaining was treated as 'family', and the minority as single. However, the timing of moves also presented difficulties since accuracy cannot be determined for less than a single decade.

Analysis of family/single movements, using the census, can only determine that family members moved during a specific decade, although movement to the same destination probably indicates that movement occurred at the same time.

Using this notion it appeared that over three-quarters of the total departures from the townships were in family units. Over one-quarter of the total migrants comprised parents in family units, unmarried family members of 15 years or over accounted for about one-fifth and the majority of the remainder consisted of children less than 15 years. The average ages of unmarried members, over 15 years of age were in their late 20s, except in Yate and Pickup Bank where the average was 23 years. Single individuals departing accounted for less than one-quarter of the total 'out-migrants'. Therefore, a significant proportion of family members was still single, which was not surprising since the expected average age of marriage for the period in these townships was over 25 years. These findings accord with those of Pooley and Turnbull, who claimed that 'the majority of young adults moved in family groupings'.[9]

Analysis has shown a correlation between the average ages of those leaving the townships and the extent to which they could be traced at a destination; the younger the age, the greater the incidence of a trace, which probably points to death being at least one reason for negative returns. Moreover, in all townships except Yate and Pickup Bank the incidence of tracing male textile workers was higher than for their female counterparts, which supports the notion that females appeared to have left a township when the actual reason was change of name through marriage. Although death and female marriage prevented identification it is also almost certain that ambiguities in both the CEBs and *LDS–RF* contributed to failure in numerous instances.

It has been shown that the occupations of people moving were mainly textile workers, the majority of whom were weavers. Those wishing to continue in weaving only needed to move short distances to nearby 'cotton towns' where rapid growth in population and textile activity was occurring and a consequent high demand for labour.

Turning to the investigation of specific destinations for out-migrants between 1871 and 1881, the main objective has been to establish whether movements were short-distance, towards 'cotton towns' and hence in search of employment. According to the Registrar Generals' marginal notes in 1871 population increases in the nearby 'cotton towns' of Oswaldtwistle, Darwen, Livesey and Witton near Blackburn were mainly due to the erection of new weaving sheds causing in-migration of workers from the surrounding areas.[10] Moreover, the census referred to the rural townships losing population, and this stated it was due to 'migration to the manufacturing districts' and 'disappearance of handloom weavers'.[11]

Migrational patterns of major outward movements relating to this study have been illustrated in cartographic format, divided into proximity zones relative to the townships of Eccleshill and Yate and Pickup Bank (Map 3.2A & B, Table 3.4).

Blacksnape and Hoddlesden have been excluded since they were districts within Darwen and the majority of movements are likely to have been between the village areas and town areas. The zoning system used classifies the townships with common boundaries to the township of study as inner zone. The next group of townships further from the study area but which have common boundaries with the inner zone are classified as intermediate zone, and townships beyond this zone but still within the county of Lancashire have been classified outer zone. For migration outside of Lancashire but within England the classification is other counties and British Isles for Ireland, Scotland and Wales. No emigrants were identified from the selected townships as leaving the United Kingdom.

Analysis confirmed the main patterns of outward movements were of a very short-distance nature, and by far the majority of destinations were within Lancashire. There was no-one relocating beyond the county boundary. Of those identified departing by far the majority were residing in nearby cotton towns, such as Blackburn, Darwen and Oswaldtwistle, these towns frequently having a

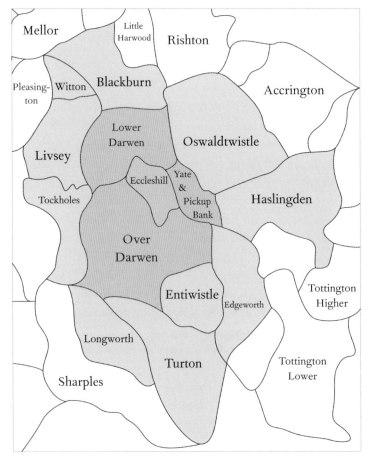

MAP 3.2A.

Key:
Reference township   Pink
Inner zone   Blue
Intermediate zone   Green

To be read in conjunction with table 3.4.

MAP 3.2B.

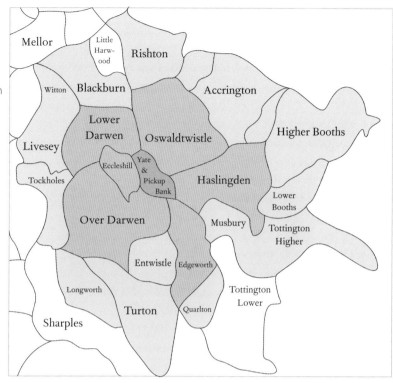

Key:

Reference township   Pink
Inner zone   Blue
Intermediate zone   Green

To be read in conjunction
with table 3.4.

Table 3.4. *Destination of Inhabitants Leaving between 1871 and 1881*

Most people
leaving the rural
communities
were moving
into nearby
towns in order
to work in the
textile industry.

	Eccleshill	%	Yate & Pickup Bank	%
Inner zone townships	Darwen	56.0	Darwen	21.1
	Lower Darwen	2.3	Ecclshill	8.7
	Yate & Pickup Bank	8.3	Oswaldtwistle	35.5
			Other	4.9
	Total for zone	66.5	*Total for zone*	70.2
Intermediate zone townships	Blackburn	12.4	Blackburn	15.3
	Oswaldtwistle	20.2	Church	2.9
	Other	0.9	Other	0.4
	Total for zone	33.5		18.6
Outer zone townships	Lancashire	0.0	Lancashire	11.2
	Other counties	0.0	Other counties	0.0
	British Isles countries	0.0	British Isles countries	0.0
	Total for zone	0.0	*Total for zone*	11.2
	Total	100.0	*Total*	100.0

Sources: CEBs and LDS-RF

common boundary with the origin township. Additionally, significant numbers moved into intermediate zone 'cotton towns'. In both inner and intermediate zone movements, occupational opportunities for working in textiles appear to have been the main stimulus. However, out-migration was not confined to declining communities alone since it also occurred at Eccleshill with its expanding population, where just over half of destinations identified in 1881 were to the nearby cotton town of Darwen. Doherty found a similar trend occurring around Blackburn between 1851 and 1871, and pointed out those migrants from the adjacent townships accounted for most of the non-native population in the town.[12] It is evident, therefore, that people from these villages engaged mainly in short-distance movements and indeed no movement from Eccleshill occurred beyond the intermediate zone boundary. From Yate and Pickup Bank 89 per cent moved to either the inner or intermediate, and the remainder to the outer zone.[13] The occupations of those traced to the outer zones were variable, the most common being colliers, domestic servants and textile workers, but they were in very small numbers. The overwhelming out-migration from the case study townships was to the cotton towns of Blackburn, Darwen and Oswaldtwistle where members of families were often engaged in some aspect of textiles manufacturing. Therefore, the findings agree with the Registrar General's notes of 1871 and the findings of other historians.

However, the above observations refer to out-migration only from the various villages, and there are no references to the possibility, indeed the likelihood of 'counter-flow', as expressed by Ravenstein, Redford, and Pooley and Turnbull. Nevertheless, there is evidence of migrational counter-flows occurring in the 'villages' concerned, since these are indicated by destinations derived from the *LDS–RF* and places of birth in the CEBs, as will be shown below.[14]

People moving into the townships (arrivals)

Whilst people were leaving the townships in the latter half of the nineteenth century there were also counter flows. In 1881, the communities consisted of between two-thirds and four-fifths of inhabitants who had arrived in the townships during the previous decade; these consisted of both those born elsewhere and return migrants (Figure 3.4 & Table 3.5).

TABLE 3.5.   *Occupational proportions of in-migrants 1871 to 1881*

People arriving in the townships were being occupied in the cotton industry at both Hoddlesden and Waterside.

Township	Agriculture	Textiles	Other	Total employed
	Arrival cohort			
Blacksnape	7.9	30.3	35.8	73.9
Eccleshill	8.8	31.1	25.0	65.0
Hoddlesden	7.4	38.4	27.1	72.9
Yate & Pickup Bank	9.2	31.2	14.4	54.7

Sources: CEBs.

FIGURE 3.4.   *Inhabitants arriving between 1871 & 1881*

Apart from people leaving the townships there was a strong influx albeit in smaller numbers than those leaving. Many of the inward movements were return migrants.

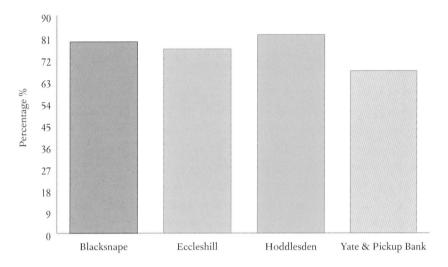

By 1881 the actual numbers occupied as a proportion of the total population at Blacksnape had increased by nearly two-fifths during the previous decade and there was a marginal increase at Eccleshill. In contrast there was a slight fall at Hoddlesden but a large fall of 30 per cent in number at Yate and Pickup Bank. However, because of variations in total decennial populations for each township in 1871 and 1881 there was only a marginal increase in the proportions occupied at the end of the decade except for Yate and Pickup Bank where the proportion fell by ten per cent. This was generally reflected in slightly larger numbers of arrivals being employed than for those departing, although this was not so in textiles with the exception of Blacksnape. Therefore, it is evident that earnings related employment opportunities were receding in textiles but otherwise increasing in most of the townships, and the following section explores this broad trend in order to establish whether it affected all occupational categories in which arrivals were engaged. Although there were strong employment attractions for people to leave these townships there were also 'pull forces' attracting people to move into both Blacksnape and Eccleshill since arrivals outstripped departures. At Hoddlesden those leaving and arriving were in virtual equilibrium whilst at Yate and Pickup Bank the numbers of arrivals represented about 86 per cent of the departures.

In agriculture, the absolute number of farms and farmers remained fairly constant between 1871 and 1881 except for Blacksnape where the small numbers more than doubled during the decade. The number of farmers arriving in Eccleshill, Hoddlesden and Yate and Pickup Bank were virtually equal to those departing, which generally indicates no more than a change in farm tenancy, but at Blacksnape arrivals outstripped departures by more than two to one. Because of census interpretational difficulties with agricultural occupations relating to farmers' family members, investigation here would be speculative and has not been pursued. Agricultural labourers entering Eccleshill and Yate and Pickup Bank were insufficient in number to replace those departing the workforce, so redesignation must have taken place. In both Blacksnape and Hoddlesden movements were negligible.

The occupationally specific nature of migration was reflected in some occupations being recruited locally whilst others, particularly those of a specialised nature were often recruited from areas where there was a reservoir of experience. Industrial occupational categories of this nature comprised extraction, general labouring, paper manufacture, iron foundry work and textiles. Characteristics of workers in each industry varied. Extractive industries were male dominated and located in all four townships; similar numbers arriving replaced those leaving between 1871 and 1881. Employment in this industry was fairly buoyant, comprising both natives and those of short-distance origin. General labourers in the 1870s increased in numbers except for those in Hoddlesden, which numerically remained the same, they were mainly male and boosted by arrivals. Employment in paper manufacture and iron foundry work occurred mainly in Eccleshill. Workers in this industry increased over the decade, although the migrational portrait was different to other occupations, nearly half had been drawn from beyond Lancashire and most of those from within county had been born in the intermediate zone.[15]

Service sector occupations were widely dispersed and this made trends and comparisons difficult. Although the total numbers for the four townships remained steady between 1871 and 1881 it was a sector displaying high mobility, and trends between the individual townships were erratic. At Eccleshill and Yate and Pickup Bank departures strongly outstripped arrivals, whilst at the latter service workers declined by nearly half over the period and this was mirrored with arrival numbers being less than half of those departing.

The major employment sector within all villages was textiles. In three of the villages the total numbers employed between 1871 and 1881 remained steady, but at Yate and Pickup Bank there was around one-third decline, and this was reflected in the numbers of cotton workers arriving being about half of those leaving. The majority of cotton workers arriving were generally in the younger age bands and dominated by females. This occupation is dealt with in greater detail at chapter 5.

Analysis of whether inward movements of people were in single units or family groups is complex as demonstrated by the following examples. First, living at Eccleshill in 1881, were the Cartridge family comprising the head occupied as a railway platelayer who had been born in London and he married a woman born in Eccleshill. They had a daughter one year old whose place of birth was given as Over Darwen. This appears in the census as a family arriving between 1871 and 1881 when the more likely scenario was that this couple met when the nearby railway line was under construction and officially opened in 1876. It is therefore feasible that the head was part of the railway labour force, the wife was a native girl and following marriage a child was born also as native but the birth was registered in nearby Darwen. If this assumption is correct then this family only accounts for one single inward movement and not a family.

Second, John Yates and his wife were both born in Oswaldtwistle, but were living in Yate and Pickup Bank by 1881. Living in the same household was a one-year-old son and mother-in-law, both born in Yate and Pickup Bank. The options are that the son was probably born after the parents' arrival, and the married couple could have arrived to live with the wife's mother, although neither the wife nor mother-in-law lived there in 1871, so either two or four people could have arrived as a family.

In spite of anomalies, the methodology used for analysing family/single movements was similar to that used for those departing between 1871 and 1881 but instead of using the 1871 census transcript, the 1881 version was substituted. The results demonstrated that the majority of arrivals were in family units similar to the departures. The cohorts arriving in Blacksnape, Hoddlesden and Yate and Pickup Bank consisted of four to five times more individuals moving in family groups than as single people whilst at Eccleshill the ratio was a staggering seven fold moving as families and most of the arrivals numerically were children. In the singles group small proportions arrived without spouse that were or had been previously married such as, widows, widowers and elderly relatives. However, the majority as expected was unmarried and mainly adolescents or young adults.

Analysis of origins for those arriving has been confined to Eccleshill and Yate and Pickup Bank for people of 10 years of age and over in order to avoid the combination of native and non-native children below this age. Also as stated above Blacksnape and Hoddlesden were excluded from this analysis since they were districts of Darwen. In addition, because origins were scattered, a summary of findings has been made and limited to townships from which most movements occurred. Arrivals born within the county were classified into four zones in a configuration similar to that used for the departure cohorts. It will be shown that this zoning classification demonstrated considerable variations between each of the two townships (Table 3.6).

TABLE 3.6.   *Places of birth of arrivals >= 10 years between 1871 and 1881.*

Place of birth	Eccleshill %	Yate & Pickup Bank %
Native	9	50
Inner zone	33	32
Intermediate zone	12	6
Outer zone	24	10
Other counties and British Isles	22	2

Sources: CEBs.

The majority of people arriving in the townships were either natives returning or those from very short distance locations.

Urban to rural movements towards the townships were less pronounced than rural to urban movement. Results for those entering the townships showed that with only one exception all of the in-migrants had been born within the British Isles,[16] and that numbers emanating from Ireland, Scotland and Wales were very small. The proportions born in counties outside of Lancashire were also relatively small, ranging from less than 2 per cent in Yate and Pickup Bank, albeit 22 per cent in Eccleshill. The higher figure in Eccleshill was due to the paper manufacturing and an iron works industry attracting specialist labour. Those arriving from the outer zone but within Lancashire varied; at Yate and Pickup Bank it was 10 per cent, but at Eccleshill around one-quarter came from scattered locations within the county. Eccleshill had local industry in contrast to Yate and Pickup Bank and this was probably the reason for the difference. Only a few arrivals came from the intermediate zones, Eccleshill experiencing the largest numbers arriving from the towns of Blackburn and Oswaldtwistle, but this only amounted to 12 per cent of the total arrivals. At both Eccleshill and Yate and Pickup Bank one-third of arrivals were from the inner zones yet they were fundamentally different, since the former was experiencing population increases and the latter declines. The largest contributors were 23 per cent from Darwen to Eccleshill and 19 per cent from Oswaldtwistle to Yate and Pickup Bank.

Although the above movements were significant, the most striking aspect regarding those arriving is the high proportion of return migrants. They were people not present in the townships in 1871 but who had been born there. Eccleshill had only one-tenth of arrivals born as natives (return migrants) but

Yate and Pickup Bank had 50 per cent. However, these numbers were again almost certainly inflated by unidentified married women. This latter aspect is an unfortunate reoccurring problem since the sources to solve the matter are not available and it is compounded by also affecting the out-migrant results.

A comparison of places of birth for the arrival cohort with those for the departure cohort between 1871 and 1881 demonstrated a changing configuration. In Yate and Pickup Bank, which experienced population decline, natives departing represented 67 per cent and at Eccleshill where population was rising it was 15 per cent of those 10 years and older in 1871. Yet, the return migrants of native birth in the smaller arrival cohort ranged from 10 per cent in Eccleshill to 50 per cent in Yate and Pickup Bank. This suggests more natives were leaving than returning in both townships. Although at Eccleshill there was increasing population and employment opportunities but Yate and Pickup Bank was of course different.

What is abundantly clear from this study is that the majority of movement in east Lancashire was hardly 'migration', but more of a short distance localised shift from a rural community to a nearby 'cotton town' in search of employment. This micro-study of migration has overwhelmingly demonstrated the dangers of large-scale generalisations used in many earlier studies. The characteristics of each of the case study townships have been shown to differ in some respects and therefore each township had its own individual portrait and uniqueness.

Daveyfield Farm, Eccleshill.
Built early eighteenth century
was a 22 acres farm in the
mid-nineteenth century.
Situated adjacent to the
Roman Road at Eccleshill.
Note the Tudor Doorway.
Listed Building.

CHAPTER FOUR

Earning a living — Agriculture

The characteristics of agriculture in east Lancashire

I N A S T U D Y O F nineteenth century Lancashire, Anderson wrote 'patterns [of agriculture]…for rural Lancashire were almost certainly not typical of agricultural areas in Britain as a whole because the whole organisation of agriculture in the Lancashire communities was very different from elsewhere'.[1] Agriculture in east Lancashire was characterised by small family run farms comprising grasslands, mainly used for feeding milk-producing cattle. Dairy produce was then sold to local inhabitants and people in nearby 'cotton towns'.

The uplands of east Lancashire have always had harsh natural conditions, never suitable for arable cultivation. The poor quality of the soil has been remarked upon over many centuries. In 1609 tenants of the Honor of Clitheroe recorded, 'extreme barrenness of that soil and coldness of that county', which was not conducive to arable cultivation.[2] Holt, who was commissioned by the Board of Agriculture to carry out a survey of agriculture in Lancashire in 1795 wrote, 'Blackburn, Clitheroe, Haslingden and similar townships, were rugged, interspersed with many rivulets, and had a thin stratum of upper soil'.[3] Binns, around mid-nineteenth century referred to the higher ground of east Lancashire as being, 'soil of a wet moory nature altering between clay, shale and peat inclined to grow rushes and heath'.[4] The Ordnance Survey map shows east Lancashire's altitudes to be mostly between 300 and 1000 feet above sea level.[5] At these high altitudes, soils are as little as two inches in depth and contain minimal nutrients.[6]

Furthermore, because of industrialisation during the nineteenth century, smoke emission from factory chimneys caused atmospheric pollution. Rain contaminated with sulphur dioxide from smoke caused acidic ground conditions, as did rain run-off from the peaty moor lands. This was detrimental even to pasture land but the use of lime increased the pH and improved soil quality for both grazing and haymaking.[7] By late nineteenth century smoke emissions were beginning to form a cloud over the east of the county reducing the already limited exposure of 1,000 to 1,100 hours of sunshine per year compared with 1750 hours in southern England.[8] In the mid-nineteenth century Binns wrote 'the summer temperature in Lancashire is 6 degrees Fahrenheit below that of London'. Timmins in the late twentieth century claimed that the soils 'were too cold, damp and acidic, and the climate was too harsh, to permit large-scale arable cultivation.'[9] The soil in Blacksnape, Eccleshill, Hoddlesden and Yate and Pickup Bank was clayey and the land, as elsewhere in east Lancashire was generally only suitable for pasturing and meadow. Nevertheless, the subsoil varied consisting of for example Coal Measures in Yate Bank but in Pickup Bank it was Millstone Grit.[10]

Although natural conditions in east Lancashire were not conducive to growing crops, the high rainfall ensured a plentiful supply of grass for pasture, and so hilly east Lancashire was destined to be predominantly pastoral farming.[11] Nevertheless, the land was sectionalised. Effectively the high extensive moors of east Lancashire grew cotton grass and heather that primarily accommodated sheep; the middle slopes below the level of the moors with thin layers of soil allowed the growth of coarse grass and formed poor to average pasture for grazing cattle whilst the lower land with more depth of soil provided better quality pasture and meadow land that could also support some arable cultivation.[12] Historians such as Thirsk have generalised that such conditions were most suitable for 'cattle and sheep rearing, sometimes with dairying',[13] and Aikin, referring more specifically to the area of study stated the 'wetness of the climate is unfortunate to the growth of corn... But is serviceable to pasturage...'[14] and with reference to Rossendale, Tupling observed 'the occupiers of land, small as well as great, had always been graziers rather than corn growers because of the exigencies of climate and soil'.[15] Therefore, the 'forests' of east Lancashire were pastoral areas and arable crops were almost limited to oats and barley, which grow in wet climates.[16]

For many centuries, agriculture in east Lancashire comprised small farms juxtaposed with domestic textile manufacture. These small farms were incapable of fully supporting the farmer and his family, so supplementary income was obtained from textiles. Fletcher commented that in 1760 the 'farmer weaver was the most widespread class of landowner (probably occupier)',[17] and the following passage appeared in a local newspaper:

> The early cotton industry in this district was closely associated with farming; spinning and weaving being carried on alongside tending the cattle and the crops.[18]

Reference to a few inventories shows the close link between farming and textile manufacture during the seventeenth and eighteenth centuries. The inventory of John Yates at Yate Bank in 1668 was valued at £35 2s. 2d.[19] His farm stock was valued at £20 19s. 4d.; just over half of the total valuation, plus stocks of woollen yarn and four wheels [spinning] indicated an engagement in textiles. The inventory of Thomas Yates of Yate Bank, deceased in 1707,[20] showed one cow and 'a pare od looms', valued at £2 15s. 0d. within a £17 15s. 8d. inventory total. Richard Rothwell of Woodhead [Yate Bank] in Rossendale died in 1711,[21] he owned three cows…s[t]erk, hay, corn, plow and a cheese press valued at £19 out of the £29 11s. 0d. total valuation. In addition there was 'one pairs of looms with all th[e] furniture to the belonging' and two wheels.

The versatility of people earning a living in these villages during the seventeenth and eighteenth centuries is further indicated in the following inventories. Randle Astley died at Eccleshill in 1641; he had interests in 'husbandary', 'wollen manufacture' and 'brewing beer'.[22] William Duxbury at Pickup Bank in 1758 possessed 'Husband Gears', seed corn, cheese press, 'Looms in the Shop and utensells'.[23] There is also evidence of farms where the owners were men of means, Davy Field Farm being an example of a substantial and spacious farmhouse, with a Tudor style doorway and a date stone inscribed 1723, see frontispiece to chapter. However the property was probably built prior to that indicated.

The above inventories along with many others provide evidence of methods by which inhabitants of the villages survived from small-scale farming or farming plus supplements, particularly textiles, prior to mechanisation in the textile industry. They were self supporting, supplying their own food from the land and animals, producing cloth for both personal use and obtaining remuneration through textile middlemen. These few examples along with the inventories of Ralph Almond, tradesman in Yate Bank valued at £307 10s. 5d. and that for William Fish, chapman at Eccleshill valued at £298 6s. 0d., also illustrates the variable wealth that existed in these rural communities. Whilst there were a few fairly wealthy chapmen, inventories show the majority of workers had to share living space with a working area and material storage.[24] What are not known are the circumstances of the proletariat living in these communities for which probate records are not extant.

From the late eighteenth century, early specialisation in textile manufacture provided higher earnings that led to population growth, which resulted in a rising market for farm produce and better opportunities for farmers. However, both Holt and Aitkin agreed that farmers remained inefficient in their approaches to business,[25] although as pointed out by Dickson in 1815 opportunities existed for selling produce, 'milk, butter and eggs' as a result of the increasing numbers of landless cotton workers.[26] While Binns observed, around the mid-nineteenth century, the closeness of textiles and agriculture was typical of east Lancashire, and quotes as an example an advertisement in the *Blackburn Mail*, September 1825 for the sale of a farm, which had a 'warehouse suitable for a manufacturer', and additionally, 'milk and butter may be disposed of in the neighbourhood'.[27] Also, Cooke Taylor who travelled through the manufacturing districts of Lancashire in the late 1830s and early 1840s observed that, many farmers lacked initiative but they had an

> ... insatiable market at their door for everything a farm produces, the very flowers in the farmers garden being convertible into money, and having the advantage besides of inexhaustible supplies of manure from the numerous manufacturing towns...villages everywhere scattered over the country to counter-balance such incentives to improvement.[28]

Furthermore, Rothwell reporting on the agriculture of the county also around the mid-century wrote, 'the district...is principally occupied as small dairy farms, there being a great demand for milk and butter; and not much adopted from the nature of its soil and climate, for arable cultivation'.[29] The minimal extent of arable land in east Lancashire compared to the rest of Lancashire and England generally is clearly shown in the 1870s Agricultural Parish Returns (APRs). In east Lancashire the emphasis was very much towards meadow and pasture cultivation.

The strong association between agriculture and textiles provided a ready-made market for the small farmer supplying dairy products to the nearby towns for which there was large demand. This allowed farming to be a profitable business, as we shall see below.

Fletcher referred to increases in farm stock and production and wrote:

> By 1860 domestic textile manufacture had well nigh dispersed and the holding, still small, produced milk and butter, not in the small amounts adequate for home and neighbours, but, with the aid of purchased feeding stuffs and heavier stocking, in the increased quantities required by the growing factory population.[30]

Therefore, contemporary views of agricultural in east Lancashire before mid-nineteenth century agree that small-scale farming was closely allied to textile manufacture and that the farming was different to farming elsewhere in England. Moreover, the views of contemporaries also imply that east Lancashire was relatively backwards with respect to agricultural organisation and so were the farmers themselves. In contrast historians have frequently considered that larger farms elsewhere to be responsible for the majority of productivity increases. For example, Chambers and Mingay considered that amalgamating farms produced 'larger and more efficient units' and small farms 'lacked the economies of scale, the technical efficiency, capital resources and flexibility'.[31] Although being criticised for backwardness, the east Lancashire farmers were unable to change either climatic conditions or terrain and there was no practical way of increasing soil thickness but nevertheless they progressed.

Small farms in east Lancashire were concentrated in an industrial sector and a part of the country that experienced significant demands for dairy produce, which these farmers were better placed to meet than farmers in arable areas. Dairying close to large cities generally was in retreat until the late nineteenth century, since cities were dependent on urban cow keepers until transportation was sufficiently developed to bring in liquid milk from a distance.[32] Instead the emergence of liquid milk production occurred in rural areas close to industrial towns. Nevertheless, Hall noted that Lancashire's farming was 'not very impressive', even by the early twentieth century, but also conceded that it could 'continue to compete with big herds at a distance, however organised they may be'.[33]

Dairy farming with a ready market in nearby towns flourished in east Lancashire, it was practicable and did not require large amounts of capital injections for improvements such as was necessary for arable cultivation elsewhere in the country. This trend continued in the second half of the nineteenth century with farmers meeting the challenge of supplying dairy produce to urban markets. This demanded extending pasture acreages, albeit often marginally, which facilitated expanding the herd. In parallel there was increased productivity achieved by both intensification and progressive specialisation, which entailed farmers purchasing special breeds of shorthorn 'flying herds' from stock merchants in other parts of the country.[34] Dickson noted that milk farms near towns in Lancashire 'buy in their cows when pretty far advanced with calf; and as soon as they drop the calves, they make a point of disposing of them [calves] to the feeders, who constantly keep a large number for the purposes of fattening them'.[35] In addition, farmers fed cattle on cheap manufactured cattle feed and used cheap or even free nutrients for feeding the pastures. These additives contributed to higher yields of milk per cow. As noted by Winstanley, 'there is plenty to suggest, therefore, that dairying in the North was both progressive and productive and that it achieved rates of increased productivity throughout the nineteenth century which matched, or even surpassed those to be found further south'. This occurrence he pointed out was, 'unlike most of the arable sector, however, there was no significant technological innovations in dairying which necessitated substantial capital investment on the part of the landlords'.[36]

The APRs for 1870s confirm that Lancashire possessed a greater proportion of permanent grass than was average for the country.[37] Fletcher found that in the early 1870s, 91 per cent of farmland in east Lancashire was under permanent grass, and consequently predominantly suited to grazing rather than arable cultivation.[38]

Cattle numbers in east Lancashire between 1870 and 1913 show that overall numbers were rising steadily until the 1890s but then they gradually declined until the Great War, at which point numbers were marginally fewer than they were in 1870.[39] However, the trends for cows and heifers were different to those for total cattle, since their numbers also increased between 1870 and the early 1890s, followed by relative stability until 1906 after which decline occurred although numbers remained significantly above those in 1870. The maintenance of milk stock numbers suggests a preference by east Lancashire farmers for milk producing cattle rather than beef. However, the rates of increase in milk cattle numbers up to the 1890s was more rapid than the rates of increase in permanent grass, the result of which could only be intensification of cattle per unit area of land.[40] This higher density farming based on dairy cattle points to farmers concentrating on milk production in order to market liquid milk and probably other dairy produce to the burgeoning urban populations created by growth in textile manufacture. In order to cope with the high intensity stocking and maintain high yields of milk production throughout the year, it became necessary to feed the land and the cattle with supplementary nourishment. Animal feed could be obtained cheaply and reduced the need for fodder production.[41] Encouragement of grass growth, feeding the cattle to increase milk production throughout the year and increasing cattle stocks with little increase of acreage or overhead costs resulted in increased productivity, profitability and innovative farming.

Other common farm animals in the east of the county were sheep and pigs. The former dramatically declined in numbers from the mid-1870s to the mid-1880s and remained at a fairly low level until World War I. In contrast, pigs increased almost continually from the early 1880s and reached a peak in 1911, but this was then followed by decline.[42]

Fletcher also noted that increased numbers of poultry assisted in affording farmers in Lancashire immunity from distress during the Great Depression, although he acknowledged milk production was of paramount importance.[43] Nevertheless, poultry was common both as free range and wholesale stocks, the former being generally linked to the kitting process where eggs, butter and cheese could be sold during the daily rounds but the larger poultry farms sold to wholesalers and retailers.[44] Hens could be kept in temporary buildings and on very small acreages, therefore very little capital was involved, furthermore it is likely, there were many kept in no more that a rear yard for family use. Both milk producers and specialist poultry-keepers in east Lancashire were able to take advantage of local market demand in the burgeoning textile towns for both eggs and poultry.[45] Fletcher concluded that, 'Associated with rising income was the growing preference for protein rather than starch, for livestock products rather than cereals and potatoes'. The major change in diet was from that of the agricultural labourer comprising oatmeal, coarse bread, cheese and fat bacon to the preference of textile workers consisting of tea with milk, white bread and butter, meat and eggs. [46]

Prosperity for Lancashire farmers was linked to growth of industry and allied consumer demands, argued Fletcher,[47] and because the population of Lancashire rose by 50 per cent between the 1860s and 1890s a proportional demand for foodstuffs could be expected.[48] During this period Wood suggested that factory based cotton wages rose by 25 per cent whilst Layton claims retail prices generally fell by 26 per cent.[49] From these figures Fletcher concluded real income in east Lancashire increased even faster than during the Golden Age, which made milk more affordable. Furthermore, at a conservative estimate, there was an 88 per cent rise in milk consumption between the 1860s and 1890s,[50] which has been endorsed by Winstanley who has shown that because of this demand from this ever-increasing market farms grew into attractive businesses, especially in the latter part of the century.[51] Moreover, Fletcher suggested 'that the demand for lamb, eggs and butter may have risen to a similar…extent'.[52] Nevertheless, in spite of increasing dairy product output there was only a small increase in the agricultural acreage of Lancashire over the last three decades of the nineteenth century. Therefore, increasing demand was supplied from intensification of the existing system,[53] and this afforded immunity to Lancashire farmers from distress during the Great Depression, which they owed to

> … the keeping of livestock, sheep, pigs and poultry: a reliance on grassland and purchased feed rather than the plough; the existence of small farms largely independent of hired labour; the presence of adjacent… markets; the practice of direct sales to the customers; and freedom of the tenant from restrictive covenants.[54]

From Fletcher's findings, it can be deduced that east Lancashire farmers were not backward, but rather they seized the opportunity to supply a nearby market demand for dairy produce. This was achieved without large capital expenditure and the engagement of large amounts of labour. More recently, Winstanley has provided a thesis on the theme of enterprise by east Lancashire farmers in the late nineteenth century and the engagement of their household members in a domestic economy. This has extended the work of Fletcher,[55] and banished the idea that family farms were 'inefficient and backward',[56] unlike the views expressed by commentators in the early nineteenth century.

Both Fletcher and Winstanley have strongly linked the survival and success of these farms to the burgeoning industrialisation and urbanisation of the nineteenth century. Winstanley has stressed the importance of survival depending upon members of farming families having to work in other occupations,[57] since farms were located close to textile towns and this provided farmers with an opportunity to put their children into factory employment, particularly weaving, in order to supplement household income.

The characteristics of agriculture in the townships

Tupling pointed out that land fragmentation in Rossendale was noticeably greater in the nineteenth century than in the seventeenth century, the causation being by parental partible inheritance to their off-spring. This resulted in families lacking sufficient subsistence from agriculture alone and needing to combine farming with domestic textile manufacture.[58] In the seventeenth and eighteenth centuries this consisted of farming comprising mixed arable, dairy, beef and sheep along with handloom weaving.[59]

Lark Hill Farm

Farm sizes in the case-study townships were typical of the area and overwhelmingly in the 5 to 50 acre category, although there were variations. In most years investigated more than two-thirds of farms were between 5 and 50 acres, which in some instances rose to a staggering 100 per cent. These proportions,

Stand Farm

Standhill Farm

Top o' the Meadow Farm

These four farms were quite small; Lark Hill Farm, Hoddlesden was situated close to the old packhorse route as it circumscribes the village of Hoddlesden to the east. In 1861 the farm income was secured from around 12 acres but five children were receiving wages from employment other than farming. By mid-twentieth century the residents consisted of husband, wife and one daughter all working the farm and dependent on farm income alone. They were milk producers supplying dairy produce by horse and milk float to some dwellings in Hoddlesden but the main outlets were in the town of Darwen. Stand Farm, Hoddlesden with 14 acres had one son and three daughters apparently working on the farm in late nineteenth century but this was clearly uneconomical. Standhill Farm, Hoddlesden had around eleven acres of land but income in 1871 was mainly dependent on the Fish families five children working outside of farming. In mid-twentieth century the farmer 'Dick' Hargreaves acquired income by using a horse and cart for moving goods locally. Top O'th Meadow Farm, Hoddlesden is situated on the old road now Harwoods Lane from Hoddlesden village to the Roman Road between Ribchester and Manchester. The 32 acres was rented in the nineteenth century to the Entwistle family who had three children working elsewhere. During the mid-twentieth century the farmer was a William Jenkinson who supplied milk by horse and milk float to many of the village houses in Hoddlesden in order to support his wife and son.

with a few exceptions, were at least equal to those found by Fletcher for the whole of east Lancashire in both 1870 and 1913 and the 70 per cent found by Winstanley for the district of Blackburn in 1881.[60] Holdings of less than 5 acres and over 50 acres were comparatively few in number.

The above estimates based on census data relate to households where the head was classed as a 'farmer'. It is clear from field investigation and O.S. maps that those occupying less than 5 acres of land usually had only a domestic property and no outbuildings.[61] This was particularly noticeable in Yate and Pickup Bank from 1871 onwards. These very small 'farms' could only support a few chickens, goats, pigs, a sheep or cow at the very most, which could have been housed in temporary wooden sheds but there is no evidence for this. Therefore, these small 'farms' were unable to provide a living for one person let alone a family, and in some respects these could hardly be called farms. However, as pointed out by Winstanley farm sizes alone 'take no account of the quality, location or productive capacity of the holdings, nor of the fact that the families…varied considerably in the degree to which they were dependent on land for their income'.[62]

Nevertheless, during the latter part of the nineteenth century opportunities

Near Scotland Farm Hoddlesden. In 1871 Thomas Duxbury was apparently managing this 17 acre farm alone.

Mid Scotland Farm, Hoddlesden. Betty Duxbury and her son were managing this farm of 15 acres in 1851, although two other sons were working as colliers and two cotton-weaving daughters contributed supplementary income.

arose for some farmers to expand their acreages in order to acquire larger incomes, particularly at Hoddlesden. During this period the village was undergoing rapid change owing to industrial developments, which led to growth of population along with housing provision for workers. These features are given detailed consideration in later chapters. Nevertheless, the impact of these changes altered the configuration of the number of farms and farm sizes although the majority remained in the less than 50 acres size band. Land required for housing and industrial development in and around the centre of the village was acquired from farmland and the abolition of a few farms. In addition the burgeoning population was being supplied with dairy produce and this encouraged farmers to expand their existing acreages and stock. Examples of this occurred at Holker House Farm, Hoddlesden where the acreage increased from 44 in 1851 to 84 acres in 1871 and between mid-century and The Great War there was also expansion at Lark Hill from 15 to 28 acres, the Valuation Book stated this farm was owned by Ranken in 1914; Stand 14 to 44 acres; Stand Hill 11 to 29 acres and Top O'th Meadow 10 to 32 acres, all three of these farms being owned by Carus in 1914. During the same period there was also change at Near Scotland Farm from 15 to 28 acres, Mid-Scotland Farm from 25 to 39 acres, Fatten House Farm 8 to 13 acres, but Far Scotland Farm was reduced from 18 to 13 acres. The first three farms were owned by the 'Ranken Exors' and the third by Rev. G. Rose[63] (Map 4.1).

Far Scotland Farm, Hoddlesden. William Yates and his wife managed this 19 acres farm alone in 1871. *Listed Building.*

Fatten Houses Farm, Hoddlesden. In mid-twentieth century James Townsend and family managed this 10 acres farm. He and his family kitted milk in the surrounding area including Hoddlesden village. They physically carried large kits of milk around the village supplying milk to each house on their round.

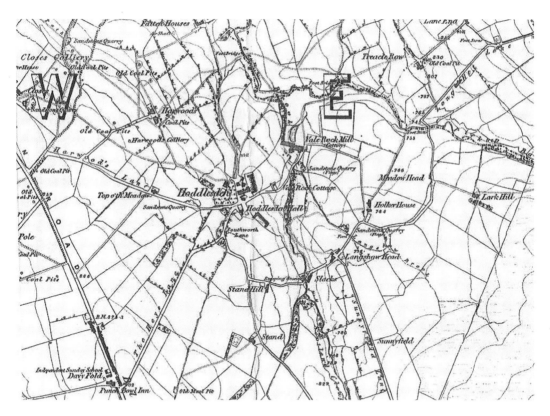

At Blacksnape, Eccleshill and Yate and Pickup Bank the picture is less clear. However, around 1914 Eccleshill had two unusually large farms for the district, namely Brocklehead with 96 acres and Manor House farm with 73 acres. The latter being situated adjacent to the Manor House noted in chapter 1. In contrast during the second half of the nineteenth century Scholes Fold Farm at Pickup Bank was reduced from 21 acres to 14 acres.

Opposite to the Handles Arms public house and adjacent to the old Manor House at Eccleshill is the Manor House Farm, which has now been converted to a residence. The census indicates that five members of the Bleazard family worked this 81 acres farm in the latter part of the nineteenth century. *Listed Building*.

Scholes Fold Farm, Pickup Bank. The farm acreage was 21 acres at mid-century but around 14 acres in 1881 and probably remained so in the twentieth century. However, during the latter period the Walsh family were supplementing farm income with a coal round encompassing delivering domestic coal to Hoddlesden and Pickup Bank from the Hoddlesden railway sidings. In addition they were engaged in delivering steam-coal to the largest factory in Hoddlesden village.

Occupiers of small farms in east Lancashire were usually tenants. From 1891, onwards the APRs provide details of either the number of owner/occupiers or those renting. During the 1890s, it was noted that at least 95 per cent of farms in Eccleshill and about three-quarters in Yate and Pickup Bank were rented.[64] Although similar details for Blacksnape and Hoddlesden are not available from this source the 1910 Finance Act Valuations show that at Blacksnape 66 per cent of the farms were rented and all of those at Hoddlesden.[65] The 1913 APR also provides a similar picture. This high incidence of renting farms was not only confined to these communities but it was widespread throughout east Lancashire.[66] The 1910 Valuation books show that no single person owned more than five farms in these villages; although most were local a few owners lived at Bolton and Preston.[67] The acreages of the total owner/occupied farmland in the selected townships were a small percentage of the entire farm acreage, except in Yate and Pickup Bank where it reached nearly one-third in 1895.

Evidence of agricultural practices in the townships before the nineteenth century is sparse. Although deeds and inventories for the seventeenth and eighteenth centuries support the existence of some upland arable farming, the impression is that it was on a very small scale and only sufficient to support local needs. An Indenture of 1771 showed that Daniel Yates, tenant of Holme Fold, Yate Bank, was only allowed to grow sufficient potatoes for his own small family. However, the Eccleshill tithe award for the mid-nineteenth century showed that there were nearly 39 acres of arable and a further 5 acres of arable and meadow combined which was about six per cent of the total farmland.[69] At Yate and Pickup

Holme Fold Farm, Pickup Bank. The date stone indicates the property had been built in 1771. The Almond family occupied this farm in 1881. It was a 10 acre farm clearly not large enough to support this family since the wife was occupied as a cotton weaver.[68]

Bank only 75 acres were tithed, 10 acres or two per cent of the total acreage was arable and the remainder meadow or pasture.[70] While sources for establishing types of cultivation in the case-study townships, even in the early nineteenth century are limited, nonetheless their histories point to mainly basic pastureland farming.

For late nineteenth century the APRs show that between 1877 and 1913 there was never more than a fraction of a percentage of land used for arable purposes, which was well below the 8.87 per cent found by Fletcher for the whole of east Lancashire in the 1870s.[71] No corn was grown and only a few potatoes in the 1870s and 1880s but none of the latter in the 1890. Cabbage was grown in 1877 and 1891 in Yate and Pickup Bank.

The case study townships were typical of east Lancashire in that land under grass was either used as fields for pasturing or meadows for producing hay in the summer and then presumably turning them into pastures following the harvesting of hay. The townships had a slight predominance of pasture over meadow acreage between the 1870s and 1913, and Yate and Pickup Bank had a larger proportion of moorland than was average for other townships in the county. The latter was mainly 'common' and largely suitable for sheep grazing,[72] and this allowed farmers who had been granted access a choice between limited dairy and sheep farming. Grasses under rotation were virtually non-existent.[73] This all indicates that farmers saw pasture farming to be the most profitable.

Cows were the most common farm animals in the townships during late nineteenth and early twentieth centuries. Here the trend was similar to that occurring in east Lancashire generally, that is an increase in cattle

Higher Grimhills Farm, Blacksnape. This was an eight-acre farm in 1851; two daughters being engaged as handloom weavers supported the household income. By 1871 the farm acreage had been increased to 17 acres, beyond this date records are not extant.

Hillock Farm, Blacksnape. At mid-nineteenth century this farm was a substantial 40 acres and had increased marginally to 50 acres by early twentieth century. At this time the farmer was a John Yates but the owner was the Rev. W. A. Duckworth.

numbers between the 1870s and 1890s but then instead of stabilising there was a decline to marginally smaller numbers in 1913 than there had been in 1877. At Eccleshill the milk stock remained steady apart from a slight fall just before the Great War, whilst Yate and Pickup Bank was exceptional since the total numbers of milking cows and heifers slowly declined from the 1870s. Here milking cows and those older than two years not in milk were in almost equal in numbers by 1913, indicating that stockbreeding became equally important to milk production, possibly because of the remoteness of the township from a cotton town. The trend at Blacksnape and Hoddlesden cannot be determined since statistics are an integral part of those assembled for Darwen, and this prevents analysis.

Intensity of cattle grazing in the townships between the 1870s and 1913 based on APR cattle numbers reveals a variation between 38 cows per 100 acres at Eccleshill and 57 cows per 100 acres at Yate and Pickup Bank, but these figures ignore the fact that grazing was also required for horses, and other animals. This intensity was much higher than the 34.4 cows per acre average in east Lancashire, in spite of the townships' higher ground and poor pastures.[74]

Milk production around 1870 averaged 433 gallons per cow per annum, according to Fletcher.[75] Therefore, the townships needed large potential outlets for disposing of liquid milk in the form of 'kitted milk'. Farmers at Blacksnape and Eccleshill could conveniently supply households in the village and parts of Darwen, farmers at Hoddlesden could supply mainly in the village itself and households at Darwen but Yate and Pickup Bank was probably less fortunate, having to compete with Hoddlesden farms but had the opportunity to supply Oswaldtwistle from Yate Bank.

Textile towns in east Lancashire were experiencing rapid population growth in late nineteenth century and there was also a *per capita* increase occurring in milk consumption at the end of the century, brought about by increasing real wages.[76] Milk production in the townships then had an increasing potential and farmers trading in direct business as producer-retailers could obtain a regular income from selling milk, and probably cheese, butter, poultry and eggs. These dairy farmers had a distinct advantage, because of the regular income, over farmers in other parts of the country engaged in rearing and fattening cattle.[77]

It is virtually impossible to plot trends for sheep stocks in the townships because of the erratic numbers stated in the APRs. From the evidence available, only a few sheep were kept in Eccleshill apart from the 1870s. Yate and Pickup Bank had very few sheep recorded and this is surprising because of the extensive moor land, which included 'rights of common' for specified farmers. Because of the nature of these returns, it is suggested that it would be dangerous to attempt conclusions without further evidence.

Between the 1870s and 1907, the trend was for a general increase in swine stock within the townships, although again numbers in records are dubious. At Eccleshill pig numbers were very small initially but then increased, whilst at Yate and Pickup Bank the figures are suspect. Nevertheless, the overall general increases indicate that there was a growing preference for pork, and since pigs could be fed on skimmed, sour or buttermilk, this was a good business combination with dairy farming.

Horses that were used specifically for agricultural purposes increased significantly in all of the selected townships until 1907 after which they fell into decline. The horses were probably used mainly for 'kitting' milk both within the 'villages' concerned and to the nearby towns, but evidence of this has not been found.

Only a few references have been found to poultry farming in the townships, but these provide evidence that it did exist. Nevertheless, distribution of hens and eggs would have made a useful addition to the milk round in addition to a few specialist egg merchants.

Although most emphasis has been placed on farmers as milk producers, there was also considerable 'mixed dairy farming'. Reference to the '1910 Field Books' compiled 1914 and 1915 indicate that whilst milk was predominantly produced for 'kitting', it was also used as a by-product for making cheese and butter.

Farmers, their families and the farm labour force

According to Wilson Fox, the small farms of Lancashire at the end of the nineteenth century were highly dependent on family labour. He wrote, 'He [the farmer] and his wife, sons and daughters work from early dawn to late at night with an industry that cannot but excite the admiration of those who witness it'.[78] Yet Winstanley has more recently pointed out the uncertainty of this assertion, 'quantifying farming's dependence on family labour, distinguishing local differences…and identifying significant changes over time are far from easy tasks.'[79]

Farmers in the townships were predominantly males, although there were a few females but these were usually designated as widows. The average ages of farmers in each of the townships, between the years 1851 and 1901, were usually more than fifty years. Only a small proportion of farmers, as expected, were under 30 years and over 65 years of age. From this we can ascertain that the majority of the farmers had a working life of less than 35 years. Less than half of the farmers were of native birth, except at Yate and Pickup Bank in some decennial years and at Hoddlesden in 1871; this indicated a high incidence of relocation. This feature was particularly pronounced in some townships where in some instances all of the farmers had been born outside of the township. At the other extreme in Yate and Pickup Bank, at least 50 per cent of the farmers were found to be indigenous.[80] In all of the townships substantial numbers of farmers had been born within five miles. However, at Eccleshill in 1871 nearly half of the farmers had been born more than 5 miles from the township and 50 per cent of these had been born in Yorkshire. In contrast, there were less than one-tenth of farmers in Yate and Pickup Bank born more than 5 miles from the township in 1851, 1871 and 1901. The incidence of movement by farmers at Eccleshill from larger distances may not have been solely related to farming but rather as an opportunity for other family members to work in other occupations. Although this investigation has supported the conclusion arrived at above that farmers were relocating at frequent intervals it is in contrast to findings elsewhere. Pooley and Turnbull stated there was 'some evidence that farmers were particularly stable – often remaining in the family farm all their lives',[81] and in reference to the hill farms above the Fylde in the mid-nineteenth century, Garnett noted, 'many families have lived in the same farm for generations'.[82]

Length of farm occupancy in the case study townships has been determined from censuses between 1851 and 1891, and the 1910 Finance Act Valuation. A few farmers lived in the township throughout a decade but then moved to a different farm. Even the same family seldom occupied the same farm for more than twenty years. Yet, if 'farmers were particularly stable',[83] as claimed by Pooley and Turnbull, then a much higher incidence of stability would be expected to have occurred in these townships.

Nevertheless, length of occupancy determined from census material alone may be misleading, since results calculated from year of arrival to year of departure would probably have shown a much longer-term. The ten year residential periods portrayed from the 1871 and 1881 censuses for example, could have meant that a farmer had taken charge of the farm in 1862 and remained at the same farm until 1890 without being detected in other census records. Nonetheless, this possible maximum still reflects greater instability than that suggested by Pooley and Turnbull. Moreover, findings showed that many farmers left the townships during the decade or died, therefore, the actual period of occupation is likely to have been of much shorter duration than this maximum possibility.

The reasons for stability or otherwise are obscure. There was no apparent linkage between stability and farm size detected since farmers that were living at the same farm in both 1871 and 1881 had similar patterns to that of all farmers in the township. Neither was there any linkage between age and stability.

The next section attempts to examine the roles of farmers and their family members in relation to the structure and characteristics of farming in the case-study townships. It was noted above that the majority of farm holdings in east Lancashire were small and essentially pasture farms. This type of farm required only a low intensity of labour, except for periods of haymaking and possibly occasional activities such as sheep dipping and shearing. During these periods it is likely that the additional help required could have been obtained from family members and friends, although the extent remains unrecorded. Higgs noted that 'because the censuses were taken in early spring they do not record seasonal agricultural activities such as harvest labour',[84] however the census does point to the labour required over the greater part of the year by stating acreage and hence the likely stocking levels, which is important to this study. The major consumption of labour was probably the twice daily milking of cows, a task unlikely to have required assistance when the number of cows to be milked was less than ten.[85] Since a substantial proportion of farms was less than 20 acres and land utilisation was never greater than two acres per cow, this translates into many dairy farms being manageable by the labour of one person.[86] Milking, kitting of milk and general daily duties could then have been comfortably performed within the daily workload of the farmer alone on these small farms. Although this occurrence is feasible, it is also possible that the workload was shared with other family members.

The censuses show that a few farmers were even able to undertake an additional occupation, the most common of which was either that of 'publican' or 'inn-keeper', and this supports the involvement of family members in farming duties. Where a second occupation was indicated most of the farms were less than 20 acres, the main exception being Belthorn Inn Farm at Yate and Pickup Bank, which was recorded as having 70 acres in 1871. It may be assumed, that part-time farmers with larger farms required assistance but this was not evident from the census. There were only twenty-five farmers in dual occupations in the combined townships in 1851 and fifteen of these were involved in the sale of alcohol (Table 4.1). In 1871, twelve farmers had two occupations and ten of these were selling alcohol. By 1891 dual occupations for farmers had declined to five but four of these were selling alcohol. Whether farming or selling alcohol was the most lucrative employment is unclear. Nevertheless, this necessity for a second occupation suggests farms did not generate sufficient income to meet the family's requirements. However, this aspect ignores employment of family members outside of farming, which generated household income, a feature to which we return below.

Table 4.1.   *Farmers in dual occupations*

Township/date	Number of farmers	Farmers/publicans	Farmers/other
1851			
Blacksnape	1	0	1
Eccleshill	3	3	0
Hoddlesden	3	3	0
Yate & Pickup Bank	18	9	9
1871			
Blacksnape	2	1	1
Eccleshill	6	5	1
Hoddlesden	2	2	0
Yate & Pickup Bank	2	2	0
1891			
Blacksnape	2	2	0
Eccleshill	1	1	0
Hoddlesden	0	0	0
Yate & Pickup Bank	2	1	1

Source: CEBs.

The table shows that farmers were engaged in occupations in addition to their farming activities, although the trend decreased between mid and end of the nineteenth century. The most common dual combination was that of farmer and publican.

On larger farms where the farmer was fully engaged, it is likely that the farmer's wife and children also made contributions. However, the extent of family involvement is difficult to determine since the census is unhelpful in providing precise occupational descriptions for family members. Designations for the farmer's spouse such as 'wife', 'farmer's wife' and 'household duties' do not provide clues regarding actual farming duties. Sheldon touring the Fylde in the early 1880s formed the view that the farmer's wife took charge of the dairy processes, but this was probably so when there was considerable labour involved in dairying that entailed cheese and butter making, but for liquid milk processing linked to kitting only, the dairy work was far less intensive. Sheldon's suggestion that there was a degree of working partnership between husband and wife,[87] no doubt still appertained in east Lancashire but the balance of activities undertaken by each partner is uncertain.

In addition to the farmer and his wife engaging in farm work, there may have been contributions by farmers' nuclear families. However, census enumeration is both restrictive and ambiguous for identifying contributions to farm work by children. Those less than 14 years of age were classified variously as 'farmer's son', 'farmer's daughter', 'scholar', 'nil', and 'half-time'. Enumerations revealed there were farmers' children, 14 years of age and upwards listed, as 'farmer's son' and 'farmer's daughter'. Yet, the extent of the children's involvement in farming is unclear. The dubious nature of the designation 'farmer's son' was demonstrated in CEB 'occupation' status. Higgs, pointing to this anomaly, stated:

> Householders were not asked to describe what the members of their households did, for how long, or where they worked, but what they called themselves. The censuses...record occupational titles rather than labour outputs.[88]

Occupational designations become even more vague when it is considered that 'farmer's son/daughter' may not even have been a description for an occupation, but rather a relationship to the farmer or possibly a disguise for unemployment. On balance, it is likely that these designations meant that offspring were possibly working in some capacity for parents, although, the consequence on smaller farms may have been that both the farmer and his children were severely under-employed. It is probable, but by no means conclusive, that family members assisted with such activities as feeding chickens and pigs, collecting eggs, partaking in milk delivery, bringing the herd from the field to the shippon for milking and other minor tasks. Nevertheless, approximations of possible labour inputs have been attempted below.

Living in farmsteads with nuclear families were a few relatives, boarders and servants. Relatives were mainly siblings of the 'head' or 'wife'. Both relatives and boarders were mostly described in the CEBs as being employed in agriculture or as servants. Boarders and lodgers were generally non-natives, although their places of birth were largely from within Lancashire, but they appeared to be unrelated to the farmers. Male relatives, lodgers and servants listed as farm servants have been presumed to be agricultural labourers and as such have been assumed to be part of the total agricultural labour force for the townships. In contrast, relatives listed as domestic servants living in the farmer's household were all females and these have been presumed to be undertaking domestic duties in the farmhouse; as such they have been excluded from an analysis of the agricultural workforce.

Not all farmers had children or extended family capable of assisting in farm work and there is evidence that some farmers recruited assistance from outside of the family. The enumeration returns show agricultural labourers living in each township, and probably employed on larger farms since they were more predominant in Eccleshill that had the highest proportion of larger farms. This township also had the largest average farm size and here the ratio of agricultural labourers was almost one per farm whilst at Yate and Pickup Bank, where the lowest average farm acreage was recorded, the ratio was one labourer to every 4 farms in 1871. By 1881 this had dwindled to 1 in 7. Although these agricultural labourers were recorded in the CEBs as living in the townships of study, however, it is by no means certain whether they were actually employed there or elsewhere.

Because of the above anomalies that have lead to complexities in assessing the contributions to agriculture by people living in the case study townships, analysis has been approached in two ways. The first endeavours to establish the likely minimum agricultural labour force as a proportion of the total labour force within each township. This has been based on the number of farmers and agricultural workers enumerated for each of the townships, although there is no assurance that the latter were actually working within the township. This assessment inevitably assumes a steady workforce for most of the year and ignores short peak periods of unusual activity such as harvesting hay. The second approach attempts to establish the maximum possible labour force in each of the townships. This calculation includes broad assumptions that a 'farmer's wife', 'farmer's son' and 'farmer's daughter' all worked on the farm in a full time capacity as did the farmers and agricultural labourers. Such assumptions cannot be verified and it is likely they give an inflated view of the farming workforce for each township. However, in the absence of better data these two approaches provide a portrait of the likely minimum and very approximate maximum degree to which agriculture was a component of the local economy. The most likely scenario is that the actual work force was about mid-way between the results obtained from the two approaches.

In approaching the minimum farming labour force it has been assumed that farmers and agricultural labourers were engaged in a full time capacity apart from the few farmers in dual occupations. These workers as a component of the total occupied populations proportions varied considerably in each township and overtime. Even with this minimal definition, therefore, analysis shows that agriculture made a significant contribution to employment in these communities.

Investigation of the potential maximum agricultural labour force demonstrated more variability between the townships. This was probably caused at least in part by variable interpretations of census requirements by heads of households or enumerators, or even both. Furthermore, whilst it is likely that farmers and agricultural labourers worked full time the work input of other nuclear family members is less clear, they may have been full-time, part-time or even made no contribution. However, full time is unlikely since wives and probably daughters had domestic duties, but any attempt at weighting the work capacity of these females would be conjecture. It is therefore highly likely that the maximum labour input of between 7 and 15 per cent of the total occupied, is an over estimation. (Table 4.2 & 4.3). Nevertheless, it is expected that family members made at least small contributions to the farming workforce beyond that undertaken by farmers, their relatives, lodgers and agricultural labourers.

These tables attempt to assess the importance of farming to the economies of the townships on the basis of the proportions of labour engaged in agriculture. The uncertainty of the involvement of the farmers' families in the farming process is described in the text. Therefore, the actual contribution is probably somewhere between the minimum and maximum labour force values shown in the two tables.

Table 4.2. *Minimum agricultural labour force.*

Township/date	Farmers	Agricultural labourers	Total min agricultural labour	Total occupied in township	% min in agriculture
1851					
Blacksnape	6	3	9	185	4.9
Eccleshill	19	4	23	304	7.6
Hoddlesden	14	4	18	327	5.5
Yate & Pickup Bank	35	4	39	731	5.3
1871					
Blacksnape	5	1	6	130	4.6
Eccleshill	16	9	25	461	5.4
Hoddlesden	15	2	17	273	6.2
Yate & Pickup Bank	35	10	45	517	8.7

Source: CEBs.
NB: Agricultural labourers include male relatives, boarders and servants.

TABLE 4.3.   *Maximum agricultural labour force.*

Township/date	Total min labour	Farmers' wives, sons & daughters	Total max labour	Total occupied in township	% max in agriculture
			(agri)		
1851					
Blacksnape	9	9	18	185	9.7
Eccleshill	23	22	45	304	14.8
Hoddlesden	18	22	40	327	12.2
Yate & Pickup Bank	39	27	66	731	9.0
	39				
1871					
Blacksnape	6	3	9	130	6.9
Eccleshill	25	10	35	461	7.6
Hoddlesden	17	12	29	273	10.6
Yate & Pickup Bank	45	27	72	517	13.9

Source: CEBs.

NB: Wives of farmers designated in the CEBs as 'farmers wife' have been included but those shown as 'wife' only have been excluded.

What is clearer is that members of farming households earned a living through working outside agriculture. By far the majority of farmers' families working away from the farm were employed in textiles, although daughters were in a greater preponderance than sons. In addition, farmers' nuclear families were engaged in a variety of sundry occupations but in numbers much smaller than those in agriculture and textiles. Sons were occupied in activities such as quarrying; clog making and repair, teaching and iron works while daughters were employed in domestic work, dressmaking and shop work. Some daughters were designated in census records as 'domestic servants'. However, the term 'servant' is ambiguous since it is not possible to determine from the census whether it meant employed in the farmhouse, working elsewhere or a guise for unemployment.

Apart from members of farming households working on farms there were agricultural labourers. These labourers comprised 'heads' of non-farming households, their sons, occasionally daughters usually engaged in dairying, and boarders living with non-farming families.[89] Within the heads' households there was evidence that a substantial number were receiving income from other family members mainly engaged in textile manufacture.[90] Therefore, these households, like farmers' households, were not entirely dependent on agriculture, but there were exceptions. Where 'heads' were the sole wage earners the reason appears to have been young parents with very young children in need of parental care.

Agricultural labourers were fairly mobile but this was usually only over very short distances. In 1871 at Eccleshill and Yate and Pickup Bank 40 per cent of these labourers had been born as natives and 40 per cent in adjacent townships. The remainder of the labourers were equally divided between those born in other parts of Lancashire and other counties of England. By 1881, the configuration had changed to over half having been born in adjacent townships, one-quarter as natives and the remainder were split between the county and other counties.

In summary quantification of the economic and social importance of agriculture in the townships cannot be precisely obtained because of limitations in the available sources. However, general indications are that farming remained important to the local economy, but these small farms seldom supported whole families. Just as farms had been dependent on supplementary earnings acquired from textiles in the eighteenth century, this dependency continued through to at least the late nineteenth century. What was different was instead of farms supplying produce for their own needs and textiles being manufactured in the home they supplied dairy produce for the 'textile towns' and family members were often employed in textile factories, although a smaller number were employed in a wide variety of occupations. Therefore, family income in small farm households in the case study townships was not necessarily derived from farm work.

Farmsteads – case studies

The above has focused on farms, farming families and the farming labour force. What now follows are examples of farmsteads within the case study townships that have been selected to illustrate the variability in size and to show particularly the small-scale nature of most farms during the late nineteenth century. Many of these farms, which are still in existence, have the appearance of a small cottage with a small patch of land attached, no barn, no shippon or any other farm buildings. Although the head of the family was designated in the CEB as a farmer with a small acreage of land, it is difficult to visualise these as farms and the 'head' was hardly a farmer. However, other farmsteads were larger as illustrated.

The construction of both farm domestic buildings and agricultural outbuildings in east Lancashire during the nineteenth century or before were fairly basic. Fletcher's description was 'farm layout and buildings [were] considered antiquated', since most were built in the late eighteenth century or before.[91] Farmsteads with outbuildings were generally designed in a layout that separated domestic and agricultural units, although a small number were constructed as an integral unit.

Two farms at Long Hey Lane, Pickup Bank both had less than three acres of

land each, during the late nineteenth century, and typical of farms in the less
than 5 acres group, but now they are used as two cottages that have been modified and refurbished.[92] These represented a quarter of the farms in this township,
although the proportions for this group in other townships were much smaller.
The left hand cottage was originally constructed as a 'two-up and three-down'
rural end-terrace farm. The original dwelling in the centre of the photograph was
a two-up and two-down mid-terrace farm, and the right hand portion a barn.[93]
One of these farms had dwindled from 6 acres in the middle of the nineteenth
century to less than 3 acres by the 1880s.[94] In the mid-nineteenth century, both
household heads were designated 'handloom weaver' and additionally one sold
beer.[95] By 1881, the 'head' that had sold beer 10 years earlier was unoccupied
but two sons and one daughter were working as cotton weavers to support the
household economy. At the other property, there had been a change of residents
to a couple, both of whom were cotton weavers. It appears that the children had
become responsible for earnings in one family and the occupants at both properties were dependent on income from textiles rather than farming. Therefore,
these families were not solely reliant on farming for income.

Stand Farm at Hoddlesden was recorded at 14 acres in 1851. This farmstead,
according to the date stone was built in 1740 and comprised the farmhouse,
now extended, with a separate barn and cattle shed.[96] [Plate 4.2, see above]
The family living there comprised the 'farmer', 'farmer's wife', three 'farmer's
daughters', the ages of which were 15, 11, 8 years old and a 10 year old son
occupied as a 'powerloom weaver'. This example illustrates the difficulties in
assessing earning contributions by farming family members, since it is unlikely

New Inn Public
House and Farm,
Pickup Bank.
Listed Building.

Date stone
over New Inn
doorway

that income from a farm of this size plus that of one probably half-time weaver was sufficient to support this family. Furthermore, whilst it is unlikely that the farmer's younger children were making a large contribution to farm work, children of five or six years could have been involved in some minor capacity. Nonetheless, a farm of this size was manageable by one person, so these data cast doubt on the census occupational descriptions.

Precise details for the New Inn Farm at Pickup Bank vary between sources. The censuses of 1851 and 1881 gave it as 15 acres and 16 acres respectively, whilst the 1910 Inland Revenue Valuation Book stated 19 acres but the Field Book showed 23 acres plus 'right of pasturage to Pickup Bank Height' (local moor land). The Field Book listed field numbers 102,109 and 112 as belonging to the farm but these totalled just less than 13 acres. Therefore, the documentation leaves the acreage in doubt. The farm buildings were separated from the combined domestic living

Garages
constructed to
replace New Inn
barn

space and public house, and according to the 1910 Field Book the outbuildings comprised a barn, shippon for 6 cows, a stable plus a further old barn and shippon. In addition to living accommodation the Inn contained a billiard room, parlour, tap room and kitchen, it was a 'Fully Licensed Free House' selling '2 barrels a week (36), 2 dozen bottles a week and about 1 gall spirits a week'.[97] The head of this household according to the census of 1851 was designated 'Farmer 15 Acres and Publican'; in 1871 'Licensed Vitular' but in 1881 he was again occupied in the dual capacity of 'farmer' and 'publican'. It is possible that this combined business could have provided a substantial family income for the head, his wife and their adopted son who was designated in the 1871 census as a 'farm labourer', but in 1881 the farm and beer house was indicated as being managed by the farmer and his wife alone. This farm was quite unique in that it was also the meeting place for the Overseers and other officers of the parish.

A farm in the 20 to 49 acre band, situated at Higher Waterside, Eccleshill, was 36 acres according to an Indenture dated about 1860 when the farm belonged to Bolton Grammar School and the Farmer was named Shorrock. Buildings at the farm were described as being in very poor condition but the land was judged to be 'in fair condition'. At the rear of the house the wall was bulging, a bed leg had fallen through a bedroom floor and the barn roof was in very poor condition. The Indenture recorded that 'corn and grain' was being grown but the area used was limited to one-third of the total acreage. The farmer was responsible

Higher Waterside farmhouse on right

Higher Waterside farm buildings

for liming and drainage of the land, including materials at his own expense.[98] It had been reduced to 24 acres according to the 1881 CEB, but in the 1910 Valuation Book it was recorded as 44 acres and in the Field Book 47 acres. This may have been the result of combining this and another farm. The Field Book describes the business as a 'Kitting Farm' and states that nearly half the land was meadow. Living quarters were detached and the outbuilding comprised a combined 16-cow shippon, a two-horse stable plus a further 4-horse stable and dutch barn; there was also a dairy and 'churning place' (presumably for butter and/or cheese).[99] In 1881 Edward Cowell and his wife were employing 1 boy plus a male farm servant (indoor) living with the family and they had two daughters working as weavers. This household received income from the farm plus income from textiles, although presumably wages and/or board had to be paid.

Holker House Farm at Hoddlesden became an unusually large farm for the townships in the late nineteenth century. The CEBs show that in 1851 there were 42 acres, in 1861 50 acres and by 1871 the acreage had increased to 84, but later reduced. A previous occupier of the farm has provided the following description.[100] The farm outbuildings consisted of 'shippon for 30 head of milking cattle and a five stalled stable. The detached farmhouse was built during the seventeenth century and was large enough to house two separate families. Therefore, here both farm buildings and living accommodation were above average in size for farms in east Lancashire. The 1851 census shows the resident farm labour force consisted of farmer and wife only; in 1861 the farmer was a widow and there was an agricultural labourer living in the farm house. Following the increased acreage in 1871 the census indicated that there was a farmer, farmer's wife, farmer's son and an agricultural labourer living at the farm, yet in 1891

Holker House Farm

the census evidence indicates that a farmer and agricultural labourer alone were working the farm. It would therefore appear that the census details understate the labour force at this later date for this relatively large farm in the district.

Viewing the evidence from these case studies it appears that farmsteads can be separated into two main components; the domestic accommodation and the agricultural buildings. The requirements for the domestic components were seldom different to any other dwellings in the district. Standards of maintenance were unlikely to be different since both were mainly rented and relied largely upon the attitude of the owner for upkeep. It was the agricultural buildings of the farms that demonstrated far greater variation, since these needed to be proportional to numbers and types of farm animals. This factor usually affected the size of barn, shippon, stabling and pigsties.

In summary this study has shown that the agricultural structure in the case study townships during the late nineteenth and early twentieth centuries was unusual; it differed markedly from that of the large farms in other parts of England and Europe that were based on agrarian capitalism and exploitation of wage labour. These large farms were occupied for generations by the same family in line with that found in the widespread study by Pooley and Turnbull.[101] Farming in east Lancashire was small-scale, pasture and less likely to run in families. However, it was not that different to farming in other parts of the country where industry had sprung up and there was a demand for dairy produce. Farms were managed by the farmer and his family and were similar to those described by Fletcher and Winstanley for east Lancashire, where the townships were situated.[102] Although farming was small scale it was dynamic in nature and linked to the growth of a thriving textile industry and real income, because of which hardships experienced in agriculture elsewhere were avoided.[103]

In summary small-scale farming developed in parallel to a capitalist industrialised urban economy experiencing population growth. These conditions generated opportunities for the small farmer to increase productivity in sales of dairy produce using scientific advances and entrepreneurial techniques that included intensification of land usage.[104] In common with other east Lancashire producer-retailers, farmers in the case study townships seem to have become aware of opportunities for selling dairy produce in the textile towns. Although these farms developed and became more profitable, they still needed supplementary earning from other household members.

Luddington Mill, Waterside

CHAPTER FIVE

The Villages as Textile Communities

P RIOR TO LATE EIGHTEENTH century the economy of rural communities in east Lancashire not only depended on small farms but also on a domestic textile industry. There is ample evidence of this both as a supplement to farming and as a single household income. Both Christopher Shorrock of Prince's Farm and William Cooper of Pinnacle Nook, Blacksnape were chapmen. Aaron Bury at Near Scotland Farm, Hoddlesden was a farmer and handloom weaver and so was the head of household at Sunnyfield Farm. At Baron's Fold Blacksnape the father of the Fish family was a handloom weaver and also built looms and John Waddicor at Drummer Stoops and his three sons were all handloom weavers as were the residents of Hillock and Far Hillock Farm. Kester Hindle of Langshaw Head was a handloom weaver and had the 'appearance of an old yeoman. He wore breeches, had a green vest, a swallow-tailed coat, and a ruffled shirt; and his beaver hat was both well worn and well brushed'.[1] Handloom weavers at the end of the eighteenth century earned good money and were clad in styles similar to the gentry.

From the outset of mechanisation in the textile industry the rural townships in this study were different in some respects to both 'model villages' and 'textile towns'; in other ways, they had similarities. During the late eighteenth and early nineteenth centuries, some rural townships like 'model villages' saw the introduction of mechanised spinning mills. They relied on a few small water-powered carding and spinning mills, each with a single employer and sited in different locations. The employers were local people, mostly yeomen, who had acquired sufficient capital to build a small mill; some of which were no larger than a single detached house or pair of semi-detached houses. This, made them different to the model villages where there was only a single mill in the area, usually a larger spinning mill with a single employer but like the rural mills, they used waterpower.

Textile industry in the townships before mid-nineteenth century

The first industrial textile site in Hoddlesden commenced around 1778 as a calico printing works besides the Hoddlesden Brook,[2] while the first small carding and spinning factory to appear in Eccleshill was erected on the bank of Waterside Brook at Grimshaw Bridge, in 1782 and powered by water wheel. But the most favoured location for the erection of early mills was beside the Hoddlesden and Tinkler's Brooks, technically in Yate and Pickup Bank, although some mills were only separated from Eccleshill by the width of Hoddlesden Brook. There were at least seven small water powered mills erected on these two stretches of water between the 1780s and c.1808[3] (Map 5.1). Old Engine or Stockclough Mill

Map 5.1. The geographical locations of the early mills in the townships using waterpower are indicated on the map along with their SD designations.

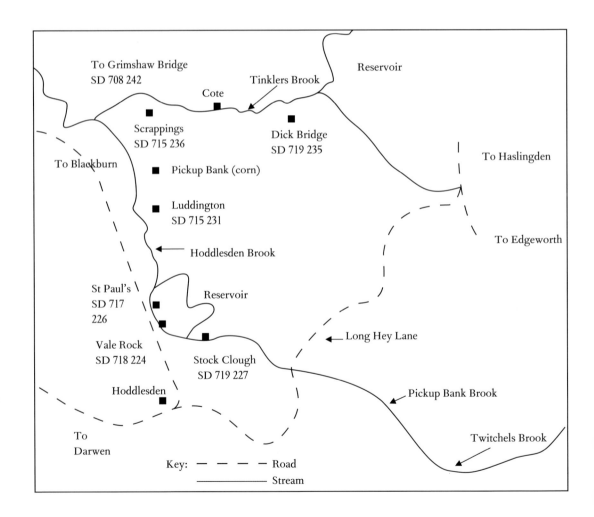

Stockclough Mill Pickup Bank. Originally a spinning mill driven by water wheel but was later converted to weaving. Most of the building is of original construction although the dormer windows have been added later as has the shutters to the left hand upper edifice.

Luddington Mill Waterside. Plate shows the mill in almost its original state except for the added porch.

The rear elevation of Luddington Mill c. 1790, which was adjacent to a stream used to turn a water wheel for operating spinning machines.

was erected in 1788 for carding; Cote Mill late eighteenth century for spinning; Scrapings Mill 1792 for carding, which survived until 1815 and at Dick Bridge there were three water-powered spinning mills built *c*.1808 by Thomas Yates of Oswaldtwistle, but the business failed in 1820. At Hoddlesden Vale Rock Mill was built for calico printing *c*.1778,[4] and sold as a going concern in 1818.[5] In 1819 George Crompton (Samual Crompton's son) applied for a new mill at Vale Rock to replace the old mill.[6] These small early mills in the townships concentrated exclusively on carding and spinning until at least 1800, and about half of them retained spinning until the first quarter of the nineteenth century and one until the 1840s. [Figure 5.1.] This was effectively a collapse of rural factory spinning in the district but until the second quarter of the nineteenth century, weaving by hand still remained highly important to these communities, therefore, there was a dramatic transition from spinning combined with weaving to reliance almost entirely towards weaving. Indeed as mills terminated spinning production, they were frequently used as weaving workshops.

Prior to late eighteenth century, domestic spinning had governed the extent of domestic production, but then mechanised spinning inventions released the constraints on yarn output. Initially the machines were small but as they were developed in size they required a large amount of power, which could be supplied by water wheels.[7] Both Thirsk and Farnie have suggested that hilly terrain and fast running streams were conducive to the installation of mechanised water-power and such streams were present in the case study townships.[8] The boundary between Hoddlesden and Yate and Pickup Bank is designated by Hoddlesden Brook originating high on the moor,[9] this stream also separates Eccleshill from Yate and Pickup Bank and there is a further separation boundary between Yate

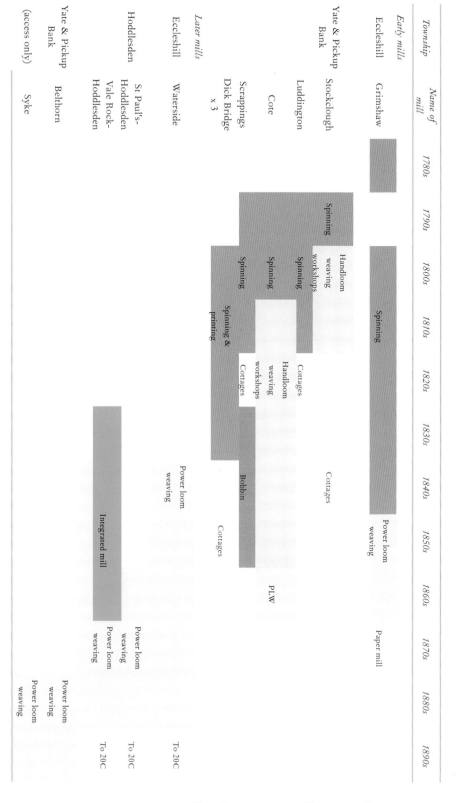

Figure 5.1 *Manufacturing processes in the townships' mills*

Bank and Pickup Bank being Tinklers Brook. The adequacy of supply by these watercourses is shown by the fact that the Blackburn Water Authority had built reservoirs connected into them by about the mid-nineteenth century. These watercourses were attractive as a power source for water wheels as noted in an advertisement in the *Blackburn Mail* in 1804, albeit for the sale of four cottages at Shorrock Fold, it reads there is 'a powerful stream, Water and efficient fall'.[10] The potential of these local streams was recognised by local people who, in the late eighteenth century, erected small water powered mills on their banks. This was in advance of urban mills. Although Blackburn became the largest textile town in east Lancashire it initially lagged behind Hoddlesden and Yate and Pickup Bank in early mechanised textile developments.

Early carding and spinning mills built in the case study townships during the late eighteenth and early nineteenth centuries were miniscule compared with the archetypal mills such as Cromford, Saltaire and those in 'cotton towns.' The actual physical sizes of mills in the townships have proved elusive since neither records nor the majority of the buildings are extant. However, Stockclough Mill is still in existence as a house with external ground floor dimensions of approximately 15 yards by 12 yards, but it has otherwise been modified. Two of the Dick Bridge mills were also converted to houses following closure. The original part of Grimshaw Bridge Mill was still in existence until recently, although it had a change of use, but it could be seen that the floor area was relatively small.[11] These examples demonstrate the very small-scale nature of some of these mills. Nevertheless, the magnitude of the workforce engaged and details of equipment in some mills provide a further perspective of size. Grimshaw Bridge Mill, Eccleshill had a labour force of only 23 in 1823. Cote Mill, Yate and Pickup Bank was a three storey-spinning mill built in the 1820s on a small patch of land with a few cottages and handloom shops but records as to who lived in the cottages have not been located. A 'For Sale by Auction' advertisement in the *Blackburn Mail* in 1807 provides some clues as to the size and type of machinery being used in two other mills at Yate and Pickup Bank. 'Calico manufactury' was noted for one unnamed mill that had a winding machine of 126 spindles capacity, three warping mills, a double carding engine, six spinning jennies and a devil. A record of the workforce required at this mill has not been located but a conservative estimate is that less than a dozen people would have been employed. The other mill, Luddington, comprised 'the new Powerful Water Wheel and complete machinery, which is of the newest and most approved', two carding engines, one 34 inch and the other 52 inch, two mules with 276 spindles each, two throstles with 144 spindles each, two double drawing heads, one fly frame with 16 spindles, one billy with 96 spindles and a devil.[12] The workforce at this mill may have been a little larger than at the last mill but only marginally so. The modest size of these mills is illustrated by comparison to a medium sized mill in the 1860s at nearby Hoddlesden that was operating 15,000 spindles and 500 powerlooms, which was similar in size to mills found in the nearby towns.[13] Therefore, the early rural mills were smaller in size, and employed fewer workers than mills in both the model villages and towns.

The owners of the small late eighteenth century mills were mainly yeomen living in or near to the townships, some of who leased their mills to local people. Both ownerships and leases were normally of short-term duration and the usage of the mills themselves was subject to change. The Hargreaves family of Haslingden built Vale Rock Mill. Grimshaw Bridge was built by William Yates of Woodhead, Yate Bank and leased to Nathen Yates, a Yate Bank chapman, living in Belthorn but the business failed in 1790; later the mill was resuscitated and had a number of owners.[14] Stockclough Mill was erected by Robert Scholes of Pickup Bank and leased to a Mary Hargreave living in nearby Hoddlesden. Luddington Mill was built by Richard Ratcliffe, yeoman of Owlett Hall, Yate Bank and leased to Robert Scholes who lived in Pickup Bank. Cote Mill was erected by William Yates, a yeoman of Yate Bank, and leased to William Turner of not far distant Helmshore, later the mill was adopted by a partnership but it finally failed in 1866. Scrapings Mill was built by John Scholes, farmer of Yate Bank.[15] Thomas Yates, yeoman of Oswaldtwistle, built the three spinning mills at Dick Bridge. The founders and leaseholders of these mills, therefore, were mainly local business people who were yeoman with interests in textiles as chapmen or farmers.[16]

Although most of the small carding and spinning mills built in the late eighteenth century were short lived and had either ceased trading or diversified by the early nineteenth century their destiny varied. Oliver and Mary Hargreaves converted Vale Rock Mill, Hoddlesden to cotton spinning in 1786. By 1814 a John Heap was occupying the mill for water-powered mule spinning. This mill was still owned by the Hargreaves family in 1819 when George Crompton (son of Samuel Crompton) leased the mill from them for use as a bleach works and extensions were added. By 1837 John Rishton had taken over the mill, which was then used for power loom weaving. At this stage major extensions were added and in the 1850s there was a new weaving shed.[17] At Yate and Pickup Bank, Stockclough Mill c.1800 was converted to handloom weaving workshops and later cottages. Cote Mill was converted in 1811 to a combination of dwellings and weaving shops. An advertisement in the *Blackburn Mail* in 1826 referring to this mill stated 'premises … are very suitable for a Print Works or Power Loom Manufactury'; and the adjacent stream has a '20 foot waterfall or thereabout';[18] this suggests a possible interest in early power loom weaving and that alternative sources of power were available, However William Turner of Helmshore resuscitated spinning at the mill during the 1820s but converted it to steam power. In 1860 four partners from Darwen adopted Cote Mill and installed 67 power looms but final failure occurred in 1866. Both Luddington and Scrapings Mills were converted to cottages in 1815. However, the 1840s, O.S., map, shows the latter as a 'bobbin shop' but the Blackburn Water Works in 1845 reported it as a cotton mill (type not indicated) occupied by Henry Baron of Balderstone near Mellor.[19] At Dick Bridge the three spinning mills were converted for calico printing but ceased trading in 1826 after which spinning was resuscitated until the mid-1850s. All this shows the vulnerability of the small early mills, which either failed or were put to other use and lacked significant impact on the villages.

It is unlikely that the owners of the small mills needed to provide accommodation for the small workforces as occurred in model villages and in some instances in the cotton towns, since employees probably lived locally and were few in number. No indications have been found of parish apprentices being engaged as in the model villages and indeed, it is unlikely that they would have been required. However, the will of John Scholes who owned Scrapings Mill showed that he also owned a fair amount of domestic property scattered around the nearby countryside and could possibly have let this to workers had accommodation been required. He also had the necessary capital to build houses had he desired. His will included copyhold messuage, barn and Tenement at Red Earth [his home] plus cottages and land in Yate Bank. Also included in the will was copyhold cotton mill, barn and tenement at Top of Copy, part of Scholes Fold, property at Edgworth, and a coal mine at Bolton-le-Moors, the valuation was 'under £300-0-0'.[20] Like other local yeoman, Scholes had no obvious personal access to external resources and no evidence has been found that he provided either housing or facilities for his workers.

In summary, the emergence of rural water powered mechanised carding and spinning mills in late eighteenth century largely replaced these as domestic processes and increased the supply of yarn for weaving. They produced a greater potential for the weaving sector, attracted more people to weaving and created a rising population over the countryside until about the second quarter of the nineteenth century, after which both the weaving workforce and population started to decline in these townships. These townships were prototypes in this mechanisation process of textile manufacture and typical of large numbers of rural communities in east Lancashire that experienced large growth in domestic weaving. The early rural mills were small, vulnerable to economic forces and there were fluctuations in ownership. However, from c.1800 rural mechanised carding and spinning declined. This demise and conversion of the mills to weaving shops and later the erection of power loom weaving sheds rather implies that spinning was a poor business to pursue in these rural locations. The abandonment of rural spinning mills was in sharp contrast to the scenario in the adjacent towns and archetypal factory villages where the size of spinning mills was increasing at a rapid rate and the power for the mills was being supplied by steam engines.[21] Model villages usually had a single employer who concentrated on the spinning process and where there was very little if any alternative employment. Additionally, mill owners in towns, usually owned one or a few mills each, and ownership was generally over a comparatively long period of time. The mills in towns and model villages were usually much more stable enterprises than the rural mills. The early rural mills did not herald the beginning of a full transformation to mechanised textile manufacture, nor did they create the conditions associated with 'factory villages' for provision of housing and amenities, as we shall see in chapter 7.

Development of large steam weaving mills from circa mid-nineteenth century onwards

The final phase of textile manufacturing or as it is sometimes termed 'full mechanisation' largely commenced in the townships about the mid-nineteenth century, and this was generally later than in towns. Additionally, there is a substantial amount of evidence to suggest that these communities were also different in other ways to urban industrial communities. By the mid-nineteenth century only marginal spinning and no carding were taking place in the townships. This was unlike the situation in most model villages where spinning mills continued to be operational. Also in parts of southern Lancashire, towns were becoming centres for spinning, production was rapidly increasing, larger spinning mills were being erected and existing ones enlarged. In east Lancashire, a much smaller amount of spinning was being undertaken and the emphasis was on the expansion of power loom weaving in steam driven mills. Power looms were replacing handlooms in towns by the second quarter of the nineteenth century, causing large declines in urban handloom weaver numbers, and by mid-century numbers were negligible.22 In these rural communities power loom weaving, however, was not introduced as rapidly as in urban centres, although by mid-century it had emerged as a factory process in both Eccleshill and Hoddlesden. These rural steam mills were larger in size than the early water powered mills and although some were in single ownership the majority was owned by partnerships or joint stock companies. They employed much larger numbers of operatives than their late eighteenth century water powered predecessors. In 1841, the Factory Inspectorate recorded that 77 per cent of textile mills in Lancashire employed more than 150 workers each, and the mills in the townships were about this size. However, urban mills built later in the century were much larger,[23] although several of the 'village' mills were subsequently extended. It is fairly evident that the introduction of these weaving factories made a dramatic impact on the working practices of inhabitants in the case study townships. Whilst these mills provided partial replacement employment for that lost by demise in the earlier cottage industry many local families sought work in nearby towns. Power loom weaving mills erected in the townships from the late 1830s onwards have been identified. At

Eccleshill, Henry Worthington built Waterside Cotton Mill in 1844 for power loom weaving (SD 715 235). This mill was described as a 'new power-loom mill', the sale of which in 1848 was made on the condition that 'steam power was completely ousting the water wheel'. By the 1880s the mill had been extended and housed 616 power looms, but business ceased in 1929.[24] The owners of Grimshaw Bridge Mill also at Eccleshill, added a two-storey extension in the 1840s and by 1850 it shifted manufacturing direction from spinning to steam power weaving, but in 1872 it was converted to a paper mill. Hoddlesden had two large mills, St Paul's (SD 717 225) and Vale Rock (SD 718 224). The former was weaving only and built in 1861 and the other spinning integrated, with weaving commencing in 1837.[25] There was no large power-weaving mill built in either Blacksnape or Yate and Pickup Bank, but on the latter's north-east boundary, Belthorn Higher Mill was built in 1861 and Syke Mill in 1854–5. The former was located in a very sparsely populated part of Oswaldtwistle (SD 717 244), and the latter at Guide near Blackburn (SD 715 249), both providing potential employment for residents of Yate Bank.[26] Therefore, whilst there was no mill in either this township or Blacksnape, the people had numerous employment opportunities for work in textiles within walking distance just as they had in Eccleshill and Hoddlesden (Map 5.2).

Jackson has pointed out that, 'it is not unreasonable to compare firms on the basis of loomage', a process that has been adopted in this section where possible.[27] Waterside Cotton Mill, subsequently solely owned by the Bullough family, had 200 looms in 1844 and engaged about 100 operatives but the mill was extended in 1880 to house 616 looms when the workforce was increased to approximately 300. Grimshaw Bridge Mill meanwhile had 120 power looms installed in the 1840s and 60 employees.[28] (Figure 5.2). The location of Belthorn Mill is just inside the Oswaldtwistle boundary.

Vale Rock Mill at Hoddlesden

Map 5.2.
Location
of Power
Loom Mills in
Townships

[Districts of Darwen]

Scale: I inch = 2 miles

comprising both spinning and weaving, which was then extended during the early 1860s to house 15,000 spindles and provide a 500 loom weaving shed.[29] Following a division of this mill into Vale Rock Spinning Mill and Vale Rock Shed (weaving), by the 1890s the spinning side comprised 4,000 mule spindles but it also had 87 power looms engaging and a workforce of about 50 operatives. In the 1950s there were 3,955 mule spindles and 138 power looms. The other part of the split business was called Vale Rock Shed and operated 352 looms from 1864 until closure in 1878. Following a fire in 1889, 400 looms were installed. When reopened in 1861, St Paul's Mill was utilised essentially for weaving in which there were 600 looms, but this capacity was eventually increased. By the outbreak of the Great War the number of looms at Vale Rock and St Paul's Mills together had increased to 1500.[30]

Figure 5.2. *Weaving mill loomage capacities and closures.*

Township	Mill	1840s	1850s	1860s	1870s	1880s	1890s	1900s	1910s	
Eccleshill	Grimshaw		120		Closed-1872 (converted to paper mill)					
	Waterside	200				616				Closed-1929
Hoddlesden	St Paul's-Hoddlesden				600				)	Operating
	Vale Rock-Hoddlesden				352				) 1500	mid-20C
Yate & Pickup Bank	Belthorn					216	252	294		Closed-1933
	Syke		200			302		Extended		Closed-1953

Sources: M. Rothwell, Blackburn Pt 1, p 37; Darwen pp 8-9, 11-12, 16-17, 22; Ribble Valley p 65; Church and Oswaldtwistle, p 43.

Details of mills on the periphery of Yate and Pickup Bank show they too were larger than the early water powered mills. Belthorn Higher Mill in Oswaldtwistle commenced weaving in 1880 with 216 looms, and by 1888, this mill had been extended to house 252 looms, probably requiring around 120 operatives.[31] Further enlargement occurred at the end of the nineteenth century to 294 looms when the numbers of operatives needed increased to about 150. Syke Mill at Guide, near Blackburn, had 200 looms mid century and was extended in 1881–2 to house 320 looms; according to Rothwell the mill employed 102 weavers with a further extension being added in 1902.[32]

Weaving mills in the townships had two main patterns of ownership. On the one hand, there were fairly wealthy private owners and on the other hand, the mills were registered companies comprising small amounts of employee stock-holdings but usually largely family stockholdings. For three years the Waterside Cotton Mill, Eccleshill was owned by three partners then one withdrew and built his own mill in Blackburn leaving James and Adam Bullough, father and son, as the sole mill owners, both lived in nearby Darwen in 1847, therefore, ownership was local. The Bulloughs also owned local land, a couple of farms, a coal mine and fireclay works.[33] The 1910 Inland Revenue Valuation Book shows that the family still owned the Waterside mill, but following James Bullough's retirement, it was leased to various people until trading ceased in 1929, most of whom were mill owners in nearby Darwen.[34]

John Rishton owned Vale Rock Mill, Hoddlesden when it was converted for steam power loom weaving in 1837. In 1836 the Place brothers arrived from Clitheroe and brought with them some workers from Clitheroe for the purpose of developing the village industry.[35] In 1840 the comparatively young Place brothers, John and Joseph, aged 29 and 32 years respectively, joined the 45 year old Rishton and became involved in the business. By 1843 major refurbishments and extensions were taking place. The 1851 census indicates the Place brothers were employing 463 workers comprising 159 men, 127 women, 83 boys and 99 girls, although not all were necessarily engaged at Vale Rock Mill.[36] Rishton left the business in 1851 but the firm still expanded and a weaving shed was added during the 1850s and by 1861 the business was employing 600 hands. The mill had 974 looms in 1862, which was a larger number than any mill in Darwen at that time. Nevertheless, Joseph Place left the firm in 1863 leaving John and his son in sole charge but the business failed a year later, resulting in closure of the mill. The firm's liabilities were £75,000 with one creditor being owed £10,000 for yarn.[37] This was a period when many mills in Lancashire were closing and a large number of cotton workers were receiving poor relief as a result of the 'cotton famine' caused by lack of raw cotton imports due to the American Civil War. Nevertheless, the Places must have been young wealthy men to have afforded such a large financial outlay and as we see in the next chapter they were also in possession of further capital investment. Following division of Vale Rock Mill into separate spinning and weaving mills the spinning side was leased for waste spinning to Holden Haworth aged 59 years in 1869 and a native of Haslingden who was also one time owner of Grimshaw Bridge Mill. By 1871 Haworth was living in Graham Street, Hoddlesden. The mill was used mainly for spinning waste that gave rise to the colloquialism 'Bump Hole'. Holden Haworth's sons managed the spinning mill following his death in 1885, and in 1901 it was registered as a family business in the name of Holden Haworth Limited, at which stage there were 4000 mules for spinning and 87 power looms. By the

1950s a family called Walsh had become the chief shareholders of the company. This business changed manufacturing direction in 1973, when part of the mill was leased to Webster Textiles to house around 50 automatic looms and another part of the building was leased by Darwen Cotton Manufacturing Company Limited for making and printing cloth. However, the company was finally wound up in 1978. James and Robert Knowles owned the other part of the split business called Vale Rock Shed from 1864 until closure in 1878. Later a group of local residents formed the Hoddlesden Manufacturing Company Limited in 1884. Parts of the premises were destroyed by fire in 1889. Following this, additional capital was raised and W. H. Place of Joseph Place & Sons became a main shareholder but the Company was wound up in 1907. During these latter stages Alexander Carus had leased the weaving shed in 1890 but eventually purchased the buildings. Some 20 years later 200 more looms were added and around 1920 there was a partial diversion into surgical goods.[38]

John and Joseph Place, having previously purchased Vale Rock Mill, erected St Paul's Mill in 1861, Hoddlesden's second mill. Following the bankruptcy of John Place the mill was purchased by James & Robert Knowles and later by Alexander Carus of Blackburn in 1882.

During most of the twentieth century this mill was locally known as Carus's Mill. The largest portion of the Mill comprised a single storey weaving shed but adjacent to Johnson Road there was a three storey section. From the third floor projected a cantilevered steel girder for hoisting cotton beams into the mill where the winding process occurred. This building had settled over time and was being supported by steel ties preventing the walls from outwards buckling.

Ownership of steam mills was much more stable than that of the early water powered mills, although not all mills remained in continuous ownership and production. Some mills in the townships were sound businesses; although they were no doubt vulnerable to trade depressions in a similar way to town mills but they otherwise appear to have provided steady employment for their respective communities. Nevertheless, the two mills in Eccleshill, however, were quite different to each other, Grimshaw Bridge having a turbulent ownership history; with frequent changes of ownership that indicate difficulties in the business while Waterside Mill was owned by the Bullough family alone for 53 years, and probably provided long periods of stability for the community. At Hoddlesden Vale Rock Weaving Mill was owned by the Place brothers for more than 20 years. The Haworth family owned Vale Rock Spinning Mill for 80 years and the Walsh family for 23 years. The Knowles brothers occupied Vale Rock Shed for 14 years and they also owned St Paul's Mill for 21 years. Alexander Carus and family later owned the Vale Rock Shed for over 70 years and then continued in partnership with Vernon & Company Limited of Preston in the name of VernonCarus Limited from 1971. Although this enterprise later failed it was put to other use, but in 2003 the mill became derelict and was finally destroyed by fire in 2008. Nonetheless, the Carus family owned St Paul's Mill for 90 years before merger with Vernon's.

In summary, steam powered weaving mills in the case study townships built from about the middle of the nineteenth century were mainly local initiatives as were their early water powered predecessors, but they were on a larger scale than the early carding and spinning mills. These weaving mills were in some respects similar to the developments taking place in the 'cotton towns' of east Lancashire, where there was also a concentration on weaving. The power weaving mills in the townships had mostly fairly stable family ownership, and in this respect were similar to model village factories, but occasionally they were owned by a partnership or a combination of family and joint stock company, which was more akin to the registered company mills in towns. Like the earlier mill owners the power mill owners usually had at least local connections, they either lived in the townships or in nearby towns and occasionally they owned mills in the nearby towns. This was reflected in migrational movements that caused the townships to become deserted during economic downturns but when business improved people returned.

The nature and characteristics of the manual textile work force in the early nineteenth century.

There is a substantial amount of evidence to suggest that the case study communities were different to some of the industrial communities previously investigated by historians, but they were typical of many other rural townships in east Lancashire that had a long history of involvement in domestic textile manufacture. Perusal of the 1660s Hearth Tax Returns, Yates Map and the 1801 census indicates that populations started to increase substantially during the late eighteenth century. Developments in cotton manufacturing processes inevitably affected patterns of employment. Centralisation of carding and spinning required a rapid and continuous growth of the textile workforce; from this cotton towns quickly emerged.

Before the mid-nineteenth century, there were many children in Lancashire, which included Rossendale, of six and seven years working an eleven-hour day, particularly in textiles. This practice had been common when textiles was a cottage industry and continued with the introduction of the factory system. Employment of very young children diminished as social reformers lobbied government to introduce restrictive legislation although in 1851 Lancashire had more working children between 10 and 14 years than any other county.[39]

Transition from carding and spinning as a domestic process to carding and spinning in small water powered mills situated in rural areas occurred from the late 1770s. Early mills producing yarn were built in Eccleshill and Yate and

Pickup Bank, where spinning and carding output capacities from mechanised processing could outperform the amounts from earlier hand production. The result was that rural hand spinners, who had been mainly women and children, eventually became redundant, although a small number may have gained employment in water driven mills.[40] Cessation of hand spinning did not necessarily cause mass unemployment since until the emergence of these mills the weaving side of the industry had been short of yarn, which restricted the size of the weaving workforce. The additional machine produced output relieved the bottleneck in spinning, encouraged expansion of handloom weaver numbers, and this opened employment opportunities for redundant spinners.[41] These early changes in production spearheaded a change from family employment in the home to individual or family employment in mills and workshops. Although carding and spinning became mechanised processes in the late eighteenth century, the weaving process continued as a cottage industry into the nineteenth century.

A decline in handloom weaving from the 1820s and 1830s caused population decline in some townships,[42] since there was very little alternative industry to which people could turn. At Yate and Pickup Bank, in the 238 dwellings there lived 233 families engaged mainly in 'manufacture and handicraft' according to the 1821 census.[43] During this period there were very few occupations apart from textiles, therefore, these statistics demonstrate the huge importance of textile manufacturing to the economy of the community. This pattern was typical of many rural townships in east Lancashire during the same period as can be seen from census statistics.

Most inhabitants in the case study communities lived within a relatively short walking distance of the nearby cotton towns of Darwen or Oswaldtwistle where alternative employment was available and this no doubt tempered the rate of decline in population. Also, losses in Yate and Pickup Bank were probably retarded by the presence of a handloom weaving workshop and also a bobbin factory. Butterworth wrote of Yate and Pickup Bank in 1833, 'Calico weaving by hand prevails and there is a mill'; the township is 'inhabited by weavers'.[44] This made the townships very different to isolated communities where there were no other employment opportunities within daily travel and where the inhabitants had to rely on a single source of employment for a living, so that they had no alternative but to re-locate.

Both Bythell and Timmins have suggested that handloom weaving numbers had declined by the mid-nineteenth century. However, there is no evidence of a dramatic collapse in handloom weaving within Eccleshill and Yate and Pickup Bank before this time, but rather a slow decline over two or three decades.

At Blacksnape in 1851 there were more handloom weavers than power loom weavers, although nearly one-third of weavers were unspecified. At Eccleshill in 1851 handloom and power loom weavers were classified in almost equal propor-

tions and the former were mainly categorised as silk weavers. At Hoddlesden half
of the weavers were designated as power loom weavers, there were only a few
handloom weavers and the remainder were unclassified as to the type of weaving
being undertaken. At Yate and Pickup Bank three-quarters of the weavers were
specified as working at the power loom and most of the remainder were weaving
either cotton or silk by hand. Therefore, the apportionment of types of weavers
in two of the townships were more carefully enumerated than at Blacksnape and
Hoddlesden by having less undifferentiated weavers (Table 5.1 & 5.2).

Table 5.1.   *Percentages of weaver types in the townships in 1851.*

Township/year	Handloom	Power loom	Unspecified	Total
Blacksnape	39.0	31.0	30.0	100.0
Eccleshill	50.3	49.7	0.0	100.0
Hoddlesden	6.0	49.0	45.0	100.0
Yate & Pickup Bank	21.0	75.0	4.0	100.0

The table shows the ratios of weaver type designations in the 1851 census.

Sources: CEBs.

Table 5.2.   *Types of weavers in case study townships 1851 to 1891.*

Township	Census occupation	1851	1871	1891
Blacksnape	Cotton weaver	0	46	69
	Power loom weaver	24	0	0
	Handloom weaver ctn	30	0	0
	Silk weaver	0	3	0
	Weaver	23	0	0
Eccleshill	Cotton weaver	0	163	230
	Power loom weaver	77	0	0
	Handloom weaver ctn	28	2	0
	Silk weaver	50	6	0
	Weaver	0	0	0
Hoddlesden	Cotton weaver	0	85	170
	Power loom weaver	70	0	0
	Handloom weaver ctn	5	0	0
	Ctn & Silk weaver	4	1	0
	Weaver	65	0	0
Yate & Pickup Bank	Cotton weaver	0	253	152
	Power loom weaver	211	0	0
	Handloom weaver ctn	8	5	0
	Silk weaver	51	2	0
	Weaver	11	0	0

The table is extracted from census data and demonstrates the decline of handloom weavers that were a combination of weavers working in cotton and silk. Also shown is the increasing numbers of mechanised weavers whose occupational descriptions were a combination of power loom and cotton weavers. The latter two terms being synonymous.

Sources: CEBs.

The towns of east Lancashire had large numbers of weavers working in mills from the mid-nineteenth century since the power loom was well established. This may be the key to the meaning of undifferentiated weaver terms such as 'cotton weaver' or 'weaver of cotton'. The 1881 census enumeration for Blackburn and Darwen was void of power loom weavers and in Oswaldtwistle there were only five power loom weavers listed, yet all three towns had an abundance of weavers working with the power loom and by this period handloom weaving hardly existed, if at all, in towns. In addition, the census only listed 15 power loom over-lookers in Blackburn and 2 in Oswaldtwistle. Therefore, since the vast majority of weavers were described as 'cotton weaver' we can be fairly certain that the local term for the occupation of power loom weaver was 'cotton weaver'. This term also appeared in the enumeration for the rural townships studied and whilst the same argument is perhaps less reliable there seems to be a good measure of justification for believing that cotton weaver and power loom weaver were synonymous by 1881. The insertion of the descriptions 'power loom' and 'hand loom' in the census, therefore, was a feature of the mid-nineteenth century and possibly no longer seen as necessary by 1881 since the vast majority of weavers were working at the 'power loom'. Furthermore, the use of the term 'cotton weaver' in the 1861 and 1871 censuses is also likely to have indicated a power loom weaver since hand weaving had probably been virtually phased out, but of this we cannot be certain. These rural townships were only a short distance from 'cotton towns', so it is likely that the same terminology was used in both, particularly as there were large-scale two-way population movements between the rural and urban areas.

The census informs us that weaving was still of paramount importance to the economy of the mid-century case study townships in spite of population decline, albeit the form was changing. By 1851, weavers represented 42 per cent of the total workforce at Blacksnape; 50 per cent at Eccleshill, 45 per cent at Hoddlesden and 53 per cent at Yate and Pickup Bank. Significant proportions of the weavers were still actively involved in handloom weaving at mid-century, although Blacksnape and Yate and Pickup Bank had experienced decline in population from the second quarter of the century. By 1851, only Eccleshill and Hoddlesden had a steam power loom mills, so power loom weavers in the other township could not have been working in the township of abode.

Having established that each of the townships still had a high degree of depend-ency on hand weaving at mid-century we now turn initially to establish the types of premises in which this type of weaving was being undertaken and then proceed to trace the extent of survival of hand weaving beyond the mid-century. During fieldwork older residents have laid claim to an upper floor-weaving workshop at Top O'th Sugar Field (once called Top O'th Lane), Pickup Bank, where, in the past, the bearings of external stone steps could be seen in the external wall.[45]

Also, at Yate and Pickup Bank and nearby Eccleshill there were handloom weaving workshops at Stockclough Mill until the 1820s and at Cote Mill until the 1850s but then power looms were installed in the latter.[46] However, there were many other farms and cottages where handloom weaving was being undertaken. For example Drummer Stoops, Blacksnape; Nursery Nook, Eccleshill, Queen Street, Hoddlesden; Height Nook, Pickup Bank, Belthorn Road, Yate Bank and others.

In 1851, the proportions of non-weaving textile occupations were small but it was noted that some occupations were beginning to emerge in larger numbers. They accounted for eleven per cent in both Blacksnape and Eccleshill, one third in Hoddlesden and 17 per cent at Yate and Pickup Bank; these included 12 winders at Blacksnape, 18 winders in Eccleshill, 30 in Hoddlesden and 38 in Yate and Pickup Bank. The latter also had 13 carders and Hoddlesden six spinners and ten overlookers.

We now turn to an investigation of the characteristics of the handloom workforce. There is ample evidence to show that the handloom-weaving labour force was not male dominated as sometimes suggested. Bythell found that the weaving workforce in the early nineteenth century comprised a large element of women and children.[47] Baines referring specifically to upland Lancashire also suggested

Top O'th Sugar Field, Pickup Bank. About fifty years ago the right hand gable end of this row of cottages had external stone steps embedded in the wall leading to the attic. It is believed that both spinning and handloom weaving were undertaken in this roof space.

Height Nook, probably built around 1783, is obviously now derelict. Height Nook was part of a census location named Height End, here fourteen handloom weavers still remained at mid-nineteenth century and four of these were engaged in silk weaving.]

Drummer Stoops. By the mid-nineteenth century there was only one handloom weaver left.

Nursery Nook. By the mid-nineteenth century there were two handlooms weavers living there.

Queen Street, Hoddlesden. By the mid-nineteenth century there were two handloom weavers both of which were silk weavers.

that large components of handloom weavers were women and children.[48] Clapham noted that it was customary for fathers and sons to work in agriculture but for mothers and daughters to work at the handloom.[49] Horn generalised, stating that where cottage industries survived, even in the third quarter of the nineteenth century, that 'it was usually women and girls who were most heavily engaged'.[50] Additionally, Timmins in a more recent quantitative piece of research focusing on hand weaving suggested that in the districts of Lancashire, which he had investigated, that women and children averaged 60 per cent of the total hand weaving workforce in 1851 and 58 per cent in 1861. Timmins' data then infers that no more than 42 per cent of the handloom-weaving workforce was adult male. Furthermore, he suggested that during the 1850s, the hand labour force was ageing with the result that the overall proportions of young handloom weavers fell and the proportions of older weavers increased. Nevertheless, in spite of decline in numbers of younger weavers, he maintained that approximately half were less than 30 years of age in 1851. Moreover, he claimed that during the 1850s the proportions of weavers in some townships fell in the 10 to 29 age range and those of 50 years plus rose from which he deduced that the 'labour force was ageing as young people turned increasingly to alternative jobs'. However, he conceded that this varied from one place to another, and that in areas where power loom weaver numbers exceeded those of handloom weavers there was a preponderance of male handloom weavers by 1861.[51]

Analyses of age and gender characteristics of the manual-weaving workforce in the case study townships have been confined to handloom weavers. This is because of doubts regarding unspecified weavers and the specific nature of power loom weavers is addressed within the next section. Assessment of whether hand weavers were an ageing group has been undertaken by initially using an age demarcation line of 45 years related to the 1851 census age data. The results showed that 71 to 79 per cent were less than 45 years and therefore not an ageing workforce in 1851. This process was then extended to those of less than 30 years and this group represented approximately one-third in Blacksnape, one-fifth in Eccleshill and two-fifths in Yate and Pickup Bank of the total handloom weavers, a result close to that found by Timmins. At Hoddlesden the numbers of identifiable handloom weavers were so small that the same exercise was meaningless. Therefore, there were more handloom weavers aged under 30 years than those aged over 45 years. By 1861 the position had changed, there were no handloom weavers at Eccleshill and only a few at Blacksnape, three at Hoddlesden but over 50 at Yate and Pickup Bank. The average ages across the townships between 1851 and 1861 also increased from the mid-30s to the mid-40s. Therefore, falling numbers and increasing average ages are approximately in line with the observations made by Timmins, indicating that younger people were leaving hand weaving for alternative work.

In 1851, the gender proportions of handloom weavers at Hoddlesden and Yate and Pickup Bank were less than two per cent in difference but females marginally outnumbered males. At Blacksnape males represented two-thirds of the total and at Eccleshill males represented three-fifths of the total. Nevertheless, in all townships there were marginally more females aged under 45 years than males but for those aged less than 30 years there was a fairly equal gender balance.

In summary, prior to the mid nineteenth century, large proportions of the total workforces in the case study townships were engaged in handloom weaving, making them highly dependent on textiles. However, after the middle of the century decline was rapid and although some townships transferred from cotton to silk weaving this only marginally prolonged survival. Following decline some townships had very little alternative employment to which the inhabitants could turn. However, in addition to employment in the townships there was industry in nearby towns where there was a large demand for weavers, albeit working at the power loom. These towns were sometimes within daily walking distance or there was the alternative opportunity to relocate. This was unlike other communities in both east Lancashire and elsewhere that experienced industrial collapse, where the inhabitants were forced to migrate.

The nature of the workforce after the introduction of power loom weaving

The mills in the case study townships provided partial replacement employment for that lost in handloom weaving, which had been the major means of income for these communities earlier in the century. The aim of this final section is to examine the changing nature of the textile workforce in the townships and particularly that of the weaving workforce during the late nineteenth century. The emergence of factory-based textile manufacturing is evident from census data. However, in the case study communities there were even higher proportions of the total workforce engaged in textiles than in towns. Census data between 1851 and 1891 indicates that over half of those returned as being employed were working in textiles, except at Eccleshill in 1871 and Blacksnape 1891. In some decennial years, the figure reached two-thirds and occasionally

Table 5.3.   *Comparative numbers of textile workers in townships >= 10 years.*

	Year	Blacksnape	Eccleshill	Hoddlesden	Yate & Pickup Bank
Absolute numbers of textile workers	1851	94	190	223	469
	1871	54	211	148	311
	1891	77	284	271	226
Textile workers as percentage of population	1851	24	31	41	40
	1871	31	33	32	41
	1891	28	41	38	43
Textile workers as percentage of all occupations	1851	53	63	72	72
	1871	53	43	57	66
	1891	46	71	66	68

Shows the large numbers of textile workers in each township and the importance of this occupation to the economy.

Sources: CEBs

more than 70 per cent (Table 5.3). Nonetheless, there was a reduction in the numbers of textiles workers at Hoddlesden in 1881, almost certainly caused by the temporary closure of Vale Rock Mill Shed in 1878. The very high intensity of textile workers in the total workforces was in contrast to just over one-third of the occupied populations shown in the same censuses for Blackburn and Burnley being shown as being engaged in cotton manufacture.[52] However, until 1861 not all textile workers were employed in factories, although there was little evidence of substantial numbers of handloom weavers, but undifferentiated weavers prevented precise counting.[53] However, the townships were paradoxically still more dependent on textiles than the towns and this high dependency on textiles meant they were even more significantly affected by economic cycles, the impact of building new textile mills, and extensions to or the closure of existing ones. This made the communities vulnerable in depression, and potentially short of labour in upturns of the economy. These features no doubt explain the substantial in and out-migration evident during the period.

Lancashire's textile workforce comprised a multitude of trades but the largest trade in east Lancashire by far was the 'weaver'. In the mid-century there had been significant numbers of handloom weavers in the case study townships but after 1851, they had generally declined to very small numbers. By the late nineteenth century over 80 per cent of the total textile workforce in each township was engaged in weaving, but by this time the vast majority was working at the power loom in factories. These proportions of weavers were even larger than those in the neighbouring 'cotton towns'.[54]

Apart from 'weavers' in the above areas there were related textile occupations such as 'clothlookers', 'overlookers' and 'taper sizers'; these were considered male occupations, with the number in each township only in single figures. Winding and warping was mainly the province of females. Winders were more predominant than warpers but even the former occupation accounted for less than 10 per cent of the total textile labour force.

A backdrop for the analysis of the nature of the textile workforce has been provided above. This noted that following the mid-nineteenth century the populations of Blacksnape and Yate and Pickup Bank were falling. Eccleshill and Hoddlesden were exceptional for east Lancashire's rural communities in that populations increased. Nevertheless, the reasons for decline were different in each township. At Eccleshill there was expansion of the Waterside Mill, whilst in Yate and Pickup Bank workers were relocating to nearby Hoddlesden where they were probably already engaged there in the mills and where one mill owner had built houses for workers.[55] This was very different to the rapid growth occurring in towns. The higher proportions of textile workers in the total occupied workforces of the townships illustrate the considerable importance of this industry to these rural communities, when placed in comparison with the workforces in towns.

The number of operatives required in a weaving mill is approximately half the number of looms at the mill. Using this ratio in conjunction with the number of textile workers living in a township provides an insight into whether when new mills were built or existing ones expanded production, workers were attracted to the locality, not necessarily as complete 'strangers' but possibly as return migrants. However, as noted above the census does not suggest employment but rather what people regarded their occupations to be. Therefore, the census descriptions may indicate an over estimation of absolute numbers actually engaged in textiles.

The 1871 CEB for Eccleshill shows that 25 per cent more people were working in textiles than the estimated number of operatives required at the two mills,[56] therefore some of these workers must have been either employed outside of the village or unemployed and merely stating what they deemed their occupation to be. Although Grimshaw Bridge Mill ceased manufacturing textiles in 1872, the addition of a comparatively large extension to Waterside Mill by Bullough in 1880 demanded an increase in the workforce. This coincided with a population increase in the village between 1871 and 1881. By 1881, the workforce required at Waterside Mill has been estimated at about 80 more than the 221 textile operatives listed in census enumeration as living in Eccleshill. The mill owners therefore probably recognised the need to draw workers from neighbouring townships, and this possibly instigated a decision for the provision of additional housing, which is dealt with in chapter 7.[57] This was unlike the situation at Grimshaw Bridge Mill where there was stagnation of the workforce.

The workforces of about 550 for the Hoddlesden Mills were not only drawn from the village but also adjacent Pickup Bank where no mill existed. The census listed 227 cotton operatives living in the village in 1851, 70 of which were power loom weavers and 65 'weavers', assuming the latter were power loom weavers this was less than an estimated number of workers required at the mills, however, there were 398 textile workers living in Yate and Pickup Bank, 211 of which were power loom weavers, and a further 24 power loom weavers were living in Blacksnape, so it is likely that there was ample labour living locally. By 1871 the number of textile workers in Hoddlesden had declined to 150 of which 85 were cotton weavers. There was also a decline in Yate and Pickup Bank where there were 306 textile workers although 253 of these were cotton weavers. The reduction in the number of textile workers between 1851 and 1871 can be explained in part by the decline in handloom weaver numbers during the period. Nonetheless, the decline in textile workers described in the censuses for both Hoddlesden and Yate and Pickup Bank is at variance to the expansion occurring at the mill. One possible explanation is that there was a trough in an economic cycle around 1871, possibly because full recovery had not occurred from the 'Cotton Famine' and the numbers actually engaged in work at the time were unusual.

Anderson pointed out in 1851 that when mechanisation had largely replaced cottage manufacture the census showed, 'The industry (textile)… employed very large numbers of women and girls, and many branches employed them to the almost total exclusion of men'.[58] But trends changed over time. There were marginally larger proportions of male than female textile workers in the townships in 1851, therefore, textiles were generally important economically for both males and females. In 1861, the census shows that the town of Blackburn had only a small predominance of females in the textile workforce, but the reverse applied in Burnley. The 1871 figures for Burnley are not available but those for Blackburn generally demonstrate increasing numbers of textile workers and an increasing preponderance of females, which increased the divide between the sexes age 20 years and over.[59] By 1881, at both Blackburn and Burnley there was a large preponderance of females, and the absolute numbers of textile workers had increased. Between 1861 and 1881 the numbers of males engaged in 'cotton' had increased by over 10 per cent but the number of females had risen by more than 50 per cent. This larger growth in female labour was mainly a consequence of growth in the mechanised textile-weaving sector. By 1881, about 64 percent of textile workers were female in both nearby Blackburn and Darwen but in Oswaldtwistle the figure was 62 per cent. This was not all that different to the gap between the sexes in the rural communities.

The following questions raised in this section are concerned with whether these townships had different age, gender and marital status profiles to each other and to those in nearby cotton towns. If there were differences, what were the reasons? Was it the isolated nature of the communities or were they features of the pace of decline in handloom weaving? There is also the additional question of the extent communities changed their age and gender compositions between the domestic industry in the first half of the nineteenth century and the later factory industry.

In order to rationalise age structures of textile workers, three working age bands were chosen; children 10 to 14 years, a working age of 15 to 34 for adolescents and young adults and older adults 35 years plus. This division highlighted that the major working age for textile operatives was between 15 and 34 years (Table 5.4). Also as expected the 5 years age band for children usually contained the least number of textile workers, although their numbers had increased by 1891. The proportions of workers in textiles between the ages 15 to 34 were much higher than the proportions in the same age groups for the total populations of the townships. However, the age profiles of

TABLE 5.4.   *Percentage age balance of the total textile workforce between 1851 to 1891*

	Age bands 1851		
	10–14	15–34	35+
Blacksnape	22	45	33
Eccleshill	17	53	31
Hoddlesden	18	61	21
Yate & Pickup Bank	16	58	26
	Age bands 1871		
Blacksnape	6	70	24
Eccleshill	13	67	20
Hoddlesden	16	64	20
Yate & Pickup Bank	16	70	14
	Age bands 1891		
Blacksnape	29	53	18
Eccleshill	14	63	22
Hoddlesden	22	56	22
Yate & Pickup Bank	19	63	18
	Age bands 1881		
Blackburn	15	48	37
Darwen	15	49	36

Shows that the major age range of textile workers in the townships was fairly young.

Sources: PP. Census England & Wales 1851, 1871 & 1891. CEBs and LDS-RF 1881.

textile workers were not too different from those in Blackburn, Darwen and Oswaldtwistle.

The youthfulness of textile workers is demonstrated by average ages, which were between 24 and 28 years. However, the analysis of age structures was generally for a period when power looms had virtually overtaken the weaving process in east Lancashire, since the average age was higher in communities such as Mellor where handloom weaving had survived (Table 5.5).

TABLE 5.5. *Average age of textile workforce and weavers in 1871*

	Textile workforce	Weavers
Blacksnape	28	25
Eccleshill	25	24
Hoddlesden	26	23
Yate & Pickup Bank	24	22

Shows that most weavers were in their early twenties.

Sources: CEBs

TABLE 5.6. *Gender ratios of weavers in 1871*

	Male %	Female %
Blacksnape	30	70
Eccleshill	41	59
Hoddlesden	35	65
Yate & Pickup Bank	45	55

Shows most weavers were female.

Sources: CEBs

Analysis of the weaver sector gender in 1871 revealed higher proportions of females than males in the townships, but females were still in slightly lower proportions than in towns, except in Blacksnape (Table 5.6). This female domination demonstrates that these rural communities experienced a gender balance in weaving during the second half of the nineteenth century similar to that reported by Bythell, Chapman, Horn and Timmins for the intensive hand weaving period in the first half of the century, when they stated that women and girls formed the larger portion of the domestic workforce.[60] In contrast, the nearby 'cotton towns' of Blackburn, Darwen and Oswaldtwistle in 1881 had a larger gender divide for weavers than the rural townships. Here males accounted for between 30 and 33 per cent, and females 67 to 70 per cent of weavers.[61] The higher proportions of male weavers in the rural townships were possibly related to the smaller number of alternative occupational opportunities to be found locally. Whereas men in the 'cotton towns' had the choice of other types of work, such as the building industry and other heavy labouring duties that often required a robust physique, to which they were generally more suited than women.

In summary the townships then were transformed from a dual economy comprising domestic textile manufacture and farming that existed well before the late eighteenth century to a largely industrial economy in the second half of the nineteenth century. During the last quarter of the eighteenth century, water-powered mills were erected, as they were elsewhere in east Lancashire, and these at least partly replaced the domestic processes of carding and spinning. These mills were instrumental in increasing the supply of yarn for weaving and hence there was an increase in the numbers of handloom weavers. These mills were often no larger than a detached domestic dwelling. Local yeomen who were either chapmen or farmers owned them, there were frequent changes of ownership, but they only engaged small numbers of workers in each mill, who were probably natives, since there has been no evidence of pauper apprentices being recruited as in model villages. These early mills had either ceased functioning or diversified to other uses by the early nineteenth century. Nevertheless, domestic weaving continued to expand until about the second quarter of the century but this was then generally followed by decline.

Following the demise of handloom weaving, survival in the townships was aided by the building of steam driven mills from around mid-nineteenth century. These were much larger than their water-powered predecessors. Mill owners employed substantial numbers of local people although on a smaller scale than those engaged in the domestic system. Nonetheless, mill employment contributed towards checking the drift of population movement away from the villages. The larger mills owners were men of means with capital far in excess of the earlier yeomen owners. Some had been local chapmen with a large clientele but most were members of capitalist families. These businesses were usually successful, of long tenure and during which time they increased capacity.

A transition occurred between employment characteristics during the domestic era and full mechanisation. The domestic system was centred on familial employment in the home but this changed with the factory system to a more disciplined regime comprising individuals. The transition was not immediate; the tendency was for young people to enter the mills, mostly as power loom weavers whilst older handloom weavers, especially males often continued to pursue their craft. The relative proportions of power and handloom weavers during the transition period are difficult to determine because of ambiguities in census descriptions. However, what is clear is that these townships were essentially weaving communities throughout the nineteenth century regardless of the type of weaving since neither spinning nor carding were ever-major occupations.

The nature of a textile workforce in the towns and townships showed that in some respects the characteristics in the latter were similar to those in 'textile towns' whilst in other respects they were different. A breakdown by gender has revealed the large predominance of females working in textiles in the towns was less pronounced in the townships, by the third quarter of the nineteenth century. In both the towns and townships, weavers formed the major component of the textile workforce. Analysis of textile workforces, revealed that the age structure in both rural and urban communities was skewed towards young single people between the ages of 15 and 24 years living with parents. After the age of 25 years, there was a large fall in numbers of textile workers in both rural and urban communities, which suggests men could earn better wages in alternative employments and females were drifting from the workforce.

Finally, the townships were fluid and essentially weaving communities; they had similarities to isolated industrial village communities and to the towns but were different in some respects to both. They may therefore be seen as hybrids of the two.

CHAPTER SIX

Other Employment and Businesses

A GRICULTURAL AND TEXTILE OCCUPATIONS have been dealt with in chapters 4 and 5. This chapter looks at the less common occupations, the most significant of which were those within the umbrella sector of extraction industries.

Coal mining

Lancashire geologically had always been an area rich in coal measures. Prior to the Industrial Revolution the output of coal was very limited, and largely a rural activity. Nevertheless, in 1877 Abram referred to coal having been extracted in our area of study for over three centuries and there is further reference in both marriage and burial register records for the seventeenth century in respect of occupations undertaken by 'coliers' and 'colegitters'. Extraction of coal from the earth developed at a slow pace, initially it was from outcrops, then sloping tunnels into hillsides, which was termed drift mining. Later, vertical shafts were dug into the ground until coal seams were reached; coal was then extracted circumferentially. These were called bell pits because of the shape of the void caused by extraction from the ground. Later, deeper shafts were sunk to reach coal at even greater depths. At the bottom of these sinkings horizontal tunnels were used to extract the coal and the tunnel roof was supported by either timber pit props or pillars of coal that were left intact for support. As mines became deeper, danger increased from environmental problems such as poor ventilation, flooding and gas explosions. Additional hazards also arose from tunnels collapsing and even the process of hauling the minerals to the surface was initially by means of a series of hazardous ladders.

 Until the early nineteenth century pits were small and only a few male miners were engaged in each, but these were often supported by women and children, the

Map 6.1.
Locations of
the numerous
collieries in the
townships are
indicated on the
map.

REPRODUCED FROM THE
1840S ORDNANCE SURVEY
MAP.

latter being as young as six or seven years and working an eleven hour day. The women and children were engaged in moving the coal underground and to the surface. Some of the tunnels were little more than two feet high and vertical movement was by climbing ladders possibly to a height of 50 feet. In 1842 the Mines Act banned the employment of all females and boys of less than 10 years from being employed in underground work. Colliery owners then started to install tramlines for trucks to be drawn by ponies. Nevertheless, following the advent of the steam engine for transporting coal both vertically and horizontally growth of the industry was rapid, the coal being used for both commercial and domestic purposes.

The Ordnance Survey maps from the 1840s onwards indicate many collieries in the vicinity of the townships (Map 6.1). At Eccleshill there was Brocklehead Colliery just to the west of Brocklehead Farm, a little further south lay Closes Colliery which was worked by the Bullough family who later owned Waterside cotton mill. Harwoods Colliery was situated on the western boundary of Eccleshill and at one time worked by John and Joseph Place, owners of Hoddlesden pipe works, while at Grimshaw there was Flash Colliery and further north Dandy Row Colliery. These collieries were small workings and employed only small numbers of miners each, although J. & J. Place were employing a workforce of 64 in 1853.[1] Another larger working, Waterside Colliery, comprised seams in both the earlier Closes and Harwoods Collieries. Adam Bullough sank a further shaft there in the early 1860s and the enterprise was extended in the 1870s to include a brick and tile works, but both closed in the 1880s. In 1872 the Eccleshill Coal Company was registered as a limited company and, following the closure of the Flash and Furnace pits, began to rework existing pits at Eccleshill and Ellison Fold; including Harwoods Colliery and possibly another section of Closes Colliery. The company began liquidation in 1877 following problems with flooding in the mine works. In the 1890s a much larger working was opened known as Eccleshill Colliery and located near Goosehouse Lane, employing around one hundred men[2] (Figure 6.1).

Many small pits were being worked at Hoddlesden before the mid-nineteenth century, but at about this time J. & J. Place commenced mining in 1838.[3] Their first major enterprise was a pit sunk near Vale Rock Mill to a depth of over 350 feet in the 1850s. The next shaft was sunk near to Holker House and eventually they were involved in working twelve pits. Two of these pits were only small. The Eccleshill one employed 32 men below ground and seven surface workers in 1916, whilst one at Top O'th Meadow, Hoddlesden employed 20 men below ground and six on the surface.[4] The last colliery to be opened and the largest was situated at Hoddlesden Moss about one mile from Hoddlesden Village; this was a drift mine in which there was an upper strata of coal and a lower strata of clay.[5] In 1861 the Places' workforce at this pit numbered 40 men but a year later it had risen to 110 men. From this pit, coal and fireclay were being transported over land by tubs on rails, initially to Old Sett End and later to New Sett End.

From the 1930s a jig road was formed between the pit at Hoddlesden Moss and Holker House which continued to the pipe work, at Hoddlesden. The line was used for transporting coal and clay to the pipe works at Hoddlesden village. This was in two sections; a continuous rope hauled the tubs from the pit to an interchange near Holker House and then a continuous chain to the pipe works. There was originally a further extension from the pipe works to Set End on the Roman Road, which travelled through a tunnel below Hoddlesden Village, commencing on the pipe works side of Graham Street and terminating in Harwoods Lane below the bus termininus. This tunnel was used during World War II as an air-raid shelter for both residents and children at the local school. By 1941 around 110 underground and 37 surface workers were engaged at the pit, but because of nationalisation in 1947 the pit was compulsorily purchased by the National Coal Board from Places and by 1953 the labour force was reduced to 103 of which 88 were colliers, but the pit finally closed in 1961 and the 99 workers became redundant.[6]

An indenture dated 1875 granted permission to mine coal beneath Hole House, Yate Bank for use at Whitebirk. At Red Earth, Yate and Pickup Bank, W. H. Shaw of Haslingden opened the Belthorn Drift Mine in the early 1890s but this was abandoned in 1963.[7] From this colliery a tram road was constructed to Ratten Row, Belthorn from which coal and fireclay were transported by aerial cable to Shaw's Brickworks at Whitebirk near Blackburn. Around 1900 a drift at Cote was developed to replace the existing one and employed about forty miners, and a third Drift was finally opened in the late 1930s at which thirty miners were engaged. From this Drift a jig road was constructed to Shaw's Brickworks at Eccleshill but alas the working were closed in 1963.[8]

Between 1851 and 1891 there were 120 to 130 coal workers living in the four villages. During this period numbers were fairly stable at Blacksnape, on the decline at Eccleshill and Yate and Pickup Bank, but quadrupled at Hoddlesden. This industry contributed

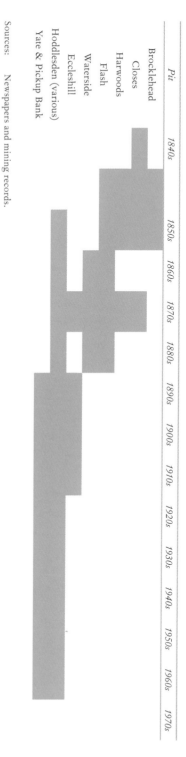

Figure 6.1. *Working periods of pits.*

Sources: Newspapers and mining records.

Pit | 1840s | 1850s | 1860s | 1870s | 1880s | 1890s | 1900s | 1910s | 1920s | 1930s | 1940s | 1950s | 1960s | 1970s

Brocklehead
Closes
Harwoods
Flash
Waterside
Eccleshill
Hoddlesden (various)
Yate & Pickup Bank

significantly to the economies of the townships (Tables 6.1 & 6.2). The increase of coal workers at Hoddlesden from about 1860 appears to be linked to the opening of Places' Pits, although there was competition for employees in the village from the textile industry.

Table 6.1. *Number of coal mine workers*

Township	1851	1871	1891
Blacksnape	31	24	32
Eccleshill	43	31	16
Hoddlesden	11	33	52
Yate & Pickup Bank	46	36	27
Total	131	124	127

Sources: CEBs.

Table 6.2. *Colliers as percentage of total employed*

Township	1851	1871	1891
Blacksnape	17	18	20
Eccleshill	14	7	4
Hoddlesden	3	12	9
Yate & Pickup Bank	6	7	6

Sources: CEBs.

The colliers at Blacksnape lived in the cottages on the Roman Road, at Eccleshill they lived mainly in the Pothouse area, in Hoddlesden largely in the centre of the village although a few lived on outlying farms. At Yate and Pickup Bank they were mostly centred in Belthorn or close by. All of the coal workers were male. In 1851 there was a boy of eight engaged in coal work at Blacksnape and two boys aged eight and nine at Eccleshill but it is not clear whether they were engaged on the surface or underground.

Clay Industries

At Hoddlesden there was a clay works owned by Joseph Place and Sons, who commenced manufacturing bricks from the clay obtained in their coal pits around 1863, they then extended the business in the mid-1870s and constructed large extensions for manufacturing other types of clay ware goods in 1887. The

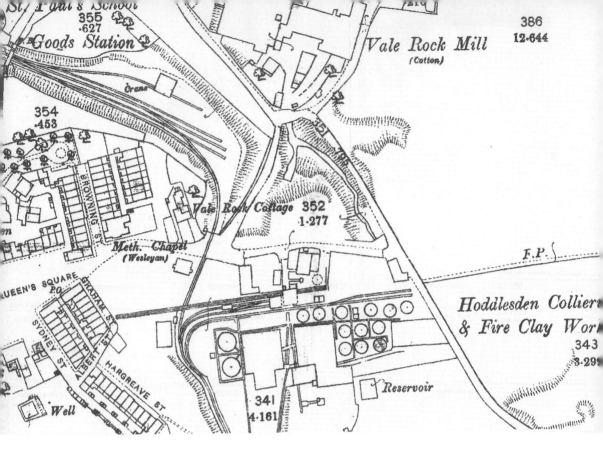

Map 6.2. Shows the location of the pipe works in Hoddlesden village with access from the railways goods sidings

Eccleshill Pipe Works, a further industry owned by the Place brothers, was situated at Goose House Bridge, Eccleshill.

Map 6.3. Shows
the location of
the pipe works
at Eccleshill with
access from the
railways goods
sidings.

Reproduced from the
1888 Ordnance
Survey map.

clay for manufacture and coal for firing the clay to form earthenware goods (mainly drain pipes) were intertwined in a combined extraction process from the various pits owned by the same company as noted above. Production at the works was later extended to a large range of fire clay drainage pipes and other earthenware materials. The clay was moulded into the required shapes and then burnt in coal-fired kilns. This business was dissolved during May 1965.[9]

The Place family opened a further works at Goose House Bridge, Eccleshill in 1892 (Map 6.3). Here they initially manufactured enamelled bricks but later

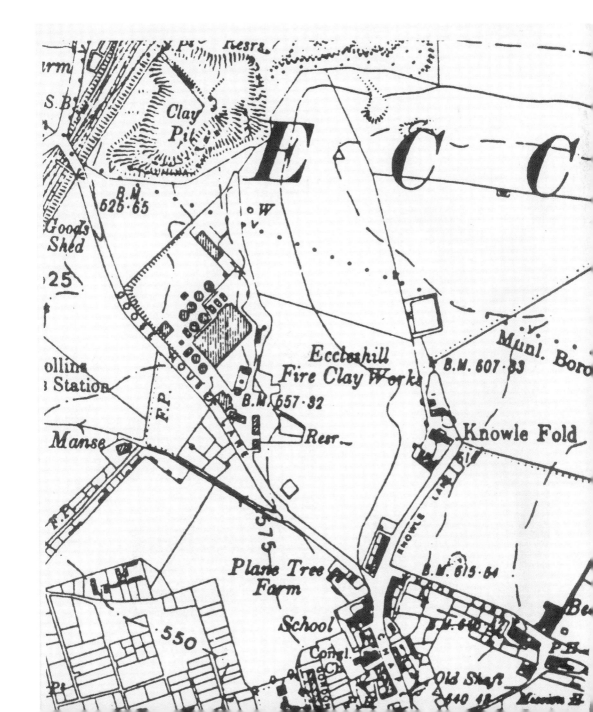

added drainpipes. The directors were two grandsons and three nephews of one
of the founder members of the business at Hoddlesden. It is evident that Places
was an important local business since the company was employing 350 workers
by 1932, although this figure probably comprises both clay workers and colliers.[10]

At Eccleshill, Shaw's Glazed Brick Company Limited started a works in 1909
with 60 employees that had been transferred from the Whitebirk Works in
Blackburn. Production comprised glazed bricks, faience and terra cotta components. Expansion of the works in the 1920s widened production to include
sanitary ware, fireplace surrounds and burial grave ornamentation and by 1926
there were 300 operatives employed at the works. The manufacturing processes
were aided by the extraction of the raw materials, coal and fireclay, from the
firm's drift mine in Yate and Pickup Bank, which was initially opened in the late
nineteenth century. By 1930 the workforce was about 500 strong, but in 1961 the

firm was amalgamated with a similar company by the name of Hathernware.[11]. Although not all employees in the mining and clay processes lived in the villages, the industries made a substantial contribution to the local economies.

To support both the local extractive and textile industries Ranken made an application to Parliament in 1864 for a branch line to be added to the Lancashire and Yorkshire Blackburn to Darwen railway line to serve Hoddlesden. This was introduced in 1876 as a goods only line and on the day of opening it was celebrated by a village party on the field behind the Griffin Public House (Ranken Arms). A further upgrade to the rail link was suggested by Adam Bullough, for passenger stations to be built at both Hoddlesden and Waterside for which he was prepared to donate land and money. The offer was never accepted, however, and the line only ever transported goods.[12]

The railway line terminating at Hoddlesden stretched for over two miles from Goosehouse Bridge near Lower Darwen to the Goods Station at Hoddlesden and was opened in stages. The larger section to Shaw's Glazed Brick works was opened for goods traffic on 23 May 1876 and extended to Hoddlesden on 2 October 1876. In 1884 the line was extended to cross Copy Lane and enter the pipe works manufacturing premises [See Map 6.2] Here sidings and loading bays were formed to facilitate transportation of the products of manufacture by the works own saddle tank steam engine. By 1950 the line from Goosehouse Bridge had been terminated at Shaw's Glazed Brick Works.[13]

Quarrying

There were many very small quarries in the townships along with a few larger ones. Extensive stone extraction in Pickup Bank took place at Twitchels (SD. 735 223), Great Hill (SD. 732 223), Gib (SD. 730 232) and at Tang Brook (SD. 722 223). In the latter quarry the stone for the Chapel at the top of Long Hey Lane was hewed around 1834. More recently these sites have been used for tipping and evidence of their existence have now been either wholly or partially destroyed. At Belthorn there was an early quarry from which the sandstone for some of the local houses was probably extracted but this site was closed in the 1840s. (SD 720 245). At Hoddlesden quarries were established near Holker House (SD. 723 222) and in Harwood's Lane (SD. 705 222). There was also a sandpit opposite Leonard Terrace at Waterside.

The numbers of personnel engaged in quarrying appears to have been very small. In the four townships in 1851 only seven quarrymen were listed in the census enumeration, in 1871 ten and in 1891 there were only two engaged in quarrying. There may have been others extracting stone from these quarries but living outside of the villages although it is unlikely they were in significant numbers. Stonemasons were in slightly larger numbers during the same period but it is not known whether they were working stone extracted locally. There were twelve men engaged as stonemasons in 1851 but only three in 1871 and seven in 1891.

Iron Works

Manufacturing of iron commenced around 1874 by the Darwen Iron Company Limited, which was established at Eccleshill and a tramway was built for transporting coal to the blast furnaces from a mine owned by the Eccleshill Coal Company. However, the Iron Company was sold in 1877 to the Darwen and Mostyn Iron Company, which became a large enterprise as demonstrated by the inventory that listed a locomotive and one hundred and eleven railway wagons. In addition during the 1880s the Ironworks engaged around one hundred employees.

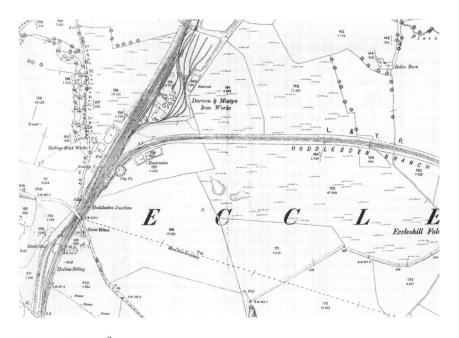

Map 6.4. Map showing the location of the Darwen and Mostyn Iron Works.
REPRODUCED FROM THE 1888 ORDNANCE SURVEY MAP.

Paper Manufacture

Manufacturing commenced in Eccleshill following the closure of Grimshaw Bridge textile mill in 1872. SD 708 242. This paper mill had a chequered history with many changes of ownership, modifications and extensions to the buildings but nevertheless, engaged a growing number of employees.

Public Services

Service enterprises in the villages comprised mainly shops and public houses. These made only a small contribution to the wage earning capacity of the community. Together they nevertheless provided food and social outlets. The nineteenth-century census for the villages states that people were engaged as 'grocer' (Table 6.3). From this we may assume that there were local food outlets and incidental sales of goods. Apart from Eccleshill and Yate and Pickup Bank in 1851 there were grocers residing in the townships in the three decennial census years analysed.

Table 6.3. *Details of shop workers*

Shop workers engaged in the villages during the second half of the nineteenth century.

Township	Name	Address	Occupation	Age
Blacksnape				
1851	Thomas Whewell	Blacksnape	Grocer	58
	John Fish	Blacksnape	Grocer	52
1871	Ralph Entwistle	Hillock	Grocer	59
	John Fish	Barons	Grocer	76
	John Riley	Blacksnape	Grocer	66
1891	Lot Wilson	Blacksnape	Grocer	60
	John Fish	Barons	Grocer & Railway Man had assistant	50
Eccleshill				
1851	Nil			
1871	Thomas Walsh	Waterside	Grocer & Draper	36
1891	Nancy Jones	Dandy Row	Grocer	34
Hoddlesden				
1851	JohnPlace	Hoddlesden	Grocer	75
	William Fish	Hoddlesden	Grocer	49
1871	William Wood	Queen Street	Grocer	26
	Henry Place	Queen Street	Grocer	48
1891	James Shepard	Queen Street	Confectioner	63
	Ben Harwood	Pleasant View	Shopman	27
	Benjamin Walsh	Harwood Lane	Co-op Manager	30
Yate & Pickup Bank				
1851	Nil			
1871	James Walsh	Moorgate	Grocer	43
	Jonathon Taylor	Belthorn	Grocer & Beerseller	62
	Jonathon Cronshaw	Davey Inn	Grocer & Publican	60
1891	George Yates	Taylor Buildings	Grocer	45
	Christopher Harwood	Top O'th Copy	Grocer	39

Sources: CEBs.

Nevertheless, there are other sources providing evidence for the existence of shops in the villages as noted below.

The Hoddlesden Co-operative Progressive Stores and Industrial Society Ltd movement commenced in 1860. Records show it then 'moved from Albert Buildings, Hoddlesden in the Parish of Darwen to 10 Harwood Road, Hoddlesden', which later became a privately owned confectioner's shop with bake house at the rear.

Harwoods Lane Hoddlesden. The right hand building was probably the first co-operative store in the village. It later became a confectioner's shop with a bake house in the basement at the rear. The edifice has now been completely redesigned from a shop front to a domestic property.

The building in the foreground is at the junction of Queen Street and Sydney Street. It was originally a co-operative store, later converted to a Conservative Club but now the village Community Centre. The extent of the building stretches from the archway to the door of the dwelling on the right of the photograph.

In 1862 the Co-operative Society continued business in a shop at the bottom of Sydney Street, which later became a Conservative Club. The rapid early success of the original business is indicated since the Hoddlesden Co-operative Progressive Stores had been offered a lease from the Hoddlesden Co-operative Land and Building Company for £300 to build a larger store and this was accepted. The new shop opened on 1 October 1862 and a celebratory Tea Party was held on the 18th of the month for members and their wives.[14]

Further evidence of the Hoddlesden Co-operative Progressive Stores being a very successful enterprise occurred in 1889 when a much larger three-story building was erected at the junction of Harwood Lane and Bayne Street.[15] The premises comprised a combined general grocery section and butchery, and a separate drapery. As a result of this development the Co-operative store that traded at the bottom of Sydney Street, which was sub-let on 31 December 1889 to Alexander Carus, Richard Herbert Eccles, William Walmesley, Thomas Howarth, James Beswick and Henry Turner, who have been presumed to be the trustees of the Conservative Club. The Co-operative Society at Hoddlesden was merged with Darwen Co-operative Society in 1957 and later sold and converted to the present Conservative Club.

This three-storey building was built in 1889 as a Co-operative Store to replace the building that is now a Conservative Club. The right hand ground floor was a general store and butchery and the left hand side a Drapery. On the upper floor were facilities for communal activities such as concerts and dancing. The house adjacent and to the left of the store was the manager's residence.

In the late nineteenth century two branches of the Hoddlesden Co-operative store were opened at Waterside, which was a combined grocers and drapers,[16] and Yate and Pickup Bank. The latter opened in 1887, at which stage it was affiliated to the Hoddlesden store at the lower end of Sydney Street.[17] Local inhabitants have claimed that the Pickup Bank store sold everything the community needed, if it was not in stock it would be ordered and quickly delivered. Apart from foodstuffs, it sold an array of hardware for both domestic and agricultural purposes.

This Co-operative Shop at Waterside was a branch of the Hoddlesden Co-operative Store. It contains a basement at the rear but the whole has now been converted to a dwelling.

Rear elevation of Waterside Co-operative Store.

The Co-operative Shop at Pickup Bank was a branch of Hoddlesden Co-operative Store. It is believed that this remote store sold almost anything including food, a limited amount of clothing and farm utensils including barbed wire. The building is now used as a domestic dwelling

The Co-operative Society that became a Conservative Club at the lower end of Sydney Street has more recently had a chequered history. In November 1978 the Club relocated to its present premises, which are now in what had been the three storey Co-op opposite the Ranken Arms. The trustees, William Jenkinson, John Walsh, Ronald Marsden and Richard Parkinson sold the building for £7000 to the trustees of Hoddlesden Youth Club and Community Centre who were namely Phyllis Jean Barton (Duckworth), Alan Wilkinson, Cyril Edward Burke and Jeffrey Eastham. The purchase was made from moneys provided by the Management Committee of the Hoddlesden Youth Club and Community Centre, whose members at that time were, David Barton, Ronald Whittaker, Rex Maynard, Leonard Hindle, Alan Wilkinson and Margaret Barnes. The committee raised monies from rental of the building and fund raising events. This even included a musical sledge going around the village at Christmas playing carols and a house-to-house collection. Credit must be given to all who made the effort to keep the project going. Around 2003/4 the then committee changed the name from the Hoddlesden Youth Club and Community Centre to East Rural Youth And Community Association, ERYCA for short. The present name is now The Carus Community Centre.

Shop Queen Street, Hoddlesden. The building with a window sun blind was a general store which has now been converted to a Fish and Chip Shop.

There were also smaller shops in Hoddlesden, one of which was in Queen Street. Living there in 1871 was a William Wood described as a grocer aged 26 years whose wife was a weaver.

Another shop was situated in Queen Square at the end of Browning Street, which had a small bake house at the rear. Henry Place, a member of the local industrial family, owned this shop.

The 1909 Finance Act Valuation also notes a shop in Albert Street but no further evidence of this has been found.[18] These were only small concerns selling a limited variety of foodstuffs, sweets and a few household requirements, but

Shop at Queens Square, Hoddlesden. The left hand portion of the building was a general store and the right hand end formed a bake house and domestic accommodation. The premises are now utilised as a Post Office and village shop.

The corner building in the foreground with blocked doorway was a Post Office on the ground floor and clogger's shop above. The now blocked doorway was the entrance to the Post Office whilst the blocked opening above was a loading door for materials to the workshop area. The building is now a domestic dwelling.

provided a useful service for the community. There was also a chip shop opened later at the back of Queen Street. At the bottom of Graham Street a Post Office was situated above which there was a Clogger's shop where local people took their clogs to be 're-shod' with iron or rubber soles.

Opposite the Co-op at Waterside there was a small corner shop at the end of Waterside Terrace, which sold groceries and odds and ends, whilst at Pickup Bank at Top O'th Copy there was a mid-terraced cottage where the resident used the front room as a small shop, selling sweets and small household items

The dwelling in the foreground is located at the end of Waterside Terrace, Eccleshill. It has had several previous uses in that it was originally a social club provided by the Bullogh family, the owners of both Waterside Mill and local collieries. Later it was used for political purposes by both the Liberals and Conservatives after which it became a village shop and has now been converted to a dwelling house.

Confirmation of businesses in the villages can be seen from the following extracts taken from the Mannex & Co. Trade Directory of Darwen for 1868:

ECCLESHILL:

Alice Hunt, Duke of York Public House.
Hy Waterworth, Handle's Arms, Public House.
James Hope, Puch Bowl, Public House.
Mary Dearden, Beerhouse.
Thomas Fielden, Shopkeeper.

HODDLESDEN:

William Entwistle: Boot & Shoe Maker, Browning Street
James Walsh: Shopkeeper, Hoddlesden Fold.
James Titherington: (Traveller), Linen & Wool Drapers.
Henry Place: Grocer & Provisions.
Richard Holden: Hoddlesden Co-operative Stores.
Elizabeth Yates: Griffin Inn (Ranken Arms), Hoddlesden.
Jsp H Place, Coal Merchant.
James & Robert Knowles, Cotton Manufacturers.

YATE & PICKUP BANK

James Howarth: Shopkeeper, Yate & Pickup Bank.
R. Holden: Shopkeeper, Yate & Pickup Bank.
Benjamin Haworth: Beer House, Yate & Pickup Bank.
Edward Houghton: Beer House, Yate & Pickup Bank.
Robert Hunt: Beer House, Yate & Pickup Bank.
R. Leach: Beer House, Yate & Pickup Bank.
William Yates: Beer House, Yate & Pickup Bank.
Holden Haworth, Cotton Spinner & Manufacturer.
Jno Ward, Innkeeper.
James Walsh, Shopkeeper.

BLACKSNAPE cannot be separated from Darwen

From Mannex Directory and census data the proliferation of premises selling alcohol has been noted. Nonetheless, just over one-quarter of premises during the period 1851 to 1891 were solely allocated to this purpose. The majority of people engaged in selling beer were in dual occupations, the second of which was usually as a farmer. Over one-quarter of those selling alcohol were classified as 'Beerseller' as distinct from 'Publican' and it may be presumed that the former restricted sales to beer only (Table 6.4).

Table 6.4.
Publicans
engaged in
the villages
during the
second half of
the nineteenth
century.

TABLE 6.4. *Details of publicans 1851 to 1891.*

Township/year	Name	Address	Occupation	Age
Blacksnape				
1851	John Yates	Rose and Crown	Victualler	37
1871	John Yates	Grimhills	Publican & Farmer 17A	17
1891	James Haslam	Crown & Thistle	Publican & Farmer	45
	John Aspden	Red Lion	Publican & Farmer	54
	?	Blacksnape	Publican	30
Eccleshill				
1851	William Lightbown	Pot House PH	Publican & Farmer 14A	45
	George Briggs	Waterside	Publican & Farmer 19A	39
	Arnold Holden	Handle Arms	Publican & Farmer 7A	36
1871	James Hope	Pot House PH	Publican & Farmer 14A	38
1891	James Ainsworth		Publican & Farmer 14A	36
	Martha Ainsworth	Handle Arms	Publican	30
	James Rostron	Duke of York	Publican	46
Hoddlesden				
1851	Richard Parker	Hoddlesden	Publican & Farmer 6A	46
1871	John Bury	East Scotland	Beerseller & Farmer 15A	65
	Yates Yates	Ranken Arms	Publican & Farmer 10A	35
1891	Millicent Yates	Ranken Arms	Publican	50
Yate & Pickup Bank				
1851	Thomas Taylor	Belthorn	Beerseller	61
	James Holden	Cat Hole	Publican & Farmer 10A	40
	Samual Jackson	Hoyle House	Publican & Farmer 13A	48
	Atherton Whittaker	New Inn	Publican & Farmer 15A	33
	Edward Sharples	Grimshaw Bridge	Beerseller & Farmer 18A	29
	Jonathon Taylor	Belthorn	Beerseller & Farmer 26A	41
	Jonathon Cronshaw	Belthorn	Publican & Farmer 50A	39
	Benjamin Walsh	Longhey Lane	Beerseller & Farmer 6A	29
	John Greenwood	Scholes Fold	Beerseller & Farmer 8A	30
	Michael Haworth	Bankfold	Beerseller & Farmer 8A	48
	John Wood	Belthorn	Publican	44
1871	Yates Yates	New Inn	Publican	48
	Rachel Houghton	Shorrock Fold	Beerseller	44
	William Yates	Belthorn	Beerseller	38
	George Brindle	Coit	Beerseller & Farmer	52
	John Wood	Belthorn Inn	Publican & Farmer 70A	64
	Jonathon Taylor	Belthorn	Beerseller & Grocer	62*
	Jonathon Cronshaw	Davey Inn	Publican & Grocer	60*
1891	John Townsend	Duke of Wellington	Beerseller	41
	Thomas Holt	Bell in the Thorn	Publican	25
	Thomas Yates	New Inn	Publican & Farmer	35
	Henry Walsh	Derby Arms	Publican	47

Sources: CEBs.

Crown and Thistle Public House, Grimhills. This hostelry is situated on the Old Roman Road that linked Ribchester to Manchester. *Listed Building.*

Red Lion Public House, Blacksnape. Another hostelry situated on the Old Roman Road that linked Ribchester to Manchester.

Handles Arms Public House, Eccleshill. Also a hostelry situated on the Old Roman Road that linked Ribchester to Manchester. In late twentieth century the business became a European food restaurant but is now a dwelling.

Blacksnape had three public houses in the nineteenth century all situated on the Roman Road passing through the village. However, details of these in census enumeration are somewhat anomalous. The present Crown and Thistle at Grimhills appears to have been variously named 'Rose and Crown', in the mid nineteenth century, later 'Grimhills' and then 'Hillock'.

A Black Lion Inn was noted in the 1881 census but this could have been either redesignated to the present Red Lion , or an earlier version of the 'Blacksnape' public house later described as the Punch Bowl Inn located nearly opposite to the entrance to Heys Lane as noted on map 6.1. It is unlikely that they were thriving businesses since their occupiers' income was supplemented by farming activities.

Eccleshill had three public houses; the Handles Arms, the Punch Bowl Inn and the Duke of York. These public houses were first mentioned in the 1881 census, but the latter should not be confused with its namesake on the same road traversing Blacksnape. The Duke of York was first listed in the 1891 census as being situated at Waterside.

The present Ranken Arms, Hoddlesden was built on the site of a sixteenth century Old Hall, that later became known as the Griffin Public House, which was described by W. T. Ashton in 1864 as having 'deteriorated into an ale

Punch Bowl Inn, Pothouse, Eccleshill. Yet another hostelry situated on the Old Roman Road that linked Ribchester to Manchester. *Listed Building.*

Duke of York Public House, Waterside, Eccleshill. Through lack of customers the business has been sold and converted to a dwelling house.

Duke of York Public House, Waterside, Eccleshill, around 1993 when it was still operating as a Public House.
Courtesy Geoffrey Cooper.

Ranken Arms
Public House,
Hoddlesden.
Listed Building.

house'.[19] The current Ranken Arms was built in 1911. In the village there were also other amenities selling alcohol but these had either a social or political attachment. The Conservative Clubs noted above sold beer and spirits, and provided indoor sports facilities such as snooker tables, darts and a congenial atmosphere. At numbers 23 and 25 Baynes Street there was a village Working Men's Club before it was relocated in Pleasant View; beer was sold in both establishments. Following the relocation of this club the building in Bayne Street was redesignated to a Liberal Club but evidence has not been found for the sale of alcohol at this establishment. These social providers, albeit marginal, created full-time and part-time work for the local inhabitants.

What is staggering from the census analysis is that it reveals that there were eleven establishments in 1851 at Yate and Pickup Bank purporting to sell intoxicating liquor. A possible reason for this may have been because packhorse routes traversed the township and there was a demand from the drivers. However, it is evident that the number of public houses declined to seven by 1871 and then four by 1891. The majority of the establishments selling liquor could hardly be called public houses, since most were dwellings where the head was also engaged in farming. Nevertheless, a few were very definitely in business as drinking houses and possibly providing overnight accommodation. The most likely of these were two designated as Inns; New Inn and the Duke of Wellington (locally known as Owd Rosins)

The right hand part of the dwelling facing was originally a Working Men's Club but then became a Liberal Club. As seen in the photograph the building is now a dwelling.

'Old Rosins' Inn, was named using the 'nick name' of John Townsend a nineteenth century landlord. This Inn was originally called the Duke of Wellington, it is located just a short distance from an old pack horse route off Long Hey Lane, Pickup Bank. It was probably built in the eighteenth century.

Hotel extension. During the twentieth century a large extension was added to convert the above Inn into a residential country hotel.

Dog Inn, Belthorn, Yate Bank. This is an old Inn in Belthorn village that was built adjacent to the old Blackburn to Haslingden Road.

An extract from the 1910 Finance Act field book describes the New Inn as a farm building separated from the combined domestic living space and public house, with outbuildings comprising a barn, shippon for 6 cows, a stable plus a further old barn and shippon. In addition to living accommodation, the Inn had a billiard room, parlour, tap room and kitchen. The 1910 Finance Act field book stated it was a 'Fully Licensed Free House' selling '2 barrels a week (36), 2 dozen bottles a week and about 1 gall spirits a week'.[20] Also carved into a stone above the entrance door we find 'New Inn, licensed dealer in foreign and British spirits, ale, beer, porter, tobacco, by order 1837' The location of public houses described as 'Belthorn' is vague but Belthorn Inn was built by Robert Yates in 1765 , other Inns were Bell in the Thorn built 1792, Derby Arms and the Pack Horse Inn built in 1820. In the nineteenth century there were no less than nine beer houses and inns in Belthorn alone, however, we must not overlook the fact that Belthorn was partly in Yate Bank and partly in Oswaldtwistle.

Pack Horse Inn, Belthorn. The Inn is situated on the Blackburn to Haslingden new road.

These villages were also serviced by an array of occupations beyond those noted above, comprising tradesmen and persons serving the community but there were generally very few in each category. Those oriented to agricultural activities were the village blacksmith and wheelwright. Others were allied to the building trades such as carpenters, joiners and plasterers. A third group of artificers was associated with household provisions, examples of which were: baker, butcher, clogger, draper, dressmaker, fishmonger, laundress, milliner, shoemaker and tailor. Providing education and pastoral care were the occasional schoolmaster, mistress and pupil teachers, vicar and sexton. Significant numbers of semi-skilled occupations were evident in all townships. In the male domain were general labourers and a few specialist labourers such as those engaged at an iron works, paper mill, pipe works and those supporting tradesmen. Females were engaged as charwomen, house-keepers, nurses and servants, although many of those designated as nurses were young girls who could have had at best no more than a very basic appreciation of nursing. There was also the village constable, engraver, paper maker, potter and several others supporting the community.

The configuration of Hoddlesden village housing changed considerably in late twentieth century. By this stage industry had virtually disappeared and a need for working-class housing for those engaged in local industry was no longer required. Instead the village housing stock was expanded to become a dormitory township for people working elsewhere and those in retirement.. This was in contrast to the satellite villages where new housing was minimal, although many properties had been either modernized or reconstructed. The twentieth century housing illustrated here is in sharp contrast to that originally built for industrial workers as will be seen in the following chapter.

CHAPTER SEVEN

Textile workers' housing

THE SHIFT FROM THE domestic system to the factory system described in chapter five created huge changes not only in working conditions but also in living conditions. This chapter seeks to explore the housing stock in the case study townships during the late nineteenth century, comparing it to the experiences in towns and model villages. Furthermore, it explains the nature of the additional housing that was provided for mill workers and analyses the extent to which occupational differences occurred between inhabitants living in older properties and those in new housing. It also looks at whether the families occupying mill houses were different in other respects from those in the rest of the village.

Workforces were inevitably dependent on housing provision as pointed out by Timmins 'the rise of factories…during the Industrial Revolution period brought a considerable demand for workers' housing'.[1] Chapman observed there had been a lack of attention to rural housing by historians and stated, 'there has been no attempt to survey the evolution of standards of accommodation … prevailing in adjacent rural areas and in industrial towns'.[2] In two of the townships investigated, factory houses were built that still survive and these have been studied by using fieldwork, evidence collected from census records, and descriptions in the 1910 Act Inland Revenue valuation and field books.

Early industrial housing built in late eighteenth and early nineteenth centuries was built in a regime lacking enforceable control of standards, hence most working-class dwellings were of a low standard. This applied to both speculative and mill owner built housing,[3] although paternalistic employers often insisted on higher standards.[4] Hole's contemporary opinion was that these circumstances continued until at least the mid-nineteenth century, and also stated that 'Social or sanitary considerations do not sufficiently weigh with the capitalist builder if they involve [financial] outlay without a corresponding return',[5] but these views were also relevant to at least some houses built by mill owners. Such conditions led to ill health and consequently demand for improvements.

Around the 1840s, both reformers and legislators lobbied for improvements to the environment, concentration being mainly on lack of sanitation, defective drainage, inadequate clean water supply and overcrowding. This debate was directed towards towns since conditions were worse there than in rural areas because of housing density and industrialisation,[6] which led to disease and high mortality, both of which resulted in economic and social costs.[7] The outcome was the Public Health Act 1848 but initial implementation was slow, spasmodic and mainly confined to individual urban authorities. Some large authorities such as Manchester and Liverpool had previously compiled their own regulatory frameworks,[8] but additionally, exceptions occurred such as at Ashton-under-Lyme where a private landowner insisted on 'good, firm and substantial buildings' when granting leases.[9] However, rural areas were excluded from the legislation.

Embodied in the 1848 Act was a provision for compilation of local building byelaws for the construction of dwellings and environmental design features.[10] Subsequently 'Byelaw Housing' regulations emerged from the 1860s, although these were not rapidly adopted, although standards of urban housing began to improve,[11] but there were exceptions. In 1909, Oswaldtwistle's Urban District Council byelaws did not include adequate standards for housing,[12] so the town was without stringent control throughout the nineteenth century.

Cotton towns in east Lancashire grew as a result of building mills and the provision of adjacent high-density housing colonies from which there was outward expansion.[13] In this respect Gaskell found that large variations occurred between towns regarding mill owned houses.[14] Joyce argued that 'the speculative builders, the small investor and the ground landlord … had a large say in determining the physical character of the factory town', but he also argued that 'Employer house-ownership was never unimportant'.[15] Walton summarised the matter, stating that 'employers' response to housing was not uniform', and this goes some way towards explaining the apparently contradictory accounts.[16] Nevertheless, by the end of the nineteenth century, ownership of urban housing by mill owners had declined, although it had been comparatively important earlier in the century.[17]

The period in which houses were built and the builder were important features. In Blackburn during the early part of the nineteenth century, mill owners built the first terraced houses for mill workers.[18] Later, speculators built long terraces of back-to-back houses and courts in congested and irregular configurations.[19] By the 1890s, factory ownership of housing had become fragmented, and Muthesius noted that by the twentieth century 90 per cent of working class houses were being rented from private landlords, although some were still factory owners.[20] Burnett suggested that the houses provided by textile factory owners were generally of a higher standard than average because their priority was concerned with attracting labour in contrast to speculators making profit.[21] When textile mills were created in sparsely populated rural areas the mill owners themselves were obliged to provide accommodation for the workforce in the form of factory villages. Most houses were to an orderly plan, but there was a good deal of variability in standards.[22] As in towns earlier housing was generally of poor quality. In the late eighteenth century the Peels built a factory village at Bury with 20 inferior back-to-back cottages,[23] and houses built at Low Moor, Clitheroe were also of poor quality.[24]

In early nineteenth century factory village housing emerged, such as the Ashworths' colonies at Eagley and Egerton, and Bazley's at Barrow Bridge. These were situated both on the periphery of Bolton and in rural environments. These mill owners and others provided variability in their housing in order to distinguish between factory floor workers, supervisors and managers.[25] Timmins

Model Village housing at Barrow Bridge Bolton including back-to-back housing for a cotton mill workforce and semi-detached and detached housing for managers.

identified at least four types of houses at Egerton ranging from small to large,[27] but also pointed out that in 1833 three-quarters of the housing was still back-to-back, although some had three rooms rather than the usual two. Even in the mid-1840s, half of the 60 operatives cottages were back-to-back. Timmins noted that:

> It is plain that the Ashworths built housing which varied widely in standard. And even if they strove to improve quality over time, a sizeable proportion of their workforce continued to live in comparatively low-quality housing, sometimes in very crowded circumstances...Whether the Ashworths provided a greater proportion of high-quality housing for their employers [ees] than other factory village owners is by no means certain.

These owners also built dwellings with different affordable family incomes in mind, although as pointed out by Timmins even families with the ability to pay higher rents sometimes opted to remain in accommodation that was over-crowded.[28] In the model villages built by philanthropists both the housing and amenities were usually above the standards of early housing in towns, where few if any amenities were provided.

In rural parts of east Lancashire, isolated houses and farms were scattered over the countryside during the pre-industrial period. From the onset of proto-industrialisation the growth of population demanded an increase in workers' accommodation. This vernacular housing was still scattered over the countryside and consisted of very short individualistic rows of cottages and occasionally folds often built in stages but in a rural setting. The scattered nature of rural housing was different to the congested urban growth that comprised back-to-back dwellings, courts and long rows of terraced housing built in colonies, and to that of compact housing in factory villages with single ownership.[29] In rural areas the majority of short rows of cottages were owned by different landlords and rented to families, although the owner sometimes lived in one of the cottages.[30]

In summary, accounts of housing standards and conditions have been subject to a certain amount of contradiction. This is partly understandable since housing standards both changed over time and their intended purpose was different. But it is evident that both town housing and industrial village housing standards improved as the nineteenth century progressed. Therefore, housing in the case study townships will be discussed in two phases. First, vernacular housing most of which was built before the nineteenth century, and second, housing provided in the townships by mill owners, mainly during the second half of the nineteenth century.

Vernacular housing in the townships

In the case study townships growth in the number of dwellings started in the late eighteenth century and continued whilst handloom weaving was expanding until about the second quarter of the nineteenth century.[31] After 1821, the number of dwellings in Blacksnape and Yate and Pickup Bank started to decline, but at Eccleshill and particularly Hoddlesden there was a continuous increase after 1841 until late in the century[32] (Table 7.1). Most vernacular properties were built, therefore, when handloom weaving was flourishing and demand decreased as handloom weaving and population went into decline.

Table 7.1.   *Housing trends in case study townships 1801-1901.*

The table illustrates the fluctuating housing stock in the townships during the nineteenth century.

Year	Blacksnape Inhabited	Eccleshill Inhabited	Hoddlesden Inhabited	Yate & Pickup Bank Inhabited
1801	Not available	72	Not available	174
1811	Not available	52	Not available	205
1821	Not available	70	Not available	238
1831	Not available	96	Not available	217
1841	65	90	48	192
1851	75	99	85	202
1861	63	106	120	207
1871	45	133	104	155
1881	63	146	93	143
1891	54	143	95	124
1901	54	77	158	133

Source: CEBs

Housing in the four communities consisted of farms and cottages before the development of working-class housing for mill workers. At Blacksnape there was ribbon development along the Roman Road, otherwise the dwellings were scattered. In Eccleshill the buildings were entirely scattered, in Hoddlesden there was a central fold with mainly scattered outlying farms, whilst at Yate and Pickup Bank there was a mixture of isolated small farms and folds. Handloom weavers occupied many of the cottages and people in the dual occupations of domestic weaver and farmer sometimes occupied farms.

These early dwellings in the townships comprised short rows of isolated cottages, small folds and farmsteads and many were of a type noted by Taylor 'some cottages with small holdings have farm buildings attached',[33] examples of which were shown in chapter 4. Even the folds were small and isolated, the largest of which was Bank Fold in Yate and Pickup Bank, where a farm has a date stone inscribed '1765' and 'Robert and Eliza Yates' and another farm '1656' and 'HKE & IGH'.[34] The 1851 census shows this Fold comprised five small farms ranging from 6 to 19 acres and 16 dwellings.

Only two exceptions occurred to the scattered configuration of dwellings; one was at Belthorn, Yate and Pickup Bank where, even in the late eighteenth century, there was an aspect of ribbon development on the west side of the road through the village, which was linked to the main road between Blackburn and Haslingden. The other exception was at Blacksnape where the 1840s Ordnance Survey Map shows the village had a string of properties arranged along the east side of the Roman Road passing through the village.

Many of these rural cottages according to census enumeration were still occupied by handloom weavers in the mid-nineteenth century.

Examples of cottages that have been formally occupied by handloom weavers' are still to be seen at Blacksnape with handloom shops at rear (SD 711 217), in Hoddlesden at numbers 2 and 4 Queen Square and at Top O'th Sugar Field (Top of Copy) with ground floor loomshops at rear, and Scholes Fold, Pickup Bank.

The census suggests that virtually all of the houses were occupied in the first quarter of the nineteenth century when handloom weaving was thriving. After this, inhabited property numbers approximately followed the proportional decline in population with a corresponding increase in uninhabited dwellings. This was in contrast to the rapid growth of dwellings in nearby town. As population declined in the townships it is likely that the poorer quality dwellings were the first to be vacated. Although housing developments occurred in the townships during the late eighteenth century with the building of handloom weavers

Bank Fold, Yate Bank. The picture is an aerial view of the Fold

Bank Fold, Yate Bank. The photographs are of one short row of cottages and one of a farmstead. The Fold must have been built in stages since there are date stones for 1656 and 1765.

Rows of cottages aliened the Roman Road at Blacksnape.

cottages the majority of these dwellings until about the mid-nineteenth century were small, scattered in nature, and the construction was uncontrolled by legislation. Early handloom weavers' cottages are still to be seen at Belthorn in Holden Street built around the 1770s, which probably had loom shops at the rear. There is also evidence of weavers' dwellings in Chapel Street, Kendle Row, Belthorn Road, Higher and Lower Fold where this Fold was also built in the 1770s. At both Blacksnape and Yate and Pickup Bank the scattered and small configuration remained the norm and very few buildings were added to the housing stock during the remainder of the century. In fact the stock later declined because of population drifting from these areas.

Many earlier dwellings in the townships have been identified as being hand-loom weavers' cottages originally, by both Rothwell in 1985 and Timmins in 1977. However, identification is now more difficult since characteristics have been at least partially masked by alterations or refurbishment and in the process badly distorted. Some older properties are to be found to be now in ruins, such as those at Height Nook and Garsden's Fold, Pickup Bank and an old farmstead at Blacksnape. These buildings illustrate the sturdy construction but unfriendly environmental conditions in which these and many other dwellings were built.[35]

Older dwellings are to be found at Dandy Row, Eccleshill, but many of the houses in the area disappeared in the nineteenth century, presumably because of out-migration brought about by the demise of handloom weaving.[36] A prime

This is a ruin of a vernacular dwelling at Height Nook, Pickup Bank, probably built 1729. A farmer who was also a handloom weaver, at one time inhabited the dwelling.

Dandy Row, Eccleshill, situated on the Old Roman Road. It can be seen that some of the cottages had offset windows and were therefore the homes of handloom weavers.

example of an ancient property is the Manor House at Eccleshill on which there is an inscribed stone 'TEF 1641' (Thomas and Elizabeth Fish).[37] [At Plate 1.2]

The oldest surviving dwellings in the centre of Hoddlesden Village are 'O'er Brig' (over the bridge, although there is no evidence of a bridge). Queens Street has two cottages at the west end (numbers 2 and 4), which were handloom weavers cottages where weaving was probably carried out in the cellar, since there are windows just above ground level for extra light and the living area floor level is entered by climbing six steps. Two dwellings to the east of these cottages were originally a single farmhouse, they have mullioned windows, which may mean that handloom weaving was undertaken as a second occupation at the farm house.

Queen Street, Hoddlesden. The first two cottages with steps to the front doors were weavers' cottages. The windows at ground floor level probably indicate that the weaving activity occurred in the basement area. *Listed Building.*

Numbers 6 & 8 Queen Street, Hoddlesden. Originally these two cottages were a stand-alone farmhouse and probably date from the seventeenth century, directly across from these dwellings, on land currently occupied by a war memorial, was the farm barn.

Slacks Cottages, Hoddlesden. At mid-nineteenth century this row of cottages comprised eight dwellings alongside the packhorse route between Blacksnape and Langshaw Head and was owned by Ranken. Also running by the cottages was a stream that led into Hoddlesden Brook across which there were stepping stones for access to Hoddlesden Village.

Langshaw Head, Hoddlesden. This Fold was originally a handloom weavers' settlement but no longer recognisable since modernisation of the properties has been undertaken.

The barn to this farm was sited in the grounds of the current war memorial. On the perimeter of the village there were cottages at Sett End, Meadow Head and Slack the latter being inhabited until the 1940s but them they were demolished. At Langshaw Head buildings have existed over several centuries. The date when the present buildings were erected is unknown but John and Mary Hindle

were living there in the 1790s and when they had the frontage refurbished in 1799 they had a date stone inserted accordingly. Holker House, Hoddlesden is the second oldest house in the whole of Darwen and was built in 1591 according to both Abram and Ashton, although the present date stone reads 1691.[38] Baron's Fold, Blacksnape also depicts older properties since a new part

The properties at Langshaw Head were probably built as shown on the date stone and occupied by the Hindle family.

Holker House, Hoddlesden. Ranken at one time owned this fine sixteenth century residence close to the old packhorse route from Hoddlesden to Pickup Bank. It appears to have had little change in the appearance of the elevations from the original. *Listed Building*

Barons Fold, Blacksnape

Date Stone

Sugar Field Farm and Cottages, Pickup Bank. Only the farmhouse to the left of the photograph is now occupied, the remaining cottages are derelict. *Listed Building.*

Lane End Farm and Cottages, Pickup Bank. Originally a farmhouse and two cottages but now converted to a single residence.

During restoration works at Lane End, Pickup Bank, a main support at first floor level was found in the form of a virtually natural tree member except for having been stripped of bark.

<small>Courtesy Mr. And Mrs. Chappell</small>

Shorrock Fold,
Pickup Bank.
Once occupied
by handloom
weavers.

was added in 1776. Some of the other older dwellings have not survived.

There were also older dwellings in Yate and Pickup Bank, such as Paddock House, above the door, 1684 is inscribed in old numerals and Scholes Fold Pickup Bank built 1725. At Lane End, the modernised building has been converted from three dwellings, the left hand one being designated as a farmhouse in the 1851 census and a further example is Shorrock Fold, which was at least three dwelling but now converted to a single property. These illustrate the small-scale nature of both dwellings and some farmhouses. A few buildings still in existence are very old, dating back to the seventeenth century, particularly in Yate Bank and were owner/occupied by yeomen. But most of the houses were handloom weavers' cottages, and therefore, working-class houses where conditions were basic, cramped and generally unhealthy.

Further details of early dwellings in the townships have been derived from 1914–15 Finance Act field books, albeit these do not indicate early nineteenth century status. Whilst these are very informative, details of the entire older

housing in the case study townships are incomplete.[39] The particulars of properties for each township vary in degrees of detail provided, presumably because
of the individual surveyor's views and observations of what was important.
Accounts were also restricted by the available space in the field books for
the section headed 'particulars, descriptions and notes made on inspection'.[40]
Although these documents provide a good cross section of information regarding
the housing for each township, there are some details of individual properties
such as the number of rooms, overall condition, terms of tenure and so forth that
have been excluded from the reports. Therefore, portraits of housing obtained
from this source can be no more than approximations, although a more informative source for the period is not available.

Both the 1914–15 Finance Act valuation books and field books show that the
vast majority of older houses in Eccleshill and Yate and Pickup Bank were rented
from landlords owning a small number of properties each, but at Hoddlesden
and Blacksnape the Ranken executors owned significant numbers of dwellings.
About two-thirds of older houses in Eccleshill that had been given a classification were freehold, some owner/occupied, but the majority rented. At Yate and
Pickup Bank only 14 per cent were freehold and the rest followed the long tradi-
tion in the Forest of Rossendale where copyhold ownership was common.[41] This
was different to the workers' houses in Blackburn where by far the majority were
long leaseholds and it was also different to many model villages such as Saltaire
where they were exclusively freehold.[42] The percentages of older owner/occupied
dwellings in the townships varied between 6 and 27 per cent of the older stock.[43]

Vernacular houses were generally built in short rows of a few stone cottages,
frequently individualistic in style and there is evidence that the houses in each
row were sometimes built in stages. They were often built into a hillside because
of the terrain, so that earth covered the lower outside wall making them subject
to excessive damp penetration. In the small number of houses that it has been
possible to survey the most common internal arrangement was either four or five
rooms; the downstairs area comprised a living/dining room, which contained the
only means of entering and leaving the dwelling, a rear scullery, and sometimes
a small parlour, all with flag floors. The upper floors usually had two bedrooms;
one of which was usually open to the stairwell.[44] The upper chambers had no
ceilings, and hence open to the underside of the roof, where rude structural
timbers could be observed.[45]

Field books give observations regarding general public health in the townships. A very small number of properties owned by the more wealthy people had
an internal hot and cold water supply. Examples were the Woodhead residence,
owned by Oliver Yates whose father was a merchant and also the residence at
Newhall Head.

In the majority of older properties at Blacksnape, Eccleshill, Hoddlesden

Woodhead House, Yate Bank. One time residence of Oliver Yates a farmer and local businessman and his father before him who was a merchant. *Listed Building.*

Newhall Head, Belthorn, Yate Bank. Probably built 1661 as indicated on the date stone. During the nineteenth century this dwelling was occupied by handloom weavers.

and Yate and Pickup Bank sanitary arrangements comprised tub toilets inside detached stone privies, often 20 to 50 yards from the dwelling, sometimes with several households sharing. Foul water was disposed of in open channels and transferred to amenable locations, whilst sewage was dumped in remote places, such as the moors.[46] Lack of efficient drainage and cleanliness of the area was a cause for concern according to the local Board of Health minutes.[47] Health standards in Belthorn are indicated by an internments section at the end of the Chapel Minute Book, which records 99 burials between 1874 and 1897, of these, twenty died less than one year of age: put another way, one in five burials was a baby.[48]

At Blacksnape, Eccleshill and Yate and Pickup Bank, water to older properties had to be either carried from a well fed by field drainage or from springs until the mid-twentieth century. Even by the mid-twentieth century, most of the older houses had only paraffin oil lamps and candles for lighting and coal fires for heating.[49] Living rooms often had a cast iron range containing a central open fire grate, on one side of which was a hot water tank and on the other, an oven for cooking and baking.[50]

From the mid-nineteenth century steam factories emerged at Eccleshill and Hoddlesden, which necessitated additional housing for the workforce. This is the focus of the next section of this chapter.

In summary, there was a wide variety of vernacular housing in the townships in the late nineteenth century, many of which had been built in the late eighteenth century or earlier. Variations occurred mainly because of the different periods of time in which the properties had been built, by different builders and for different purposes and different classes of people, but the majority were built for families engaged in manufacture, especially weaving. Because of the period when the dwellings were built, they were not subject to legislation for either quality or standards and this is reflected in the appearance of those properties still in existence where original construction is evident.

These earlier dwellings in the townships had their own individual characteristics; hence, they were different to the uniform configuration of dwellings in most model villages, and there were no back-to-back, court or high-density housing as in towns. In the countryside, dwellings were more spaciously positioned. Rural houses generally had more space inside than early dwellings in towns and sanitary arrangements, although shared basic tub toilets were an improvement on privvy middens. Factory village housing at the lower end of the quality range was generally inferior to rural housing. However, at the upper end of the quality range it appears that factory village housing was just as good or even better than older rural housing, particularly the housing intended for managers and senior workers.

Industrially linked housing

Workers' housing was often provided when mills were opened or enlarged, whether it was from already existing stock or needing to be built. To meet this requirement three fundamental reasons have been identified for employers providing housing. Firstly, it has been suggested that it was a means of attracting a workforce, secondly, paternalistic ideologies motivated the provision of both housing and amenities and thirdly, the existing stock was in very poor condition. Rural 'mill housing' built in the late nineteenth century appears to have been influenced by the whims of the mill owners or the builder for standards of design and construction. Despite national legislation and local regulations, rural areas escaped enforcement of building control during this period. Whilst the 1875 Public Health Act gave local authorities powers to inspect property, condemn unsanitary or overcrowded premises, the control was limited to urban areas. Even the 1890 Housing of the Working Classes Act was more concerned with urban than rural housing. It was not until the Housing Town Planning Act 1909 that systematic surveys of rural housing became obligatory.[51]

Three of the four townships noted above had small early water-powered mills but these mill owners probably had no need for building houses or to provide amenities because of the small numbers they employed. However, it must not be overlooked that the owners of these early mills had considerable competition for a workforce from a thriving cottage weaving community, who were accommodated in dwellings locally. Nevertheless, it is presumed that at least some mill workers lived locally and there was little need if any to draw labour from elsewhere. Although no records of mill owned houses have been found linking them to early mills it would be dangerous to discard the possibility.

When large steam driven power loom mills were built in Eccleshill and Hoddlesden the owners had the advantage of operating in settlements that were at least already or partly established; yet, they clearly considered it necessary to both purchase some of the existing stock and supplement it by building additional houses close to their mills. At Eccleshill and Hoddlesden houses were not built at the same time as the mills, but were deferred until extensions were added.

Following the building of Waterside Cotton Mill at Eccleshill in 1844, the census enumeration for 1851 shows only three houses in the township were uninhabited and that no new houses were being built. The 1861 census showed nine houses in the process of erection and by 1881 the actual number of new houses had increased by 39. The 1881 census showed two new rows of dwellings, named Victoria Buildings and Waterside Terrace in Eccleshill, which were indicated in the 1914–15 Valuation Book (VB) as belonging to Bullough the owner of Waterside Mill.[52] The absolute combined number of dwellings in these two rows varies according to the sources consulted. The 1914–15 VB records 38 houses, the 1880s O.S. Map shows

Mill Workers' houses, Waterside. Eccleshill. They are Victoria Buildings (below) and Waterside Terrace (top). The plan of Victoria Buildings forms a dog-leg comprising twenty dwellings.

Nursery Nook, Eccleshill. People living in these cottages mostly worked at the nearby Paper Mill.

36 houses and the 1881 CEB lists only 34 houses. Field observation has indicated 36 houses with no obvious indications of change from original construction. It has been assumed that 36 new mill houses were erected as Waterside Terrace and Victoria Buildings close to the mill and three others were possibly built by a speculator.[53] It appears that this mill owner built houses needed because of extensions to the mill, noted above,[54] that demanded an increase in the workforce. In addition to these 'mill houses', the Bulloughs purchased five older type houses and three farms in nearby Yate and Pickup Bank, although it is uncertain whether they were linked to mill use.[55] Nonetheless mill houses made a substantial contribution to the total housing stock.[56]

Other than Waterside Mill in Eccleshill, there was also a smaller mill at Grimshaw Bridge. The 1910 survey shows that the mill owner had purchased four older type cottages at Nursery Nook and three at Grimshaw Bridge.[57] However, the 1871 census shows five cottages at Nursery Nook, although none was indicated at Grimshaw Bridge in any of the nineteenth century enumerations or on the First Edition of the 25 inch O.S. Map. Whatever the actual number of mill-owned older houses, it was very small and there is no evidence that the mill owners built new properties. In any event, the mill had a very unstable ownership pattern, changing hands many times over the period when it was being used for manufacturing textiles.

Prior to 1841 the economy of Hoddlesden had been more agricultural than industrial but this changed as the century progressed. Almost half of the dwellings supported a farmer, although the attached acreage cannot be determined from the census, subsequent censuses indicated that a good proportion of farm acreages were very small and incapable of providing adequate subsistence. From the mid-century the number of farmers declined but houses in the township generally increased for the remainder of the century.

The 1841 census for Hoddlesden indicates that 47 dwellings existed, which included cottages and farms.[58] The Ordnance Map surveyed in 1844 shows that Hoddlesden was beginning to develop as an industrial area since as noted above a cotton mill, quarries and collieries had been established.[59] Prior to this time

Upper Browning Street, Hoddlesden. Built 1844 by Mr O. Hargreaves to house mill workers at the local cotton factory.

Oliver Hargeaves had purchased half of the land in Hoddlesden for £3804 in 1825,[60] at about the same time that the Place brothers were extending Vale Rock Mill. This landowner then built Hargreaves Street and Browning Street, which are shown on the 1840s map, to accommodate mill workers; these were of superior quality to those already existing.

Hargreaves Street, Hoddlesden. Built 1844 by Mr O. Hargreaves to house mill workers at the local cotton factory.

Griffin crest mounted on the houses in Upper Browning Street and Hargreaves Street.

Both Upper Browning Street and Hargreaves Street were symmetrically built around a pedimented central feature, which bears the family crest of the Hargreaves, a Griffin.

Both Browning and Hargreaves Street comprised two houses in the central feature with four more on each flank. In Lower Browning Street there were nine houses. The dwellings in both Upper Browning Street and Hargreaves were substantially built properties. At each end of both streets there are stones built into the gables with the inscription 'MDCCCXLIV EDIFICAVIT O. HARGREAVE', meaning 1844, Built, O. Hargreave.

Hargreaves crest mounted on the houses in Upper Browning Street and Hargreaves Street

By mid-century Hoddlesden was still a relatively small village but the census enumeration schedule for 1851 shows an increase in the number of properties in the village to 78. However, precision should not be assumed on these census statistics since many anomalies are to be encountered with census data. Examples to be found are the number of dwellings in a street often change from one census to another, possibly because they were unoccupied on census night and this has not been recorded; dwellings and particularly farms have not been noted in some censuses and there are many other examples. Typical conflicts in the census are to be found for Browning Street 1871 – 17 dwellings, 81 – 17, 91 – 19, 1901 – 19 and the 1910 Finance Act Valuation shows 19 houses. For

Lower Browning Street, was built by Joseph Place, the local industrialist.

Hargreaves Street we find the census for 1871 – 16 houses, 81 – 10, 91 – 11, 1901 – 11 and the 1910 Valuation shows 10 houses. Scrutiny of the nineteenth century Ordnance Survey maps indicate that there were no changes in the numbers of properties in each of these rows of houses during the period.

In 1861 the Hoddlesden Co-operative Land and Building Company was formed with twelve directors, the purpose being to buy and sell land on which to build houses. They included the Rev. G. W. Reynolds, W. B. Ranken, Adam Bullough, John and Joseph Place (chairman). In the following year they put out a tender for eight houses, which was accepted on 4 February 1862. At the same meeting two directors were reported to have resigned and Adam Bullough and Fielding Clapham were appointed as replacement directors and two years later Henry Place accepted a directorship, he was a local grocer and may have been related to J. and J. Place, the local industrialists. In May 1862 the directors agreed that when the houses were complete they would be let to J. and J. Place at 3s. 4d. each per week, effectively from 4 October 1862. On 7 May 1863 a tender for a further seven cottages was accepted and by September of the same year there was discussion regarding gas fixtures and meters indicating that the village had a gas supply service. Neither the rent nor the location for these houses were specified although the top and bottom dwellings were to be allocated three tubs of coal and the other five two tubs of coal; the size of tubs and frequency of delivery were not stated.[61]

The Co-operative Building Society, in which the Place brothers held shares, built two terraces in Baynes Street from the 1860s. There are eleven dwellings in the upper terrace, although the three at the top of the row appear to have been

Graham Street, Hoddlesden. These houses formed a left hand flank to the Post Office and Conservative Club buildings. They were erected during the latter part of the nineteenth century and were inhabited by people working at the local cotton mills.

Sydney Street, Hoddlesden. These houses formed a right hand flank to the Post Office and Conservative Club buildings. They were erected during the latter part of the nineteenth century and were inhabited by people working at the local cotton mills.

Albert Street, Hoddlesden. Appears to have been built very late in the nineteenth century. There were originally five houses in this short row, in which there were people with a mixture of occupations.

St Paul's Terrace, Hoddlesden. These houses appear to have been built in the 1880s according to census data. The occupants were essentially working in textiles.

Clifton Terrace, Hoddlesden. These houses appear to have been built in the 1880s according to census data. The occupants were essentially working in textiles.

Bayne Street, Hoddlesden. These two rows of houses formed Upper Bayne Street and Lower Bayne Street. According to census data building was staggered from the 1860 onwards. Most of the dwellings housed cotton workers but there were also occupants in other employments.

Carus Street and Alexander Terrace, Hoddlesden. The two rows were built in the early twentieth century and were the last houses to be built that were essentially for housing textile workers. No further houses were built until the 1970s at which time they were erected as speculative accommodation as opposed to local workers housing.

added at a later date. The upper row is of a better quality having larger rooms, an enhanced edifice and dressed stone surrounds to windows and doors, the lower row having stone surrounds to windows only. By 1861 another 30 dwellings had been built in Hoddlesden. Further additions occurred later with the erection of Graham Street and Sydney Street with seven houses each, in Albert Street there were five houses, at Pleasant View there was a terrace of seven houses, St Paul's Terrace has now eighteen houses, Clifton Terrace has now eleven houses and in the 1890s Bayne Street was virtually complete. Between 1907 and 1911 the Co-operative Society built Carus Street (later Avenue) and Alexander Terrace. Alexandra Carus paid the Society to have these terraces named after him, which were later adopted by the Carus Brothers as the property of St Paul's Mill Company. These houses were probably the most substantial in the village at the time due to progressive developments in legislation. Alexander Carus was living in Hoddlesden Hall by 1920 and had realised his wish of becoming squire by purchasing the estate in 1920 for £26,000, which consisted of around 800 acres and comprised 14 farms and some houses in the village.

Ownership of the village houses and farms can be found in the 1910 Finance Act Valuation books which provide information relevant to the field surveys carried out around 1914 and they also provide extracts from earlier Poor Rate levy. These documents show that major property owners were Ranken Executors with 26 per cent, the Carus family with 29 per cent, the Co-operative Land and Building Society owned 11 per cent and Joseph Place who was also a director of the latter owned a further 5 per cent. In terms of specific rows of dwellings the Co-operative Land and Building Society owned Graham Street, Sydney Street and one-third of Queen Street. The Ranken Executors owned the other two-thirds of Queen Street along with houses at Slack, Hoddlesden Fold, Meadow Head, Langshaw Head, together with over half of the farms and other scattered properties. In addition the executors of Ranken also owned seventeen houses on the Blacksnape Road. The Carus family owned one-third of Bayne Street, half of Browning Street, Hargreaves Street, St Paul's Terrace, Carus Street and Alexander Terrace.[62]

Carus Street is unusual as an elevated row comprising eleven dwelling with an adjoining house at the upper end at the junction of Carus Street and Chapman Road. In front of each property is a small garden traversed by 12 stone steps in which there is a quarter-spaced landing. Alexander Terrace comprises 15 houses, although the end house at the bottom of the terrace appears to have been added later. This is a fine row of well-built houses, which have course stone fronts and the doors and widows have dressed stone surrounds. At the front of the houses there are lawns about 30 yards long. It is more than likely that all of these home owners built houses for a workforce to live, but it also likely that both the Carus family were motivated to build them as mill houses and Joseph Places as industrial houses but the Co-operative Land and Building Society and Ranken are more likely to have been speculators. This is indicated by a Society directors' motion that the company members should have a preference for their occupation.[63]

In terms of the villages' utility services there is evidence that a main sewer was in existence at Hoddlesden in 1863 since the directors of the Land and Building Society arranged for a connection. In addition there was to be emptying of ash pits and in 1890 closets were built in Albert Street.[64] A gas supply was also being supplied to the village in 1901 since gas back boilers were being installed.[65] This completed the village development based on industrial needs until the dormitory accommodation programmes from the 1960s added around a further 300 dwellings. However, the Land and Building Society were selling working class houses in 1955 at about half the price of the directors valuation and on 22 May 1957 it was moved at a General Meeting that the Company should be wound up.[66]

Apart from mill houses for workers there was the occasional residence built for people with means. In 1861, the present Hoddlesden Hall was built by William Baynes Ranken but it was known as 'The Cottage'. This was a stone structure with cellars, outbuildings and stables and in advance of any modern dwellings in Hoddlesden.[67] The Hall was located in a secluded area of the village and access was by a tree-lined drive. It was gradually extended over time, part of which was enhancement by a large lounge just over 23 feet by 19 feet, excluding bay window, in keeping with a design seen by Mrs Ranken on a trip to Malta. An alternative view is that the image was founded in Australia. The room was large with big French windows overlooking the landscaped gardens on two sides. The 'Hall', located at SD 716 224, has now been converted to four apartments.

In some respects the above Hall was a replacement for the old sixteenth century Hall that had been located on the site of the present Ranken Arms, which is shown on the 1840s Ordnance Survey map. The old hall survived until 1864, and in 1825 it was reported by Baines the Lancashire historian that the building was large but plain,[68] albeit later it was described as having 'deteriorated into an ale house', called the Griffin. A Ralph Marsden who owned most of the land in Hoddlesden around the sixteenth century was living there in 1597. The residence remained in the Marsden family until 1733 at which time it was bequeathed to two daughters, one of which married a George Hargreaves. Oliver the grandson of George inherited half of the estate belonging to the village and purchased the other half in 1825 as noted above. Oliver married twice but was without issue and on his death in 1858 the estate was bequeathed to William

William Bayne Ranken 1829–1889. Inherited the Hoddlesden estate and became a benefactor to both the School and Church in Hoddlesden.

Hoddlesden Hall. Built for William Baynes Ranken, known as the local squire. A fine building within its own grounds containing landscaping, lawns, kitchen garden and stables. In more recent years the buildings have been divided into four separate compartments. *Listed Building.*

Ranken's grave where he was interred in the burial ground of St Paul's Church Hoddlesden.

Alpine Villa, Harwoods Lane, Hoddlesden. Located beside the Old Road from Hoddlesden to Sett End. Built late nineteenth century and generally occupied by either professional people or factory owners.]

Baynes Ranken, the son of his second wife but by her first marriage.

He came to Hoddlesden the following year at the age of twenty-nine, having previously graduated at Trinity College, Cambridge, was a 'Barrister-at-Law' and owned a London residence. Ranken was a wealthy man even prior to the windfall and was highly influential in developing the village of Hoddledsen.[69] He lived in the village for the remainder of his life and was finally interred at the local Parish Church. Joseph Place, local industrialist also built the detached residence, named Alpine Villa at Harwoods Lane in 1863. This dwelling too reflected status. Although mill owners at Eccleshill and Hoddlesden built new houses and purchased older ones they contributed very little in the way of amenities, like their predecessors they did not demonstrate the paternalistic tendencies found in the model villages; and there is only a minimal amount of evidence for any contribution.[70] This evidence amounts to a social club at Eccleshill, built as an end property to Waterside Terrace and owned by Bullough the mill owner; he also made donations to religious institutions. Ranken too gave generously to Church of England local school and Church. This was however very different from some factory villages where paternalistic employers sometimes provided extensive amenities, which included sports facilities, places of worship, schools and even almshouses and hospitals.[71]

At Yate and Pickup Bank, it was not so much the reasons why employers built houses but rather the reasons why they did not. Mills were located just outside of the township's boundary, mostly no further than the width of a stream or road from the boundary and some of these mill owners built houses in these townships. Within Yate and Pickup Bank, there was only one mill with a small number of power looms surviving by the mid-nineteenth century,[72] and the workers must have either lived in older accommodation or outside of the township, but even this small enterprise failed in 1866. One mill owner in adjacent Hoddlesden built several terraces of substantial houses as noted above, some of which were inhabited by people relocating from Pickup Bank.[73] Therefore, although Yate and Pickup Bank had no mills or no new mill houses, there was fairly easy access to nearby housing and employment opportunities.[74]

Analysis of who provided housing in these communities during the latter part of the nineteenth century has demonstrated that provision was not uniform. At Blacksnape there were very few additional houses built in the post vernacular period. Bullough's the mill owner provided housing for mill workers in Eccleshill. Whilst at Hoddlesden there was an inverted semblance of trends to those in cotton towns where by the end of the nineteenth century mill owners in towns were shedding their housing stock and there was a reliance on speculators to provide workers houses. At Hoddlesden speculators had built houses to be occupied by textile employees and by the end of the nineteenth century and the beginning of the twentieth century it was the mill owners that provided this function. The experience in Yate and Pickup Bank was not all that different to Blacksnape.

In summary, the reasons for mill owners building houses in the case study townships seems to have been to attract workers in order to supplement the workforce already in existence when mills were expanded. In model villages when mills were built on green field sites, employers had to attract an entire workforce. This involved the provision of an entire housing stock, and possibly amenities, which were often linked to paternalistic ideologies, albeit the latter was sometimes exaggerated. In the 'cotton towns', most houses in early nineteenth century were built by factory owners to attract workers but later in the century by speculators for profit. Nevertheless, the prime reason for building mill houses in rural areas, model villages and by speculators in towns was profit, although the circumstances were different.

Characteristics of mill housing

In order to assess the quality of mill housing, in terms of external fabric, internal layouts, facilities and services, reference has been made to two sets of documents along with fieldwork. Firstly, the 1910 Act Inland Revenue valuation and field books have been consulted, since these are the earliest records that have been found for placing the houses in context. The valuation books provide addresses and an estimate of gross annual value based on earlier poor rate levy, which was related to rental. These valuations have been used to classify properties within townships and make comparisons between mill and non-mill owned dwellings. Moreover, the 1910 field books provide details of some internal layouts. Secondly, estate agents' particulars of houses currently for sale provide further details. Although this source stipulates particulars currently appertaining, some original aspects have remained unchanged throughout the life of the property. These agents' particulars have been supplemented with fieldwork to detect alterations and extensions.

The mill houses were generally of a standard design when built in each individual township. Fieldwork revealed that façades were unlikely to have been changed from original construction, but some internal layouts had been rearranged and services improved from when the properties were first built. Exceptions to standard designs occurred in the end property at Waterside Terrace Eccleshill indicated above originally as a social club as noted above, and two houses either side of the obtuse dog-leg in Victoria Buildings, Eccleshill.

The general environmental conditions of mill houses in the countryside during the late nineteenth century were generally better than in towns because of open spaces and less pollution, although because of industrialisation in Hoddlesden, the level of atmospheric contamination from the cotton mills and pipe works was probably very similar to that in towns. In model villages, mill owners building houses at the same time as those in the townships, usually paid higher regard to both waste disposal and sanitation than in the townships. Therefore, the general environment in which mill houses were built in the townships appears to be a hybrid between the towns and model villages.

The external structures of all village mill house frontages were built in coursed stone and openings were dressed with stone sills and lintels only; rear walls were in random rubble but of better quality than in vernacular houses. Although the houses at Eccleshill had coursed stone frontages, the standard was of lower quality than houses built particularly in the early twentieth century at Hoddlesden; All roofs were covered with thin slates instead of the earlier heavy flagstones and the internal roof space was enclosed with a bedroom ceiling adding better thermal insulation than the open space below the rafters in older dwellings.[75] Nevertheless, mill houses in the townships in order of aesthetic appearance and quality of construction were Eccleshill the lowest and Hoddlesden the highest standard. Therefore, mill housing in these townships followed the style and external construction used for many east Lancashire town houses built during the same period, except that the rear structural walls in towns were often built of brick; although in nearby Blackburn a large proportion of housing had all external walls constructed entirely in brickwork.

Housing belonging to the mills had access at both front and rear, similar to byelaw houses in towns, this was unlike the single access of their rural predecessors and urban back-to-backs. Windows were larger and higher than in older properties, giving enhanced daylight and allowing the use of sliding sash frames that opened to the external air for improved ventilation. Most mill houses had their own back yard, which led to either a narrow rear passage or back street, where refuse could be collected and coal delivered. The only exceptions were a few houses in the upper terrace of Victoria Buildings at Waterside, Eccleshill where there was a rear entrance but no rear yard since the wedge shaped land did not permit sufficient space. In the rear yards at Eccleshill there was a tub privy and provision for ash storage. At Hoddlesden the houses built from the mid nineteenth century onwards had rear yards with access from a back road.[76] In the yards were tub toilets but these were later replaced by water closets. Transportation to the village generally was by horse and cart from Darwen crossing the Blackburn to Edgeworth Roman Road and there was also a goods branch railway line as noted above. At Waterside Terrace, Eccleshill, the road had been made good at the mill owner's expense.[77] Otherwise comments in the field books reported the highways in all townships as being generally in 'very bad repair', but all of the mill houses had front pavements similar to those in towns.

Utility services were non-existent at Blacksnape and Yate and Pickup Bank until about the mid twentieth century but at Waterside the mill owners laid services to mill houses. Cold water from the mill was piped to a sink in the houses and piped gas was supplied. As Hoddlesden was part of Darwen there was not the same reliance on the local mills for services since they enjoyed municipal service provision. Nevertheless, Joseph Place & Sons provided the first electric lights in Hoddlesden.[78] Services to the mill houses were not all that different to some working-class housing in both Blackburn and Oswaldtwistle since by the end of the nineteenth century, the towns still had nearly 50 per cent of houses with toilet tubs.[79] Model village dwellings built in the latter part of the nineteenth century usually had better services than both the towns and townships, with water closets and piped water provided to every house and other services were as good.[80]

The numbers of rooms and ground floor internal space in the mill houses have been studied by fieldwork and estate agents' particulars. Victoria Buildings and Waterside Terrace, Eccleshill were similar in area with about 400 square feet of ground floor internal space each. Those in Hoddlesden varied in ground floor interior space from just over 300 square feet in Browning Street, although the central properties in both upper Browning Street and Hargreaves Street projected beyond the façade of the remaining frontage of the row and were therefore a little larger in floor area and at Alexandra Terrace the interior floor space was nearly 500 square feet.

The mill houses at both Eccleshill and Hoddlesden had fewer rooms than most of the older dwellings, particularly farmsteads. Most were two-up, two-down, and in this regard typical of many rows of houses in the nearby cotton towns. However, the rooms in at Alexandra Terrace, Hoddlesden were more spacious than those in Eccleshill and the remainder of the village. The original layout of the ground floor in the above mill houses comprised a front room of over 200 square feet in area, which was larger than most working-class houses in towns but the back room or scullery was around 150 square feet and therefore comparable with those in towns houses.[81] As a barrier to the exposure of weather, there was a vestibule in some houses that also added a degree of privacy, which was in advance of many town houses. At Eccleshill the upper floor had two bedrooms of 160 and 114 square feet respectively, again a little more generous than most in weaving towns, both bedrooms having separate access from a landing with balustrade.[82] At Hoddlesden bedroom space also varied from that in towns; for example in Browning Street the houses had two bedrooms of 180 and 80 square feet respectively and at St Paul's Terrace the two bedrooms were 200 and 60 square feet respectively. In contrast the three bedroomed houses at Alexandra Terrace, were 195, 102 and 64 square feet in area, which demonstrates the large variation in sleeping accommodation available in the village. These houses had the same number of rooms as very late nineteenth century town houses but marginally more internal floor space than most town houses. Heating arrangements in all of the case study houses appear to have been satisfactory for the period with a fireplace in every room, similar to most houses in towns.

Both older and mill houses in these townships were almost exclusively freehold, and rented to the occupants; the owner/occupied percentages being Blacksnape 22, Eccleshill 16, Hoddlesden 13 and Yate and Pickup Bank 9. The exception was at Eccleshill where Victoria Buildings was all freehold but at Waterside Terrace the surveyor only provided a classification for three houses, one freehold and the others leasehold, this appears unlikely in this row of mill houses.[83]

The 'Gross annual value' of all houses in the townships has been extracted from the 1910 valuation books, this value has been deemed to be roughly proportional to the size and quality of properties at the time when valuation occurred. At Blacksnape the average value of the housing stock was just over £3 12s. od.; Eccleshill £6 to £7. In Hoddlesden about £8 5s. od. and at Yate and Pickup Bank about £5 0s. 0d. These average valuations may be contextualised further in that the percentages of houses in Blacksnape and Yate and Pickup Bank below a gross annual valuation of £6 were 94 and 66 per cent respectively. In contrast at Eccleshill and Hoddlesden the houses in the same category were 21 and 18 per cent respectively. In the two latter townships the housing stock had benefited from both the addition of speculative and mill housing developments but also the improvements in legislative control. Using this overview, the mill houses have been placed in a further context. At Eccleshill the mill houses had a gross annual valuation, marginally above average for the township. The superior quality of housing in Carus Street at Hoddlesden was £9 15s. 0d. and Saint Paul's Terrace was £8 14s. 0d. and therefore both of these rows of houses were deemed to be above average for the village, however, both Browning Street and Hargreaves Street were valued at £6 10s. 0d. and hence deemed to be below average when surveyed in 1914. The highest standard of housing was found to be in Alexander Terrace where the factory owners not only supplied a high standard of dwelling but also furnished these properties with long flowing gardens. It is interesting that these valuations coincide with recent observations made during fieldwork. Therefore, both mill and speculative housing in the case study townships, like houses in model villages, were widely variable and the quality where applicable was clearly dependent on mill owners' judgements. Nevertheless by and large the houses were an improvement on pre-nineteenth century rural dwellings that suffered from improvisation and lack of legislative control.

In summary, mill and speculative housing in the townships had similar characteristics to working-class houses in towns. Different standards of housing between the townships appear to have been related to the timing of construction. It is possible that mill owners and speculators took a lead from what was occurring in towns. Comparisons with housing in industrial villages are almost impossible because of the diversity of building at the time.

Characteristics of people living in purpose built mill houses

The numbers of textile workers living in new mill-owned houses in the townships represented a significant percentage of the total textile workforce, although the houses at Eccleshill only represented a relatively small proportion of the total stock. Between 1881 and 1901 circumstances changed since the total textile workforce in Eccleshill declined by around half but at Hoddlesden the workforce increased by more than two-fold. A further factor was the Eccleshill housing stock remained fairly constant with mill housing representing just over one-fifth of the total stock. In contrast at Hoddlesden the stock increased during the two decades after 1881 largely because of speculative building and so the proportion of mill houses declined from around 30 per cent of the total stock to about 20 per cent. However this changed again at the beginning of the twentieth century with the construction of houses in Carus Street and Alexander Terrace. The Co-operative and Building Society built these two rows but both appear to have been later purchased by the owners of Carus Mill and in this respect became mill houses.[84]

Investigation of the inhabitants living in mill houses between 1881 and 1901 has provided an indication as to the purpose for building the houses. The census shows that between three-fifths and three-quarters of people living in these houses were 10 years of age or over. Among the over 10s almost three quarters were working in textiles at Eccleshill and between two-thirds and four-fifths of textile workers were engaged as cotton weavers. At Hoddlesden there were smaller proportions working in textiles but two-thirds of these were engaged as weavers (Table 7.2). At Eccleshill between 1881 and 1901 the majority of mill owned houses

TABLE 7.2.   *Inhabitants living in mill houses*

Township	Year	Total occupants	% Occupants >=10 yrs	% Occupants>= 10 yrs working in textiles	% of textile workers that were cotton weavers
Eccleshill	1881	175	67	70	67
	1891	165	77	72	80
	1901	136	76	74	68
Hoddlesden	1881	63	63	40	63
	1891	249	74	54	63
	1901	265	75	61	68

Sources: CEBs

had a textile worker living there, but in 1901 three houses were without textile workers. In 1881 and 1901 at Hoddlesden there were five houses in both decennial years without textile workers but in 1891 the entire mill owned houses had at least one person engaged in a textile occupation. Therefore, it was largely textile workers and their families that occupied mill houses.

Most inhabitants living in mill houses at Eccleshill in 1881 were incomers, 26 per cent only were natives, of these incomers 24 per cent had been born in Oswaldtwistle, 20 per cent in Yate and Pickup Bank, and the remainder were from scattered locations. By 1891 the configuration had changed somewhat; there were no natives living in the mill houses and the majority had been born in cotton towns; over fifty per cent were from Darwen, 28 per cent Blackburn and nearly 15 per cent Oswaldtwistle.[85] Thirty per cent of natives reappeared in mill houses in 1901 with a corresponding proportion having been born in Darwen and 24 per cent in Yate and Pickup Bank. It seems rather strange that no natives were living in mill housing in 1891 but the figure relating to Darwen was high and so the possibility arises as to whether there had been some confusion between place of birth and registration district. At Hoddlesden in 1881 there was an almost even distribution of 20 per cent between those born native at Darwen and Yate and Pickup Bank. In 1891 there was more diversification with 25 per cent born native, 32 per cent from Darwen and 17 per cent from Yate and Pickup Bank. Natives were in even smaller proportions in 1901 at 11 per cent, Darwen contributing nearly 40 and Yate and Pickup Bank 15 per cent. Some of the incomers were from towns beyond easy daily travel; hence, the mill houses were attracting 'outsiders' but whether they came direct from their place of birth or in staged movements is unknown.

During the late nineteenth century between a third and a half of heads of households living in mill houses were engaged in cotton manufacture.

Not everyone employed and living in mill houses worked in textiles, some had other occupations and this sometimes included the 'head' of households. Nonetheless, analysis of household occupations for those living in mill owned houses indicates a strong association with textiles for family income. The available enumeration data indicates that between three-fifths and nine-tenths of 'heads' in mill houses were working in textiles, except at Hoddlesden in 1881, and that significant proportions were senior workers (Table 7.3).

TABLE 7.3. *Heads of mill owned households*

Year	Village/ Street	Total occupied heads in township	Total occupied in cotton	% in cotton	Heads occupied and living in mill houses	% of total heads in township living in mill houses	Absolute Nos. occupied in cotton	% of heads in mill houses occupied in cotton
1881	Eccleshill	128	42	33	29	23	24	83
1891	Eccleshill	119	59	50	26	22	22	85
1901	Eccleshill	76	38	50	31	41	27	87
1881	Hoddlesden	89	30	34	13	15	5	38
1891	Hoddlesden	135	52	39	38	28	23	61
1901	Hoddlesden	158	61	39	45	28	28	62

Sources: CEBs

The remainder were occupied variously in extraction, service work, and some had no occupation given, although the latter were largely female and accounted for at least 80 per cent of the unemployed (Table 7.4).

TABLE 7.4. *Occupations of occupants living in mill houses.*

By far the major occupations of those living in mill houses were employed in cotton manufacture during the late nineteenth century, hence the incentive for mill owners to provide accommodation for workers.

Occupations	Eccleshill			Hoddlesden		
	1881	1891	1901	1881	1891	1901
Textiles	82	91	76	15	102	122
Extraction/labourers	3	6	3	8	30	21
Domestic	4	1	4	4	4	10
No occupation given	23	22	15	7	37	48
Total	112	120	98	34	173	201
% of total occupied in textiles	73	76	78	44	59	61

Sources: CEBs

* Workers on the land have been excluded from this table because of the problematic enumeration described in chapter 4

The precise occupational status of heads of households engaged in textile manufacturing is also interesting. Although the numbers of workers in each township were small and trends tended to be erratic, when the figures were aggregated for mill houses in the townships the results showed that about one-quarter of heads were engaged in supervisory capacities compared with less than ten per cent across the entire townships. These results clearly suggest that mill owners gave some preference when letting households to those in senior occupational positions, since the census shows a high proportion of overlookers were living in mill houses. It is also evident from census enumeration that a substantial number of heads had family members working in cotton. Had this not been so it is unlikely they would have been allocated a mill house, and this generally applied whether or not the head was employed in a factory. However, in both townships, most mill households had a head working in textiles and the remainder of heads had at least one household member working in a factory.

Not surprisingly, it was found that the majority of textile workers living in mill houses were cotton weavers. In 1881, two-thirds of the textile workers living in mill houses at both Eccleshill and Hoddlesden were cotton weavers almost equally divided between the sexes and there were a few female winders and warpers. In addition a few males were engaged in non-weaving occupations such as overlookers and there were engineers working in the cotton mills. It is fairly evident that the major means of income into mill houses was derived from cotton weaving, probably at the local mill, and that the provision of these houses also benefited the employer long term. Unfortunately, records are not extant to inform us whether these people living in factory houses actually worked in the local mill but it is likely.

In summary all of the mill houses contained at least one textile worker. The majority of these were in-migrants, although this included return migrants. Heads in mill houses were often in-migrants, engaged in textile supervisory occupations and a significant number had family members working in textiles as cotton weavers most of whom were aged between 10 and 25 years. This implies they had been attracted by an offer of work and that the major source of income in mill houses was derived from working in cotton manufacturing.

We have now traced the ever-changing scenes in these east Lancashire rural townships. The rugged barren wastes used as hunting grounds prior to disaf-forestation were later transformed by landowners seeking to increase income and poor families attempting survival through a dual economy of farming and domestic textiles. From the late eighteenth century mechanisation in textiles evolved and by the mid nineteenth century there was full mechanisation of the industry causing a transformation from domestic textiles to factory manufacture. Later the textile industry export trade declined and these communities, having experienced strong dependency on the cotton trade, found themselves unable to earn a wage locally. Since this period these settlements have developed into dormitory townships. Nevertheless, people clearly find the communities desirable places in which to live and consequently there is a dearth of unoccupied properties.

Notes

CHAPTER ONE: THE EARLY YEARS

1   T. Newbigging, *History of the Forest of Rossendale* (Rawtenstall, 1893*)*; G. H. Tupling, *The Economic History of Rossendale* (Univesity of Manchester, 1927); W. Farrer & J. Brownhill, *Victoria history of the County of Lancaster (VCH)*, vols. 2 & 6, (Dawson, Cannon House, Folkstone, 1991 & 1992).

2   J. Aspden, *Historical notes on Hoddlesden Village* (unpublished, no page numbers).

3   Aspden, *Historical notes*; Tupling, *The Economic History*, pp. 166–8.

4   Tupling, *The Economic History*, pp. 12–3.

5   Farrer & Brownhill, *VCH*, vol. 6, p. 280.

6   Farrer & Brownhill, *VCH*, vol. 6, p. 454.

7   For a detailed history of the Forest of Rossendale see Newbigging, *History of the Forest*; Tupling, *The Economic History*; W. Farrer, *The Court Rolls of the Honor of Clitheroe* (Emmott & Co., Edinburgh, 1897–1913), vols. 1–3 (Emmott & Co., Manchester, 1897).

8   A. Duckworth, *Darwen's Day* (Calderprint, Burnley, 1993), no page numbers.

9   Farrer, *The Court Rolls*, vol. 2, p. 524.

10 Farrer & Brownhill, *VCH*, vol. 6, p. 280. A vill is a tract of rural land similar to a parish.

11 Farrer & Brownhill, *VCH*, vol. 6, p. 273; A. Crosby, *A History of Lancashire*, (Phillimore, Chichester, 1998), p. 46; Tupling, *The Economic History*, p. 3.

12 Farrer & Brownhill, *VCH*, vol. 6, p. 273; Crosby, *A History*, p. 46; Tupling, *The Economic History*, p. 3.

13 Tupling, *The Economic History*, pp. 31–2.

14 Agistment, during the period, referred more particularly to the proceeds of pasturage in the king's forests.

15 Tupling, *The Economic History*, pp. 32–34 & 41.

16 Newbigging, *History of the Forest*, p. 279; Tupling, *The Economic History*, pp. 3–4.

17 TNA, E 179/130/28, Lancashire Poll Tax, 1379, documents 1 and 2.

18 M. Postan (ed.), *Cambridge Economic History of Europe* (1966 edn.), pp. 561–2.

19 Newbigging, *History of the Forest*, p. 69 & 95.

20 Farrer & Brownhill, *VCH*, vol. 2, p. 458 & vol. 6, p. 280; Crosby, *A History of Lancashire*, p. 58.

21 Tupling, *The Economic History*, pp. 71–3.

22 Farrer, *The Court Rolls*, vols. 2, p. 425.

23 Newbigging, *History of the Forest*, p. 96. A list of Greaves can be found in this reference at pp. 97–107.

24 Newbigging, *History of the Forest*, pp. 88–90.

25 Tupling, *The Economic History*, pp. 42 & 373–7.

26 Tupling, *The Economic History*, pp. 44 & 49.

27 Tupling, *The Economic History*, p. 50.

28 Tupling, *The Economic History*, pp. 76 & 235.

29 Farrer & Brownhill, *VCH*, vol. 6, p. 280; Farrer, *The Court Rolls*, vols. 3, p. 438.

30 J. G. Shaw, *Darwen and its People* (T.H.C.L. Books, Blackburn, 1991), pp. 552–5.

31 Tupling, *The Economic History*, p. 98.

32 Tupling, *The Economic History*, p. 109.

33 Tupling, *The Economic History*, p. 115.

34 Tupling, *The Economic History*, pp. 127–8.

35 Tupling, *The Economic History*, p. 148.

36 Tupling, *The Economic History*, p. 151.

37 Tupling, *The Economic History*, p. 154.

38 Farrer & Brownhill, *VCH*, vol. 6, p. 280; W. A. Abram, *A History of Blackburn, town and parish* (Toulmin, Blackburn Times, 1877), p. 761.

39 Aspden, *Historical notes*.

40 Tupling, *The Economic History*, p. 79.

41 W. King, 'The Economic and Demographic Development of Rossendale c.1650–1795', unpublished Ph.D. thesis, University of Leicester, 1979, pp. 14–5, 18–9 & 143–5.

42 King, The Economic p 300–1. The core areas were Bacup, Goodshaw, Haslingden & New Church.

43 Lancs. C.R.O/PR/2059/14 & King pp 300–1.

44 Lancs. C.R.O., Hearth Tax Return 1666, MF1/27 (E179/250/6,8–9.) Folio 250–1. The numbers exonerated and non-exonerated for hearths in 1666 were 51. Using 4.5 as the average number of persons per household the approximate population was 230, compared with 26 dwellings in 1630 and an estimated 120 inhabitants. Farrer & Brownhill, *VCH*, vol. 6, pp. 269–275 & 280. For a more detailed account see this reference.

45 Tupling, *The Economic History*, p. 167.

46 Tupling, *The Economic History*, p. 168.

47 Tupling, *The Economic History*, pp. 166–8.

48 Lancs., C.R.O., PR 3016 (M/F 8/12-22), Haslingden (1772) & LPRS 45, Newchurch (1705–7); Tupling, *The Economic History*, p. 177.

49 Tupling, *The Economic History*, pp. 171–2.

50 A. J. L. Winchester, & A. G. Crosby, *England's Landscape: The North West* (Collins, London, 2006), pp. 57–8.

51 Farrer, *The Court Rolls*, vol. 3, pp. 15, 328, 408–13.

CHAPTER TWO: A PERSPECTIVE OF INDUSTRIALISATION AND POPULATION IN EAST LANCASHIRE

1 R. J. Morris, 'Urbanisation' in R. J. Morris and R. Rodger, *The Victorian City* (London, Longman, 1993), pp. 43–4.

2 M. Berg, *The Age of Manufactures 1700–1820* (Routledge, London, Second Edition, 1994), p. 98.

3 P. Hudson, *Regions and Industries: a Perspective on the Industrial Revolution in Britain* (Cambridge University Press, 1989), p. 25.

4 A. P. Wadsworth & J. De. Lacy Mann, *The Cotton Trade and Industrial Lancashire 1600–1780* (Manchester University Press, London, 1965), pp. 170–1.

5 J. K. Walton, *Lancashire: A Social History 1558–1939* (Manchester University Press, 1987), p. 62. It should be noted that these figures only represent imported raw cotton. During this period mixtures of cotton and other fibres inflated production to approximately double.

6 G. H. Tupling, *The Economic History of Rossendale* (University of Manchester, 1927), p. 203, quoting Newbiggin who claimed that no cotton goods were made in Rossendale before 1770; M. B. Rose, *The Lancashire Cotton Industry: A History Since 1700* (Preston, Lancashire County Books, 1996), p. 3; Wadsworth & Mann, *Cotton Trade*, p. 278.

7 D. A. Farnie, *The English Cotton Industry and the World Market, 1815–1896* (Oxford, Clarendon Press, 1979), p. 4. Claims that the cloth trade grew initially as a supplement to farming income but later as a major industry; Tupling, *Economic*, p. 177–8. He concluded that half of the endeavours of Rossendale were towards textile manufacture.

8 G. Timmins , *Four Centuries of Lancashire Cotton* (Lancashire County Books, 1996), p. 89.

9 B. L. Mitchell and P. Deane, *Abstract of British Historical Statistics* (Cambridge University Press, 1962), pp 177–8, shows that raw cotton imports were 2,318,000 lb in 1750 and had risen to 3,612,000 lb by 1770; J. D. Marshall, *Lancashire* (David and Charles, London, 1974), p. 60.

10 G. Timmins, *The Last Shift: Decline of Handloom Weaving in Nineteenth-century Lancashire* (Manchester University Press, 1993), pp. 71 & 76; S. Schwarz, 'Economic Change in north-east Lancashire, c.1660–1760', *THSLC*, vol. 144, (1995), pp. 79–80.

11 Walton, *Lancashire Social*, p. 104; Timmins, *Last Shift*, p 25, quoting Bythell, pp. 41–2, 44–48 and 63–5.

12 Farnie, *The English Cotton Industry*, p. 52; J. Thirsk, 'Industries in the

Countryside', in F. L. Fisher (ed), *Essays in the Economic and Social History of Tudor and Stuart England* (Cambridge University Press, 1961). Thirsk claims that the terrain of Rossendale allowed streams to be dammed with ease and at a minimum expense for this type of semi-engineering work.

13 O. Ashmore, *The Industrial Archaeology of Lancashire* (Newton Abbot, David & Charles, 1969), p. 40; Oliver M. Westall in J. W. A. Price, *The Industrial Archaeology of the Lune Valley*, Centre for North-West Regional Studies; K. L. Wallwork, 'The Evolution of an Industrial Landscape: The Calder Valley, Lancashire from c.1740–1914', unpublished Ph.D. thesis, University of Leicester, 1966. He draws attention to the high rainfall on high ground adjacent to the Calder Valley. The water was used initially for providing waterpower in the countryside but later power generation in urbanised areas such as Darwen and Blackburn, p. 18.

14 Wallwork, 'Evolution', p. 20.

15 According to Mr Alan McEwen of H. A. McEwen, Boiler Makers of Keithley, the water wheel was only capable of generating about 12-horsepower, which was small compared to steam power. A. Crosby, *A History of Lancashire* (Chichester, Phillimore, 1998), p. 76.

16 Ashmore, *Industrial Archaeology*, p. 44.

17 The Leeds and Liverpool Canal was fully completed in 1816. There was a good Turnpike Road system in operation by the late eighteenth century and railways were operative from the 1830s as an alternative and efficient means of transport.

18 Crosby, *History of Lancashire*, p. 76. The Burnley area had its own sources of coal, which were distributed to Colne and Accrington. Blackburn was on the extremity of coal seams and coal was quickly worked out. The fuel required in the Blackburn area was then obtained from the Wigan area via canal barges and later rail. Farnie, *English Cotton*, p. 46; J .Whitley in A. Crosby, *Leading the Way: A History of Lancashire's Roads* (Lancashire County Books, Preston, 1998), p. 167. It has been pointed out by Mr Brian Maden, ex-colliery manager, that a further reason for bringing coal from Wigan was that east Lancashire coal was of inferior quality for raising steam in mills.

19 G. W. Southgate, *English Economic History* (London, Dent, 1952), p. 119; R. L. Hill, 'Hargreaves, Arkwright and Crompton: why three inventors?', Copy of Conference Paper, *TH* (1977), pp. 114–26.

20 Hill, 'Hargreaves, Arkwright', p. 34.

21 Hill, 'Hargreaves, Arkwright', pp 36–9; Southgate, *English Economic*, p. 119.

22 Timmins, *Last Shift*, pp. 28, 37–9 and 87–8. It has been estimated that there were 240,000 British handloom weavers of cotton in the 1820s but by the mid-1830s the number had been reduced to 200,000.

23 Wallwork, 'Evolution', p. 64.

24 Timmins, *Last Shift*, p. 19.

25 Timmins, *Last Shift*, pp. 20–22.

26 A. J. Taylor, *Concentration and Specialization in the Lancashire Cotton*

Industry, *EcHR* (1949), p. 117. Estimated the number of looms in Lancashire in 1835 to be 90,000.

27   D. Bythell, *The Handloom Weavers* (Cambridge University Press, 1969), p. 105.

28   Wallwork, 'Evolution', p. 64. The *Blackburn Mail*, 6 May 1829, commented on poverty in the town caused by economic recession.

29   Taylor, 'Concentration', p. 117.

30   Timmins, *Last Shift*, pp. 12 & 22. The mill was small and contained 96 looms.

31   Mitchell, *Abstract*, p. 372. The increasing use of power loom production is demonstrated by increasing raw cotton imports during the 1830s that increased a further 25% in the 1840s. Timmins, *Last Shift*, 20–22. In 1835 the number of looms in Lancashire accounted for 57% of the British total but by 1850 the proportion had risen to 71%. Walton, *Lancashire*, p. 199.

32   Farnie, *English Cotton*, pp. 4 & 46.

33   Timmins, *Last Shift*, pp 26–8. For details of his calculations see Timmins, *Last Shift*, pp. 36–42 and Appendix A1. The estimation of 168,000 hand weavers in Lancashire in 1821 was 70% of the 240,000 total for Britain suggested by Wood.

34   Wallwork, 'Evolution', p. 53.

35   Farnie, *English Cotton* pp. 4 & 46.

36   Bythell, *Handloom*, pp. 53 & 267; Wood, *History of Wages*, pp. 127–8.

37   Timmins, *Last Shift*, pp. 20 & 184.

38   PP., 1826/7 (231) v, QQ. 1962–3. William Fielden, J.P., of Blackburn told the emigration committee in 1826 that, 'handloom weaving in that district [was] almost at an end as a means of subsistence'.

39   *Blackburn Mail (BM)*, 2 December 1826 & Bythell, *Handloom*, p. 238. In 1826, poor relief was given to 1400 people in Cliviger and 1353 in Briercliff from populations of 1500 and 1611 respectively.

40   PP., 1837/8 (167) xviii, pt 1, Q. 2863. Alfred Power, Assistant Poor Law Commissioner reported to a select committee that, 'handloom weavers of cotton has been for some time a diminishing class, very considerably for some years in Lancashire but there is at present a large number of persons in various parts of Lancashire employed in handloom weaving...'

41   PP., 1833 (690) vi, QQ. 10172–4. Report from James Grimshaw, spinner and manufacturer at Barrowford, who stated that handloom weavers in the Colne district were on the increase. W. Cooke Taylor, pp. 71, claimed that 'the number in Rossendale is as great has it ever had been,' in 1842. PP., 1840 (314) x, Q. 4861, in Bythell, *Handloom*, p. 258. In 1840, Henry Ashton who owned mills in Turton reported that he had employed handloom weavers, 'all we could bargain with'.

42   Timmins, *Last Shift*, p. 91.

43   Walton, *Lancashire:* p. 109.

44   PP., 1835 (341) xiii, QQ. 1759–60. Robert Gardener a spinner and handloom manufacturer in Lancashire stated that handlooms had not been manufactured in ten years prior to 1835. PP., 1833 (690) vi. Q.

3976. ﹍﹍﹍ in Bythell, *Handloom*, p. 258. In Clitheroe, James Thomson, a cloth printer reported that in 1833, his firm had 'many dyers, washers and labourers in our works that were formerly handloom weavers'.

45   Bythell, *Handloom*, p. 266, quoting PP., 1837/8 (174) xviii, Q. 3294. Alfred Power, Assistant Poor Law Commissioner claimed in 1837 that, 'the worst part of Lancashire with reference to the distressed handloom weavers is about Colne, Burnley and Padiham … the number of handloom weavers in cotton has been materially reduced'.

46   *BS*, 23 June 1838.

47   Timmins, *Last Shift*, p. 112.

48   Wood in Timmins, *Last Shift*, p. 28.

49   *BA*, 24 September 1859, in Bythell, *Handloom*, p. 259, 'if the old men, mostly handloom weavers, would work constantly, they might earn sixteen shillings per week; but it seems they are pretty much their own masters, and do not work much on Monday'.

50   Timmins, *Last Shift*, p. 118; D. Bythell, *Sweated Trades: Outwork in Nineteenth Century Britain* (London, Batsford, 1978), p. 38; Bythell, *Handloom*, p. 266.

51   Percentages vary according to whether minimum or maximum numbers are used, since census enumerators failed to distinguish clearly between different types of weavers.

52   Timmins, *Last Shift*, p. 118.

53   Timmins, *Last Shift*, p. 187. Handlooms were less harsh on natural fibres and setting up for fancy cloths was easier than with power looms.

54   Timmins, *Last Shift*, p. 11.

55   *BS*, 1 August 1838. Report by George Dewhurst of Blackburn.

56   Timmins, *Last Shift*, p. 110; Timmins, *Made in Lancashire: A History of Regional Industrialisation*, p. 185.

57   Timmins, *Last Shift*, p. 142.

58   Timmins, *Last Shift*, p. 136–7; Timmins, *Made in Lancashire*, p. 185. Census 1871, III, pp. 423 & 426. Census 1911, X, I, p. 208.

59   Timmins, *Last Shift*, p. 136.

60   J. Mokyr, *The Economics of the Industrial Revolution* (Allen and Unwin, London, 1985), p. 230 referring to Deane and Cole, 1962.

61   N. L. Tranter, *Population and Society 1750–1940* (Longman, London & New York, 1985), p. 35.

62   A. Redford, *Labour Migration in England 1800–1850* (Second Edition, Manchester University Press, 1964), pp. 38–9; Timmins, *Last Shift*, pp. 24–5; Wadsworth & Mann, *Cotton Trade*, p. 312.

63   Gregory King's hearth tax calculations multiplied by 4.5 births per marriage gives a population for Lancashire of 196,100; E. C. K. Gonner, 'The population of England in the eighteenth century', *RSSJ*, vol. 86. Gives a higher figure of 207,090: W. Smith, *An Historical Introduction to the Economic Geography of Great Britain* (London, Bell, 1968), p. 153. Lancs. CRO, Hearth Tax Return 1666, MF1/27 (E179/250/6,8–9.). The number of hearths in 1666 was Eccleshill 36 and Yate & Pickup Bank 51.

64 R. Lawton, 'Population trends in Lancashire and Cheshire from 1801', *THSLC*. 114 (1962) p. 191. He shows that between 1700 and 1750 population in England and Wales increased 9 per cent, Cheshire 23 per cent but Lancashire 83 per cent; and between 1750 and 1800 the figures were 41, 51 and 134 per cent respectively.

65 Schwarz, 'Econonmic', pp. 78–9.

66 Walton, *Lancashire*, pp. 78–9. In Rossendale the change to a lower age of marriage took place at an earlier date than in many other places and this was reflected in both a rising birth rate and reduction in the intervals between births from the beginning of the eighteenth century. Marshall, *Lancashire*, p. 53, has shown that many townships in the early eighteenth century had large proportions of weavers, and this was a point at which early marriage occurred.

67 H. J. Habakkuk, *Population Growth and Economic Development since 1750* (Leicester University Press, 1974), p. 8; Hill, 'Hargreaves, Arkwright', pp. 5–6.

68 M. S. J. Parker & D. J. Reid, *The British Revolution 1750–1970: A Social and Economic History* (Poole, Blandford, 1972), pp. 4–5.

69 Timmins, *Last Shift*, pp. 24–5; J. T. Swain, 'Industry before the Industrial Revolution: north east Lancashire c.1550–1640' (Manchester, 1986); W. King, 'The economic and demographic development of Rossendale c.1650–1795', unpublished Ph.D. thesis, University of Leicester, 1979, pp. 14–5, 18–9 and 143–5. He claims Rossendale housed 1000 inhabitants in the mid-sixteenth century, which then increased to about 3000 – by the mid-seventeenth century with a further increase to between 10,000 and 11,000 by the 1770's. Schwarz, 'Econonmic'. Timmins, *Made in Lancashire*, p. 36.

70 Marshall, *Lancashire*, p. 66.

71 Habakkuk, *Population*, p. 36.

72 Habakkuk, *Population*, p. 14; Tranter, *Population*, p. 49 referring to M. Drake, 'Marriage and population growth in Ireland 1750–1845', *EcHR.*, xvi, 1963–4.; N. F. R. Crafts and N. J. Ireland, *A simulation of the impact of changes in the age at marriage before and during the advent of industrialisation in England*, PopSt., 30, 3, 1976; Wrigley & Schofield, *Population* (London, 1981).

73 Hudson, *Industrial*, p. 141.

74 Tranter, *Population*, p. 103; Habakkuk, *Population*, p. 40.

75 Marshall, *Lancashire*, p. 53. The parish registers of Newchurch in 1705 and Haslingden in 1722 indicated that more that one-third of the total recorded were weavers.

76 Walton, *Lancashire*, pp. 78–9. In Rossendale, the birth rate rose from less than 30 per 1000 in 1716 to nearly 41 per 1000 in 1731. The intervals between births fell from 27.8 months in the 1720s to 22.3 months by the early 1780's. Timmins, *Made in Lancashire*, pp. 37–8, quoting King.

77 Schwarz, 'Econonmic': Lawton & Pooley, *Britain 1740–1950:* p. 30; Redford, *Labour migration*, p. 18; Hopwood, *History*, pp. 6–7. Shows weavers' wages increased from 8*s.* in 1770 to 25*s.* per week in 1800 but

by 1820 they had declined to 9s. per week. These values can only be taken as trends since wages varied between districts and with the type of cloth woven. T. E. H. Capper, 'The Rise and Decline of Industrial Colonies at Backbarrow, Cark-in-Cartmel and Low Wood', unpublished M.A. dissertation, University of Lancaster, 1969, Chap 4, p. 6 & fn. 42; Wood, *History* p. 127. Claims there were 184,000 weavers in 1806 rising to 240,000 by 1820 or a 30% increase during which time there was a 47% increase in population.

78 R. K. Fleischman, *Conditions of Life among the Cotton Workers of South East Lancashire 1780–1850* (Garland, London, 1985), p. 260, quoting Parliamentary Papers. Walton, *Lancashire*, p. 124.

79 Marshall, *Lancashire*, p. 51.

80 Walton, *Lancashire*, p. 110.

81 Timmins, *Last Shift*, p. 44. Examples provided are Newchurch-in-Pendle 82%, Colne 68%, Blackburn parish 55%, Burnley 36, Haslingden 49% and Padiham 42%.

82 Lancs. CRO. M/F DRB 2/11, Bishops Transcripts, St Mary, Blackburn. About 4% of the entries excluded occupations. Timmins deduced a figure of 55% for Blackburn Parish between 1818–21, p. 44.

83 Walton, *Lancashire*, p. 124.

84 1841 CSR; PP. 1852, vol. lxxxvi, Census of England and Wales, 1801–1851, Population (7).

CHAPTER THREE: DEMOGRAPHIC
CHARACTERISTICS OF THE TOWNSHIPS

1 1851, CSR, vol. 7, p. 49.

2 1871 CSR, p. 24.

3 R. Lawton, 'Population changes in England and Wales in the later nineteenth century: An analysis of trends by Registration Districts', *TransInstBritGeogr*, 44 (1968), pp. 55–74.

4 C. Pooley and J. Turnbull, *Migration and mobility in Britain since the 18th century* (ULC Press, 1998), p. 24. Have illustrated the difference between net and gross migration by using the example of 1000 in-migrants & 900 out-migrants giving a net-migration of 100 people but a gross movement of 1900 individuals.

5 J. T. Danson & T. A. Welton, 'On the population of Lancashire and Cheshire and its local distribution during the fifty years 1801–51', Pt. 3, *THSLC*, vol. 11, 1859, p. 41.

6 Pooley and Turnbull, *Migration*, p. 24.

7 Number employed in 1871: Blacksnape 71, Eccleshill 343, Hoddlesden 264 and Yate and Pickup Bank 467. Numbers employed in 1881: Blacksnape 165, Eccleshill 408, Hoddlesden 258 and Yate and Pickup Bank 369.

8 CEBs.

9   Pooley and Turnbull, *Migration*, p. 76.

10   1871 CSR; Doherty, 'Short-distance migration', pp. 84–5.

11   1871 CSR.

12   Doherty, 'Short-distance migration', p. 222.

13   In the area known as Belthorn there were approximately equal numbers of houses in Yate and Pickup Bank and Oswaldtwistle and in a few instances a single house were straggled across the boundary. This presents a methodological problem in defining study areas since inhabitants moving to the opposite side of the road of the ribbon layout would be identified as a migrant.

14   Ravenstein, 'The laws of migration' (1889), pp. 286–9; Redford, *Labour migration*, p. 186.

15   The numbers of paper and iron workers combined from Lancashire but more than 5 miles from Eccleshill and Yate and Pickup Bank were 33. In addition, there were 25 from outside of Lancashire including 8 from Ireland and Scotland. Only 4 arrived from within 5 miles of Eccleshill and Yate and Pickup Bank.

16   One ex-British Isles resident had re-located from America and was living in Eccleshill as part of a nomadic family.

CHAPTER FOUR: EARNING A LIVING – AGRICULTURE

1   M. Anderson, *Family structure in Nineteenth Century Lancashire* (Cambridge University Press, 1971), p. 79.

2   J. T. Swain, 'Industry before the Industrial Revolution, North-East Lancashire c.1550–1640', *ChetSoc*, vol. 32 (1986), quoting Holt; PRO. DL.5/19 fol. 395, p. 34.

3   J. Holt, *General view of the Agriculture of the County of Lancaster* (David and Charles Rept, Newton Abbot, Rpt. 1969 of 1795 Ed.), p. 8.

4   J. Binns, *Notes on the agriculture of Lancashire: with suggestions for its improvement* (Dobson and Son, Preston, 1851), p. 12.

5   1840s, 6 inch, Ordnance Survey map.

6   Personal knowledge of agricultural conditions in the area.

7   Swain, *Industry Before*, chap 3, quoting Rodgers.

8   The report of the land utilisation survey of Britain, Pt. 45, Lancashire, 1941, p. 53.

9   G. Timmins, *The Last Shift* (Manchester University Press, 1993), p. 46; Binns, *Notes on the Agriculture*, p. 12.

10   W. Farrer & J. Brownhill, *Victoria History of the County of Lancaster*, vol. 6 (Dawson, Cannon House, Folkstone, 1991), p. 280.

11   Swain, *Industry Before*, p. 34.

12   H. King, 'The Agricultural Geography of Lancastria', *JMGS*, 1927–8.

13   Swain, *Industry Before*, p. 34, refering to J. Thirsk, *Farming regions of England*, p. 4; T. W. Fletcher, 'Economic development of agriculture

in east Lancashire', unpublished M.Sc. dissertation, University of Leeds, 1954. Appendix 1, p. vi. East Lancashire totals: 1870 – 48,174 cattle, 51,837 sheep; 1911 – 46,266 cattle, 39,002 sheep & 1951 – 54,140 cattle, 41,547 sheep.

14 J. Aiken, *A description of the country from thirty to forty miles round Manchester* (David & Charles, Newton Abbot first published 1795, 1969 Ed), p. 8.

15 G. H. Tupling, *The Economic History of Rossendale* (University of Manchester, 1927), p. 146.

16 J. D. Marshall, *Lancashire* (David and Charles, London, 1974), PP 34–7.

17 Fletcher, 'Economic', p. 56.

18 *Darwen Advertiser* (DA), 13 October 1988. This article was a flashback to a report in the *Blackburn Mail*, September 1825.

19 Lancs., CRO./WCW, John Yates, Yate Bank, 9 November 1668.

20 Lancs., CRO./WCW, Thomas Yates, Yate Bank, 2 December 1707.

21 Lancs., CRO./WCW, Richard Rothwell, Rossendale, 18 June 1711.

22 Lancs., CRO./WCW, Randle Astley, Eccleshill, 29 April 1641.

23 Lancs., CRO./WCW, William Duxbury, Pickup Bank, 18 February 1758.

24 Evidence of shared working and living space is indicated by the listing of inventory items room by room.

25 Aiken, *A description*; Holt, *General view*, PP 56–7 and 71

26 R. W. Dickson, *General view of the agriculture of Lancashire* (Sherwood, London, 1815), p. 545.

27 Binns, *Notes on the agriculture*, p. 12, quoting the *Blackburn Mail*.

28 J. Caird, *English agriculture in 1850–51* (Longnan, Brown, Green and Longmans, London, 1852), p. 265.

29 W. Rothwell, *Report of agriculture in the county of Lancaster* (Groombridge, London, 1850), p. 20.

30 Fletcher, 'Economic', p. 56.

31 J. D. Chambers and G. E. Mingay, *The Agricultural Revolution 1750–1880* (Batsford, London, 1966, Reprint 1984), pp. 92 & 96.

32 M. Winstanley, 'Agricultural and Industrial Revolutions: reassessing the role of the small farm', Claus Bjorn (Ed.) *The Agricultural Revolution reconsidered* (Landbohistorisk Selskab, Odense, Denmark, 1998), pp. 96 & 99.

33 A. D. Hall, *A Pilgrimage of British farming, 1910–1912* (Murry, London, 1913), p. 235.

34 Winstanley, 'Agricultural and industrial', p. 104.

35 R. W. Dickson, *General view*, p. 545.

36 Winstanley, 'Agricultural and industrial', 104.

37 Fletcher, 'Economic', p. 64. Extracts from the APRs in 1870 show that the percentage meadow and pasture in England to be about three-fifths of the total agricultural land compared with two-thirds in Lancashire.

38 APRs average of 1870, 1874, 1875. Fletcher, 'Economic', p. 128.

39 Fletcher, 'Economic', p. 102.

40   Fletcher, 'Economic', pp. 65 & 103. Cattle per 100 acres: England and Wales 16; Lancashire 29 and east Lancashire 34.4.

41   T. W. Fletcher, 'Lancashire livestock farming during the Great Depression', *Agricultural History Review*, vol. 9 (1961), p. 21.

42   Fletcher, 'Economic', p. 103.

43   Fletcher, 'Economic', p. 37.

44   C. B. Phillips and J. H. Smith, *Lancashire and Cheshire from AD 1540* (Longman, London, 1994), p. 238.

45   Phillips & Smith, *Lancashire, p. 238*; T. W. Fletcher, 'Lancashire livestock', pp. 26–7.

46   Fletcher, 'Lancashire livestock', p 21.

47   Fletcher, 'Economic', p. 22.

48   Between the 1871 and 1881 censuses the population of Lancashire rose by 39% and east Lancashire 40%.

49   G. H. Wood, *The history of wages in the cotton trade during the past hundred years* (Sherratt, Manchester, 1910), p. 128; W. T. Layton, *An introduction to the study of prices* (Macmillan, London, 1912), p. 150.

50   Fletcher, 'Economic', Appendix, PP x and xi. The statistics are for stocks of milk cattle, increasing average yields and numerous references to consumption between 1870 and the end of the century.

51   Winstanley, 'Industrialization', p. 173.

52   Fletcher, 'Economic', pp. 21–2 and 95.

53   Fletcher, 'Economic', p. 22. The small change of acreage may have been merely a result of change from customary measure to statute acre.

54   Fletcher, 'Economic', p. 37.

55   Fletcher, 'Economic'; 'Lancashire livestock'; T. W. Fletcher, 'The Agrarian Revolution in arable Lancashire', *Transactions of the Lancashire and Cheshire Antiquarian Society.* 72 (1962); Winstanley, 'Industrialization', pp. 157–195.

56   Fletcher, 'Economic', pp. 113–4; Winstanley, 'Industrialization', pp. 157–195.

57   Winstanley, 'Industrialization', p. 161.

58   G. H. Tupling, *The Economic History of Rossendale* (University of Manchester, 1927), pp. 161 & 227.

59   J. Abbott, Pictorial History of Hoddlesden (1985).

60   Winstanley, 'Industrialization', p. 171.

61   O.S. map 1880s.

62   Winstanley, 'Industrialization', p. 163.

63   CEBs; Lancs., CRO, DVAC 1/2/5 & 6, The Finance (1909–1910) Act , Valuation Books.

64   The APRs prior to 1891 do not provide details of owner/occupancy.

65   LCRO., DVAC 1/2/5 & 6, The Finance (1909–1910) Act , Valuation Books.

66   APRs, 1913.

67   The main owners of farms were: Eccleshill; Mr J. Hodgson of Bolton, five farms; Yate & Pickup Bank; Mr O. Yates, Yate Bank, four farms, one being his personal dwelling.

68 Lancs., C.R.O., DDH 780 Lease Holme Fold, Yate Bank. Tenant, Daniel Yates, 177.

69 R. J. P. Kein & R. R. Oliver, *The tithe maps of England and Wales* (Cambridge University Press, 1995). Lancs., CRO. *List of Enclosure Awards*. Lancs., CRO. DRB 1/69. Eccleshill Tithe Award 1843 showed 38A and 3r of arable only and 4A, 3r and 48p of arable and meadow combined. This was less than 6% of the township's farmland.

70 Lancs., CRO. DRB 1/218 Tithe Award 1848.

71 Fletcher, 'Economic', p. 64. TNA. MAF 68/532.

72 W. G. Hoskins and Dudley L. Stamp, *The common lands of England and Wales* (Collins, London, 1963), p. 295.

73 TNA., MAF 68/, Abstract of Lancashire parish returns of acreage of crops and of livestock – 1870 & 1880.

74 These figures ignore grazing required by other animals.

75 Fletcher, 'Economic', p. xxviii.

76 Fletcher, 'Economic', Appendix, pp. x, xi & xxiv. Between 1871 and 1901 the population of Blackburn increased by 42.6% and Darwen by 66%.

77 Winstanley, 'Industrialization', p. 173.

78 PP. 1894 (C 7334) xvi, pt 1, Appendix A1 and A2. Reports by Wilson Fox (Assistant Commissioner) of the Garstang District of Lancashire and the Glendale District of Northumberland, pp. 565–6

79 Winstanley, 'Industrialization', p. 81.

80 CEBs.

81 C. Pooley and J. Turnbull, *Migration and mobility in Britain since the 18th century* (ULC Press, 1998), p. 62.

82 J. Garnett, 'Prize report on the farming of Lancashire', *JRAS* (1849), p. 18.

83 Pooley and Turnbull, *Migration*, p. 62.

84 E. Higgs, 'Occupational censuses and the agricultural workforce in Victorian England and Wales', *EconHR*, xlviii, 4 (1995), p. 704.

85 Following discussions with farmers it is estimated that one person could have milked 10 cows in two hours based on the then current yields. Consideration of the number of cows is more important than the acreages of farms since there was a high utilisation of the land.

86 The pasture acreage per cow in the case study townships was generally around two to three acres.

87 J. Sheldon, *Lancashire cheese-making and dairy farming* (n.p., repr. From *Preston Guardian*, 21 Sept, 5 Oct and 2 Nov, 1895), p. 6.

88 Higgs, 'Occupational censuses', p. 704.

89 Daughters working as agricultural labourers were described in the census as 'Dairy maid (ag lab)'.

90 CEBs.

91 Fletcher, 'Economic', p. 56.

92 Photograph taken by writer in 2004.

93 The 1851 CEB shows that a handloom weaver of silk occupied the centre portion of this terrace.

94 1851 CEB; Map created from CD, Disc 2, *First Edition 25 inch*

Ordnance Survey maps of Lancashire 1888–1893, produced by Digital Archives, Warrington in conjunction with Lancashire Record Office.

95   The 1851 census shows the head's occupation to be a 'farmer and beer-seller'. This was also the residence of great, great grandfather who my ancestors have informed me was also a handloom weaver of silk.

96   Inspection of building and discussion with current owners.

97   TNA., IR 58/9065 Field Book – Yate & Pickup Bank, folios 189 and 190.

98   Bolton Library Archive, ZJA 601–2, Waterside Farm, Eccleshill.

99   TNA., IR 58/9064 Field Book – Eccleshill, folio 2.

100   I am grateful to Mr J. Hacking for the information tendered.

101   Pooley and Turnbull, *Migration and mobility*.

102   Fletcher, 'Economic'; Winstanley, 'Industrialization'.

103   Fletcher, 'Economic'; 'Lancashire livestock'; 'Agrarian'; Winstanley, 'Industrialization'.

104   Winstanley, 'Industrialization', PP. 171–81

CHAPTER FIVE: THE VILLAGES AS TEXTILE COMMUNITIES

1   *Blackburn Weekly Telegraph*, 14 February 1914, report of interview with William Fish (old resident of Blacksnape).

2   M. Rothwell, *A Guide to the Industrial Heritage of Darwen including Hoddlesden, Yate and Pickup Bank, Eccleshill and Tockholes*, (Bridgestone Press, UK, 1992), p. 11.

3   W. G. Hoskins, *The Making of the English Landscape*, (Penguin Books, Harmondsworth, 1981), p. 222. The first water-driven factory in Lancashire was erected in Chorley in 1777.

4   Rothwell, *Darwen*, pp. 9 & 11.

5   *BM*, 6 February, 1818.

6   J. Abbott, *Pictorial History of Hoddlesden* (1985), pp. 5 & 14.

7   See chapter 2 for illustrations.

8   J. Thirsk, *The Rural Economy of England* (Hambledon Press, London, 1984); D. A. Farnie, *The English cotton industry and the world market, 1815–1896* (Clarendon Press, Oxford, 1979).

9   Personal local knowledge.

10   *BM*, 11 January 1804, p. 3.

11   Rothwell, *Darwen*, pp. 8–9; Personal observation.

12   *BM*, 22 April, 1807, p. 1.

13   Rothwell, *Darwen*, p. 11.

14   Rothwell, *Darwen*, pp. 8–11.

15   Rothwell,, *Darwen*, p. 9.

16   Rothwell, *Darwen*, p 9, 71–72. This writer is not specific with his references but he states generally that the information was extracted from local newspapers in Blackburn Library from 1793, Trade Directories, Fire Insurance Policies and Records, Yates Engine Lists,

    Darwen Local Board Rates, Corporation Rates and Valuation Lists in Blackburn Museum.

17 Rothwell, *Darwen*, p. 11.

18 *BM*, 29 January, 1826, p. 3. Stockclough Mill is locally referred to as 'Old Engine'. It has now been converted to a house and this demonstrates the smallness of some of the early mills.

19 Rothwell, *Darwen*, p. 9.

20 Lancs. CRO. WCW, C681, John Scholes, Yate Bank, Yeoman, 30 Nov, 1812.

21 CSRs; B. R. Mitchell and P. Deane, *Abstract of British Historical Statistics* (Cambridge University Press, 1962). The population increases in both the towns and townships approximately correlates with rapid increase in raw cotton imports into Britain in the early nineteenth century.

22 G. Timmins, *The Last Shift* (Manchester University Press, 1993), p 112.

23 J. K. Walton, *Lancashire: a social history 1558–1939* (Manchester University Press, 1987), p. 108.

24 These quotes were recorded in the Darwen Advertiser as a flashback on 27 March 1920.

25 Rothwell, *Darwen*, pp. 8, 11–2.

26 Rothwell, *Blackburn Pt. 1*, p. 37; M. Rothwell, *A guide to the industrial heritage of Church & Oswaldtwistle including Belthorn, Knuzden and Stanhill* (Bridgewater Press, 1993), p. 8.

27 K. C. Jackson, 'Enterprise in some working-class communities: Cotton Manufacture in North East Lancashire 1880–1914, *TH*, vol. 37, No. 1 (May 2006), pp. 52–81.

28 *Barrett's directory of Blackburn, Accrington, Darwen and Clitheroe* (Barrett, Preston, 1897), p. 477, shows Adam Bullough as a Cotton Manufacturer in Eccleshill.

29 *Preston Herald* 21 November 1863. In 1863 the Vale Rock Mill provided a tea party for workers and friends at which there was an attendance of 600 people.

30 Rothwell, *Darwen*, pp. 11–12.

31 D. Hogg, *A history of Church and Oswaldtwistle 1860–1914*, vol. 2 (Accrington and District Local History Society, 1971), p 70. Belthorn Higher Mill closed 1933.

32 Rothwell, *Blackburn Pt 1*, p 37; Rothwell, *Church and Oswaldtwistle*, p. 43. Syke Mill closed in 1958.

33 *Barrett's directory of Blackburn, etc.* (1897), p. 477, shows Adam Bullough as a Cotton Manufacturer.

34 Lancs. CRO. DVBX 1/3/3, 1910 Inland Revenue Valuation Books. This reference shows the mill was being leased to N & J Eccles , Darwen in 1914. CEB 1881.

35 J. Aspden, *Historical notes on Hoddlesden Village* (unpublished, no page numbers).

36 CEBs.

37 *The Times*, 1 July 1864.

38 Rothwell, *Darwen*, p. 11–12.

39 A Crosby, *A History of Lancashire*, (Phillimore, Chichester, 1998), p. 103.

40 S. D. Chapman, *The Cotton Industry in the Industrial Revolution* (MacMillan, London, 1972), p. 64. In the eighteenth century, Chapman has claimed that a hand spinner required 50,000 hours to process 100 lbs of cotton. The early mules took 2000 hours and the Water frame only a few 100 hours.

41 G. H. Tupling, *The Economic History of Rossendale* (University of Manchester, 1927), pp. 177–8; Timmins, *last*, p. 25. D. Bythell, *The Sweated Trades* (London, Batsford, 1978), pp. 42–4.

42 This is explained in chapter 3.

43 PP. 1822 vol. xv, Census of Great Britain: Abstracts of Answers and Returns 1821, p. 152.

44 Harris Museum, Preston. BA1/B/63. Baines M.S.S, Lancashire Parishes, Blackburn Parish, 1833, 'Butterworth note books and maps', vol. 2, No. 7, pp. 8, 638 & 643.

45 SD 726 229.

46 Rothwell, *Darwen*, p. 8.

47 Bythell, *Handloom Weavers*, pp 60–2.

48 E. Baines, *History, Directory and Gazetteer of the County Palatine of Lancaster*, vol. 2 (William Wasles & Co, Liverpool, 1824, reprinted 1968), p 494.

49 J. Clapham, *An Economic History of Modern Britain: Free Trade and Steel 1850–1886*, (Cambridge, 1932), p. 180.

50 P. Horn, 'Victorian villages from census returns', *LocaHist*, vol. 15, (1982), p. 26.

51 Timmins, *last*, pp. 120–2. During the 1850s the 10 to 29 years age group declined from 51% to 38% whilst the 50 years of age and over group increased from 14 to 20%.

52 PP. Census of England and Wales, 1862, vol. 11; *Ages, condition as to marriage, occupations and birth-places of the people*, H.M.S.O., [C-5597, 1863], pp. 635, 639, 643 & 645. PP. 1873 Census of England and Wales, Ages, Condition…of the People 1871 (H.M.S.O., London, C872) Census of England and Wales, 1881, vol. 3, *Ages, condition…of the people*, [C-3722, 1883], pp. 355 & 360.

53 Numbers annotated in the census as handloom weavers were; Eccleshill 12%, and Yate and Pickup Bank 7%. Undifferentiated, denoted as 'cotton weavers': Eccleshill 2%, and Yate and Pickup Bank 26% although it is likely that in the last two townships there were power loom weavers because of requirements in the village mills.

54 The proportions of the total textile workforce engaged as weavers were: Blackburn 68%, Darwen 69% and Oswaldtwistle 61%

55 This relocation would have shortened walking distance and avoided traversing very bad underfoot conditions.

56 Rothell, *Darwen*, pp. 8, 16–17. The numbers of operatives working in the mills are based on this source.

57   In 1871, 210 textile workers were listed in the census as living in
      Eccleshill and about 100 were needed at Waterside Mill and 60 at
      Grimshaw Bridge Mill. In 1881, 221 textile workers were listed but
      Rothwell claimed 300 operatives were required at the Waterside Mill
      alone mill in the 1880s. In 1871 the population of Eccleshill was 633
      and 768 in 1881

58   Anderson, *Family Structure*, p. 22.

59   Census of England and Wales, 1871, *Population*, No: 18, Irish
      University Press Series, pp. 423 & 426. Census of England and Wales,
      1881, vol. 3, *Ages, condition as to marriage, occupations and birth-places
      of the people*, [C-3722, 1883], p. 360. The actual numbers of female
      cotton workers in Blackburn in 1861 were slightly in excess of males
      but in Burnley male numbers exceeded those of females. In 1871
      figures for Burnley were not included in the census tables.

60   Bythell, *Handloom*, pp. 60–1; Timmins, *Last Shift*, pp. 119–20.

61   1881 British Census and National Index, England, Scotland, Wales,
      Channel Islands, Isle of Man and Royal Navy, The Church of Jesus
      Christ of Latter-Day Saints, 1999. The percentage of male cotton
      weavers in Blackburn, Darwen and Oswaldtwistle were 33, 32 and 30
      respectively.

CHAPTER SIX: OTHER EMPLOYMENT AND BUSINESSES

1   *Preston Guardian*, 19 March 1853.

2   M. Rothwell, *A Guide to the Industrial Heritage of Darwen including
      Hoddlesden, Yate and Pickup Bank, Eccleshill and Tockholes*
      (Bridgestone Press, UK,1992). p. 62–3.

3   Ann Stokes currently living in Darwen is a descendant of Joseph
      Place. She has undertaken considerable research into the family
      history.

4   Letter from British Coal, Stoke-on-Trent to Mrs A. Stokes, dated 4 July
      1989.

5   J. Nadin, *East Lancashire Mining Memories*, (Tempus, Stroud, 2008),
      pp. 117–8.

6   Rothwell, *Darwen*, p. 64–5.

7   BL, loose sheets, G. Hartley, History of Shaws Glazed Brick
      Company Limited and Family.

8   Rothwell, *Darwen*, p. 63–4.

9   Letter from Company House to Mrs A. Stokes, dated 12 March 1990.

10   *BT*, 14 March 1932.

11   BL, loose sheets; Hartley, History of Shaws; *DN*, 6 November 1926.

12   J. Aspden, *Historical notes on Hoddlesden Village* (unpublished, no page
      numbers).

13   TNA, Rail/1005/474, Hoddlesden Branch Lancashire & Yorkshire
      Railway; TNA. AN 13/1711, Hoddlesden Branch Lancashire &

Yorkshire Railway.

14   DL, K7, Hoddlesden Cooperative Land and Building Company
      Minutes 1861 to 1957; TNA, BT 31/3331/19778, No. of Company:
      19778: Hoddlesden Cotton Manufacturing Co. Ltd.

15   Lancs, CRO. DDX 2075, Darwen Cooperative Society.

16   Barrett's directory of Blackburn & District 1881 (Barrett & Co, 1881,
      Preston).

17   CWS Directories 1940 and 1951.

18   Lancs, CRO. DVAC 1/6, Darwen, The Finance (1909–10) Act,
      Valuation Book

19   W. T. Ashton, *The Darwen Valley of the past*, (1932).

20   TNA. IR 58/9065 Field Book – Yate & Pickup Bank, folio, 189 and
      190.

CHAPTER SEVEN: TEXTILE WORKERS' HOUSING

1   G. Timmins, 'Housing quality in rural textile colonies, c.1800–1850:
      The Ashworth settlements revisited', *IndArchaeolRev*, XXII: 1, 2000.
      p. 21.

2   S. D. Chapman, 'Workers' housing in the cotton factory colonies,
      1770–1850', *TH* vol. 7 (1976), p. 112.

3   G. Timmins, 'Housing quality', pp. 29–35. The Ashworths' built
      back-to-back houses at Egerton and Bank Top near Bolton; F. Collier,
      *The Family Economy of the Working Classes in the Cotton Industry 1784–
      1833* (ed) R. S. Fitton (Manchester University Press, 1964), pp. 33–4.
      The Peels built 20 back-to-back houses for cotton workers at Burr Mill
      Bury with earth floors, no water and no refuse disposal.

4   Some accounts of early housing for managers such as Bazely's at
      Barrow Bridge and Ashworths at Edgerton and Eagley suggest they
      were subject to paternalistic control and above average in standard.
      However, Timmins has revisted the latter settlements and cast some
      doubt on earlier accounts. The writer visited Bazely's back-to-back
      housing also at Barrow Bridge and considers these not to be of a high
      standard. Timmins, 'Housing quality'; D. O'Connor, *Barrow Bridge,
      Bolton, A model industrial community of the nineteenth century* (Bolton
      Central Library, undated).

5   J. Hole, *The homes of the working classes with suggestions for their
      improvement* (Longmans Green, London, 1866), p. 8.

6   J. Withers, *Report on the sanitary condition of the Borough of Blackburn*
      (Douglas, Blackburn, 1853), p. 7; B. R. Mitchell and P. Deane,
      Abstract of British historical statistics (Cambridge University Press,
      1962), p. 57. Withers, strongly opposed the unhealthy living conditions
      and compared the death rate in 1851 of 27.16 per 1000 in the town with
      a national figure of 22 per 1000 in England and Wales

7   J. Burnett, *A Social History of Housing 1815–1985* (Second Edition,

Methuen, London, 1986), p. 11.

8   S. Muthesius, *The English Terraced House* (Yale University Press, London, 1982), pp. 33–6. Some large urban authorities compiled their own legislation before the 1848 P. H. Act was introduced. Examples are: Birkenhead in 1843, Manchester 1844, Nottingham 1845, Liverpool 1846.

9   Burnett, *Social*, pp. 93–5.

10 J. K. Walton, *Lancashire: A Social History 1558–1939* (Manchester University Press, 1987), p. 313–4. Local byelaws usually demanded features such as improved height of rooms, minimum window size and apertures opening to outside air.

11 G. W. Southgate, *English Economic History* (Dent, London, 1952), p. 283.

12 Bye-Laws, Oswaldtwistle District Council, 1909. The 1875 Public Health Act attempted to bring in uniformity with regard to health and safety of buildings but attention to the legislation by urban authorities was varied. Even after the 1936 Public Health Act there was a wide variation of interpretation between local authorities.

13 Burnett, *Social*, p. 10.

14 J. D. Marshall, 'Colonisation as a factor in the planting of towns on north-west England' in H. J. Dyos (ed) *The Study of Urban History*, (Edward Arnold, London, 1968), p. 22; P. Gaskell, *The Manufacturing Population of England* (London, 1833), pp. 41–6. In Oldham he claimed 'there was a conspicuous absence of houses connected with mills'; at Bury there was 'a large number of mills with associated housing and [the town] was also surrounded by numerous industrial settlements'; in Rochdale over half the mill owners owned houses but only a small number each.

15 P. Joyce, *Work, Society and Politics* (Harvester Press, Brighton, 1980), p. 121–3.

16 Walton, *Lancashire*, pp. 199–200.

17 D. Beattie, *History of Blackburn* (Carnegie, Lancaster, 2007), pp. 102–18.

18 D. Beattie, *Blackburn – The development of a Lancashire cotton town* (Ryburn Publishing, Halifax, 1992), pp. 51–2; Joyce, *Work*, p. 121–2.

19 Joyce, *Work*, p. 121–3; Beattie, *Blackburn – The Development*, p. 52–3. Gaskell estimated that: 'the number of houses owned by industrialists was between 10 and 12 per cent of the total' in the towns of Blackburn and Darwen, in the second quarter of the nineteenth century. By mid-century Joyce estimated, 20 per cent of the houses in Blackburn were owned by textile employers and in Darwen, Eccles Shorrock, a single textile employer, alone owned 12 per cent of the housing stock. After mid-century employer housing ownership started to decline, although by the 1860s and 1870s both Joyce and Beattie found that housing in Blackburn owned by textile employers still represented around 13 per cent of the total housing stock.

20 Muthesius, *The English*, p. 17.

21 Burnett, *Social*, p. 81–3.

22 Burnett, *Social*, p. 12. Mill housing was built at Cromford, Belper and Styal. In the early nineteenth century, the Ashworths commenced building dwellings at Bank Top and Egerton near Bolton, as did Bazely at Barrow Bridge, Bolton. In the latter part of the nineteenth century villages were built at Saltaire, Bournville and Port Sunlight.

23 Collier, *Family*, pp 33–4. The Peels' cottages had earth floors, no water supplies or refuse disposal, and hence very poor quarters for the workers.

24 O. Ashmore, 'Low Moor, Clitheroe: a nineteenth century factory community', *TLCAS.*, lxxiii and lxxiv, (1963–4), p. 141. The majority of dwellings were assessed at £1 in the 1827 Rate Book demonstrates the poor quality. Timmins, 'Housing quality', p. 24; shows the cheapest Ashworths' houses at Egerton were rated at just over £2 and the highest were rated at just over £10 in 1866.

25 Remarks made by official guide during tours of Barrow Bridge. Senior workers such as overlookers had bigger and better houses, some with gardens. B Meakin, *Model factories & villages: ideal conditions of labour and housing* (Fisher Unwin, London, 1905), pp. 421–2.

26 S. M. Gaskell, 'Housing estate development 1840–1918, with special reference to the Pennine towns', unpublished Ph.D., thesis, University of Sheffield, 1974, p. 63; Burnett, *Social*, p. 161. Back-to-back housing with 2 floors = 450 ft2; Bye-law housing minimum = 570 ft2 and 2 up and 2 down terrace = 760 ft2. Timmins, 'Housing quality', p. 24 & 35.

27 Timmins, 'Housing quality', pp. 29–35. Boyson, *Ashworth Cotton*, p. 118.

28 D. O'Connor, *Barrow Bridge*; Timmins, 'Housing quality', pp. 29–35; Joyce, *Work*, p. 123.

29 For a fuller description see Marshall, 'Colonisation'.

30 Lancs. CRO., DVBK 1/3/3 Eccleshill and Yate and Pickup Bank. The Finance (1909–1910) Act , Valuation Books.

31 Lancs. CRO. MF 1/27, 1666 Hearth Tax returns; Darwen Library, *Yates map of Lancashire, 1786*; Census Statistical Tables 1801 to 1841.

32 Census Statistical Tables 1841 to 1901.

33 R. F. Taylor, 'A type of handloom-weaving cottage in mid-Lancashire', *IndArchaeol*, vol. 3, No. 4 (1966), p. 254.

34 W. A. Abram, *A History of Blackburn, Town and Parish* (Toulmin, Blackburn Times, 1877), pp 763–4.

35 Personal recollections and recent photographs.

36 *Blackburn Weekly Telegraph*, 14 February 1914, report of interview with William Fish (old resident of Blacksnape).

37 Abram, *A History of Blackburn*, p. 598.

38 Abram, *A History of Blackburn*, p. 507.

39 B. Short, *Land and Society in Edwardian Britain* (Cambridge University Press, 1997), pp. 65–7.

40 Surveys for the case study townships were undertaken in 1914 and 1915.

41 Comments apply to houses only where the surveyor had recorded the

owner's interest and not to the total properties in the townships.

42 The Lancashire Land Registry at Warton has supplied the information for Blackburn and I am grateful to the Saltaire Museum for reference to Salt's estate.

43 Percentages of owner/occupation were: Eccleshill 27% and Yate and Pickup Bank 14%.

44 A few local residents have kindly allowed internal inspections of their properties but the small number cannot be taken as typical, although it is probable the remainder were of a similar configuration.

45 During restoration, an upper floor structural member was exposed at Lane End, Yate and Pickup Bank. The member was clearly the trunk of a tree with forked main boughs at the end.

46 At mid-twentieth century, these channels could still be recognised as making their way to local watercourses. Toilet tubs were emptied weekly on the nearby moors.

47 Darwen Borough Local Board of Health Minutes 1854–1869 (Darwen Library, ref: NO9).

48 Lancs., CRO, URBE 1/2/1 Minutes Belthorn Independent Chapel from 1873.

49 Personal recollections.

50 Personal recollections and conversations with older inhabitants.

51 Burnett, *Social*, pp. 137–8.

52 CEB 1881; Lancs, CRO. The Finance (1909–1910) Act, Valuation Book, DVBK 1/3/3 Eccleshill and Yate and Pickup Bank.

53 CSRs.

54 See, chapter 5.

55 Lancs. CRO. The Finance (1909–1910) Act , Valuation Books, DVBK 1/3/3 Eccleshill and Yate and Pickup Bank. Lancs. CRO. O.S. map-sheet 62 NE & NW Lancashire, Scale 25 inch to 1 mile, surveyed 1892; 1881 CEB, Eccleshill. There were 20 dwellings in Victoria Buildings and 16 in Waterside Terrace.

56 CSRs; Beattie, *Blackburn – The development*, p. 53, quoting from Joyce, *Work, Society*. The 36 factory houses represented 29% of the total of 123 inhabited houses and farms in Eccleshill in 1881, which was above the 13% factory owners' houses in Blackburn in the 1870s.

57 Lancs. CRO. The Finance (1909–1910) Act, Valuation Books, DVBK 1/3/3 Eccleshill and Yate and Pickup Bank

58 CEB.

59 O.S. map – sheet 71 Lancashire, Scale 6 inch to 1 mile, surveyed 1844.

60 DL/C82/HOD, J. Aspden, *Historical Notes on Hoddlesden Village* (unpublished, no date), p. 1.

61 DL, K7, Hoddlesden Cooperative Land and Building Company, p. 15, 24, 43 and 57.

62 Lancs, CRO. DVBK 1/2/1-6 Darwen; DVBK 1/3/3 Eccleshill and Yate and Pickup Bank. The Finance (1909–1910) Act , Valuation Books.

63 DA, K7, Hoddlesden Cooperative, p. 81.

64 DA, K7, Hoddlesden Cooperative, p. 84 and 168.

65   DA, K7, Hoddlesden Cooperative, p. 203.

66   *DA*, K7, Hoddlesden Cooperative, p. 279.

67   Estate Agents particulars.

68   E. Baines, *History, Directory and Gazetteer of the County Palatine of Lancaster*, vol. 2 (William Wales & Co., Liverpool, 1825, reprinted 1968).

69   Aspden, *Historical notes;* www.lancashire Towns/Hoddlesden .

70   TNA. IR. 58/9091. At Eccleshill the end property of Waterside Terrace was provided by Bullough the factory owner as a Conservative Club.

71   TNA. IR 58. The Finance (1909–1910) Act, Field Books. Eccleshill and Yate & Pickup Bank, IR 58/9064.

72   Rothwell, *Darwen*, p. 9. Cote Mill, Pickup Bank.

73   Quotes from the ancestors of people who currently live or have lived in Hoddlesden.

74   Although the mill in Hoddlesden was only just over the boundary with Pickup Bank the paths and cart roads to be negotiated were in a deplorable condition, particularly in winter months. TNA, ED 21/8865 – A School Inspector's Report referring to Yate & Pickup Bank in 1877 stated that, 'The footpaths are as bad as they can be'.

75   Some rear walls in the townships mill owners' terraces were constructed in random rubble.

76   Fieldwork.

77   TNA. IR. 58, The Finance (1909–1910) Act, Field Books. Eccleshill and Yate & Pickup Bank.

78   *Darwen News*, 6 December, 1884, p. 8.

79   *Annual report of the health of Blackburn 1893–4* (Toulin, Blackburn, 1894), pp. 70 & 76. Hogg, *History of Church and Oswaldtwistle* , p. 47.

80   Remarks by official guide at Saltaire.

81   Room sizes exclude space for stairs, walls, vestibules and lobbies.

82   Estate agents' particulars.

83   TNA. IR. 58, The Finance (1909–1910) Act, Field Books. Eccleshill and Yate & Pickup Bank, IR. 58/9064, 9065 & 9066.

84   Lancs, CRO, DVBK. The Finance (1909–1910) Act , Valuation Books.

85   CEBs.

Bibliography

Primary Sources

1. Manuscript Sources

A. NATIONAL ARCHIVES

AN 13/1711, Hoddlesden Branch Lancashire & Yorkshire Railway.

BT 31/3331/19778, No. of Company: 19778: Hoddlesden Cotton Manufacturing Co. Ltd.

IR 18/4025, Tithe File Eccleshill.

IR 18/4345, Tithe File Yate & Pickup Bank.

IR 58, The Finance (1909-1910) Act, Field Books. Eccleshill and Yate & Pickup Bank, IR. 58/9064, 9065 & 9066.

IR 133, The Finance (1909-1910) Act, O.S. Valuation Maps. CIII. 2 (IR 133/7/49), XCV. 14 (133/7/43) and XCV. 11 (IR 133/7/40)

MAF 68/532, Abstract of Lancashire Parish Returns of Acreage of Crops and of Livestock – 1877.

MAF 68/760, Abstract of Lancashire Parish Returns of Acreage of Crops and of Livestock – 1881.

MAF 68/1330, Abstract of Lancashire Parish Returns of Acreage of Crops and of Livestock – 1891.

MAF 68/2242, Abstract of Lancashire Parish Returns of Acreage of Crops and of Livestock – 1907.

MAF 68/2584, Abstract of Lancashire Parish Returns of Acreage of Crops and of Livestock – 1913.

Rail/1005/474, Hoddlesden Branch Lancashire & Yorkshire Railway.

TNA, E 179/130/28, Lancashire Poll Tax, 1379, documents 1 and 2.

TNA. 1910 Finance Act, O.S. Valuation Maps for Lancashire:
    CIII. 2 (IR 133/7/49)
    XCV. 14 (IR 133/7/43)
    XCV. 11 (IR 133/7/40)

B. Lancashire County Record Office
Agriculture land classification map, sheet 95, 1961
DDH 780 Lease Holme Fold, Yate Bank.
DRB 1/218, Yate and Pickup Bank Tithe Map and Schedule.
DRB 2/11, St Mary, Blackburn, Bishops Transcripts 1821.
DVAC 1/2/5 & 6, Hoddlesden; The Finance (1909-1910) Act, Valuation Books.
DVBK 1/3/3, Eccleshill and Yate and Pickup Bank; The Finance (1909-1910) Act, Valuation Books.
DDX 2075, Darwen Co-operative Society.
Greenwood's map – 1818.
Hand List of Enclosure Awards.
MF1/27 (E179/250/6,8-9.). Hearth Tax Return 1666, folios: Eccleshill 245; Mellor 224; Tockholes 221 and Yate and Pickup Bank 250-1.
O.S. map-sheet 71 Lancashire, Scale 6 inch to 1 mile, surveyed 1844.
O.S. map-sheet 62 Lancashire, Scale 6 inch to 1 mile, surveyed 1846.
O.S. map-sheet, Scale 25 inch to 1 mile, surveyed 1892, 1912 and 1932. (Eccleshill, LXX.12 & LXXl.9; Yate & Pickup Bank LXX1.9)
O.S. – Landranger map, 103, Blackburn, Burnley and surrounding area, Scale 1 : 50,000, 1991.
PR/2059/14.
PR 3016 (M/F 8/12-22), Haslingden (1772) & LPRS 45, Newchurch (1705-7);
RDBL 2/2/2, Yate and Pickup Bank-Rating Survey 1913.
RDBL 3/4/6, Lancashire County Council, Report of County M.O.H., Blackburn District, 12 October 1949.
URBE 1/2/1. Minutes Belthorn Independent Chapel from 1873.
WCW, Wills and Inventories for Eccleshill, and Yate and Pickup Bank.

C. Blackburn Library
Census Enumerators' Books 1851 to 1891.
Hennet's map of Lancashire – 1828-29.
Hartley, G., *History of Shaws Glazed Brick Company Limited and Family* (loose sheets).
Annual report of the health of Blackburn 1893-4 (Toulin, Blackburn, 1894).

D. Darwen Library
Census Enumerators' Books 1851 to 1891, microfilm copies for Eccleshill and Yate and Pickup Bank (accessed digitally for 1881).
Yates map of Lancashire, 1786.
K7, Hoddlesden Co-operative Land and Building Company Minutes 1861 to 1957.

E. Harris Museum, Preston
BA1/B/63, Baines M.S.S, Lancashire Parishes, Blackburn Parish, 1833, 'Butterworth Note Books and Maps'.
J. Sheldon, *Lancashire cheese-making and dairy farming* (n.p., repr. From Preston Gaurdian 21 Sept, 5 Oct and 2 Nov, 1895)

2. Printed Sources

A. ACCRINGTON LIBRARY
Bye-Laws Oswaldtwistle District Council, 1909.

B. BLACKBURN LIBRARY
Annual Report of the Health of Blackburn 1893-4 (Toulin, Blackburn, 1894).
Mannex's, *History, Topography and directory of mid-Lancashire* (Bailey &
   Thomson, Preston, 1854).

C. BOLTON LIBRARY
B916TUR and Reserve Stock 800.343BRA, *The Brandwood facsimilii papers*.
ZJA 601-2, Waterside Farm, Eccleshill.

E. MANCHESTER CENTRAL LIBRARY
1841, Registrar General 3rd Annual Report 1841 (London, Clowes.).
1853, Registrar General 14th Annual Report 1851 (London, HMSO.).
1853, Report of General Board of Health, Over-Darwen 1851 (London,
   H.M.S.O.).
1898, Health Report for Darwen 1891 (Darwen, Council Officers).
1906, Registrar General 14th Annual Report 1906 (London, HMSO.).

F. PARLIAMENTARY PAPERS
PP. 1801-1802, vol. vi, Census of Great Britain: Abstracts of Answers and
   Returns 1801.
PP. 1812, vol. xi, Census of Great Britain: Abstracts of Answers and Returns
   1811.
PP. 1822 vol. xv, Census of Great Britain: Abstracts of Answers and Returns
   1821.
PP. 1826/7 (231) v, QQ. 1962-3; Migration Committee.
1833 vol. xxxvi, Census of Great Britain: Abstracts of Answers and Returns
   1831.
1834 vol. xx, Factories Inquiry.
PP. 1837/8 (167) xviii, pt 1, Q. 2863; Select Committee.
1840, 639, xxiv, Report on the Condition of the Handloom Weavers.
PP. 1852, vol. lxxxvi, Census of England and Wales, 1801-1851, Population (7).
PP. 1853, vol. lxi, Census of Great Britain, Population 9, Ages, Civil
   Condition, Occupations & Birth Places 1851 (IUP).
PP. 1861, vol. i, Census of England and Wales, Population Tables, Ages,
   Occupations 1861.
PP. 1862, vol. ii, Census of England and Wales, Ages, Condition as to
   Marriage, Occupations and Birth-Places of the People 1861 (H.M.S.O.,
   London, C 5597)
PP. 1873, Census England and Wales, Population 18, 1871, Pt. 1 (Irish
   University Press, C. 872).
PP. 1872, vol. i, Census England and Wales, Population Tables, Counties 1871
   (H.M.S.O., London).

PP. 1873 Census of England and Wales, Ages, Condition as to Marriage, Occupations and Birth-Places of the People 1871 (H.M.S.O., London, C872)

PP. 1883, vol. i, Census England and Wales, Counties, Population 1881 (H.M.S.O. London).

PP. 1883, vol. iii, Census of England and Wales, Ages, Condition as to Marriage, Occupations and Birth-Places of the People 1881 (H.M.S.O. London, C 3722).

PP. 1883, vol. iv, Census of England and Wales, 1881, *General Report*, lxxx.

PP. 1893, vol. iii, Census of England and Wales, Ages, Condition as to Marriage, Occupations and Birth-Places of the People 1891 (H.M.S.O. London, C 7058).

PP. 1894, vol. xvi, pt 1, apps A1 and A2. Reports by Wilson Fox (Assistant Commissioner) of the Garstang District of Lancashire and the Glendale District of Northumberland (H.M.S.O. London, C 7334).

PP. 1904, vol. iii, Census of England and Wales, 1901, Condition as to Marriage, Occupations and Places Birth-Places of the People (H.M.S.O. London).

PP. 1914, vol. x, Pt 1, Census of England and Wales, Occupations and Industries 1911 (H.M.S.O. London).

G. CONTEMPORARY NEWSPAPERS
Accrington Times
Blackburn Mail
Blackburn Standard
Blackburn Times
Blackburn Weekly Telegraph
Darwen Advertiser
Darwen News
Manchester Mercury
Preston Guardian
The Times

H. ORAL EVIDENCE
North West Sound Archive. No 17. Walker H., Farms in Rossendale, in Bolton Library.
North West Sound Archive. No 18. Walker H., Farms in Rossendale, in Bolton Library.
Lancashire Textile Project, Tape 78/SC/1, Mr J. Cooke, Retired Mill Manager, interviewed by Mary Hunter, 9 December 1978. Lancashire Textile Project, Tape 78/SC/1, in Blackburn Library.

I. ELECTRONIC SOURCES
Archer S., *LDS Companion: User's Guide*, Archer (Dartford), 1999.
1881 British Census and National Index, England, Scotland, Wales, Channel Islands, Isle of Man and Royal Navy, The Church of Jesus Christ of Latter-Day Saints, 1999.
Disc 2, *First Edition 25 inch Ordnance Survey Maps of Lancashire 1888-1893*, produced by Digital Archives, Warrington in conjunction with Lancashire Record Office.

3. Contemporary Published Printed Sources pre 1914

A. BOOKS

Abram, W. A., *A history of Blackburn, town and parish* (Toulmin, Blackburn Times, 1877).

Aiken, J., *A description of the country from thirty to forty miles round Manchester* (David & Charles, Newton Abbot, First Published 1795, 1969 Ed).

Baines, E., *History, directory and gazetteer of the County Palatine of Lancaster*, vol. 2 (William Wales & Co, Liverpool, 1825, reprinted 1968).

Baines, E., *The history of the County Palatine & Duchy of Lancaster*, (ed.), Harland J. (George Routledge, Manchester, 1870).

Baines, E., *History of the cotton manufacture in Great Britain* (1966 reprint of 1835 Edition).

Barrett's directory of Blackburn & District 1881 (Barrett & Co., 1881, Preston).

Barrett's directory of Blackburn & District 1891 (Barrett & Co., 1891, Preston).

Barrett's directory of Blackburn and District 1888 (Barrett, Preston, 1888).

Barrett's directory of Blackburn & District 1900 (B Barrett & Co, 1900, Preston).

Barrett's Directory of Blackburn, Accrington, Darwen and Clitheroe (Barrett, Preston, 1897).

Binns, J., *Notes on the agriculture of Lancashire: with suggestions for its improvement* (Dobson and Son, Preston, 1851).

Caird, J., *English agriculture in 1850-51* (Longman, Brown, Green and Longmans, London, 1852).

Chapman, S. J., *The Lancashire cotton industry* (University of Manchester, 1904).

Clarke, A., *The effects of the factory system* (Grant Richards, London, 1899).

Cobbett, W., *Rural rides during 1821-32*, vols. 1 and 2 (Reeves and Turner, London, 1893).

Collier, F., *The Family Economy of the Working Classes in the Cotton Industry 1784-1833* (ed.), R. S. Fitton (Manchester University Press, 1964).

Dickson, R. W., *General view of the agriculture of Lancashire* (Sherwood, London, 1815).

Farrer, W., & Brownhill, J., *Victoria history of the County of Lancaster*, vols. 2 and 6 (Constable & Co., London, 1911).

Gaskell, P., *The manufacturing population of England* (London, 1833).

Hall, A. D., *A pilgrimage of British farming, 1910-1912* (Murray, London, 1913).

Hole, J., *The homes of the working classes with suggestions for their improvement* (Longmans Green, London, 1866).

Holt, J., *General view of the agriculture of the county of Lancaster* (David and Charles Rept, Newton Abbot, Rpt 1969 of 1795 Ed).

Layton, W., *An introduction to the study of prices* (MacMillan, London, 1912).

Marsden, R., *Cotton weaving: its development, principles and practise* (G. Bell and Sons, London, 1895).

Meakin, B., *Model factories & villages: ideal conditions of labour and housing* (Fisher Unwin, London, 1905).

Newbigging, T., *History of the Forest of Rossendale* (Rawtenstall, 1893).

Radcliffe, W., *Origins of the new system of manufacture* (Lomax, Stockport, 1828).

Returns of owners of land 1873, vol. 1 (H.M.S.O. 1975).

Rothwell, W., *Report of agriculture in the county of Lancaster* (Groombridge, London, 1850).

Solly, Rev. H., 'Industrial villages: A remedy for crowded towns and deserted fields', *Society for Promoting Industrial Villages*, No. 1 (1884).

Taylor, W. C., *Notes of a tour in the manufacturing districts of Lancashire* (Duncan & Malcolm, London, 1842).

Toynbee, A., *Industrial Revolution of the 18C in England* (Longmans, Green & Co., London, 1908).

Radcliffe, W., *Origins of the new system of manufacture*

Whittle, P. A., *Blackburn as it is: A topographical, statistical and historical account* (H. Oakey, Preston, 1852).

Withers, J. *Report on the sanitary condition of the Borough of Blackburn* (Douglas, Blackburn, 1853).

Wood, G. H., *The history of wages in the cotton trade during the past hundred years* (Sherratt, Manchester, 1910).

B. ARTICLES

Abram, W. A., 'Social conditions and political perspectives of the Lancashire workman', *Fortnightly Review* (Oct, 1868).

Bowley, A. L., 'Rural population in England and Wales: A study of the changes of density, occupations and ages', *Journal of the Royal Statistical Society*, vol. 77, No. 6 (May 1914), pp. 597-652.

Danson, J. T. & Welton, T. A., 'On the population of Lancashire and Cheshire and its local distribution during the fifty years 1801-51', *Transactions of the Historic Society of Lancashire and Cheshire*, vol. 9, Pt. 1 (1857), pp. 195-212.

Danson, J. T. & Welton, T. A., 'On the population of Lancashire and Cheshire and its local distribution during the fifty years 1801-51', Pt. 3, *Transactions of the Historic Society of Lancashire and Cheshire*, vol. 11 (1859), pp. 31-70.

Danson, J. T. and Welton, T. A., 'On the population of Lancashire and Cheshire and its local distribution during the fifty years 1801-51', *Transactions of the Historic Society of Lancashire and Cheshire*, vol. 12, Pt. 4 (1860), pp. 35-74.

Garnett, J., 'Prize report on the farming of Lancashire', *Journal of the Royal Agricultural Society*. (1849), pp. 1-51.

Harrison, W., 'The development of the turnpike system in Lancashire and Cheshire', *Transactions of the Lancashire and Cheshire Historic Society*, vol. 4 (1886), pp. 80-92.

Ravenstein, E. G., 'Birthplaces of the people and the laws of migration', *Geography Magazine*, 3 (1876), pp. 173-7, 201-6 & 229-33.

Ravenstein, E. G., 'The laws of migration', *Journal of the Royal Statistical Society*, 48 (1885), pp. 167-235.

Ravenstein, E. G., 'The laws of migration', *Journal of the Royal Statistical Society*, 52 (1889), pp. 241-305.

Rew R. H., 'An inquiry into the statistics of production and consumption of milk and milk products in Great Britain', *Journal of the Royal Statistical Society*, vol. 55, No. 2 (1892), pp. 244-86.

Sheldon, J., Lancashire cheese-making and dairy farming (n.p., repr. *From Preston Guardian, 21 Sept, 5 Oct and 2 Nov, 1895).*

Wood, G. H., 'The statistics of wages in the United Kingdom during the nineteenth century (Part xv): The cotton industry', *Journal of the Royal Statistical Society*, vol. 73, No. 1 (Jan, 1910), pp 39-58.

Wood, G. H., 'The statistics of wages in the United Kingdom during the nineteenth century (Part xviii): The cotton industry', *Journal of the Royal Statistical Society*, vol. 73, No. 3, (Mar, 1910), pp 283-315.

Wood, G. H., 'The statistics of wages in the United Kingdom during the nineteenth century (Part xviii): The cotton industry', *Journal of the Royal Statistical Society*, vol. 73, No. 4 (Apr, 1910), pp 411-434.

Wood, G. H., 'The statistics of wages in the United Kingdom during the nineteenth century (Part xix): The cotton industry', Sect v, changes in the average wage of all employed, with some account of forces operating to retard the progress of industry, *Journal of the Royal Statistical Society*, vol. 73, No 6/7 (June, 1910), pp 585-633.

4. Secondary Sources

BOOKS, PAMPHLETS, ARTICLES AND THESES, POST 1914

a) Books and Pamphlets

Abbott, J., *Pictorial History of Hoddlesden* (1985).

Addison, W., Sir, *The old roads of England* (Batsford, London, 1980).

Albert, W., *The turnpike road system of England 1663-1840* (Cambridge University Press, 1972).

Allen, R. C., 'Agriculture during the industrial revolution', in R. Floud, & D. McCloskey (eds.), *The economic history of Britain since 1700*, vol. 2 (2nd Ed, Cambridge University Press, 1994).

Anon. *The history of Haslingden Grane*, (ed.), A. Crosby (No publisher or date).

Anderson, M., *Family structure in nineteenth-century Lancashire*, (Cambridge University Press, 1971).

Anderson, M., *Approaches to the history of the western family 1500-1914* (Basingstoke, 1980).

Anderson, M., 'The social implications of demographic change', in F. M. L. Thompson (ed.), *The Cambridge social history of Britain 1750-1950* (Cambridge University Press, 1990).

Armstrong, W. A., 'The interpretation of the census enumerators' books for Victorian towns', in H. J. Dyos (ed.), *The study of urban history* (Arnold, London, 1968).

Ashmore, O., *The industrial archaeology of Lancashire* (David & Charles, Newton

Ashton, W. T., *The Darwen Valley of the past*, (1932).

Abbot, 1969.

Aspen, J., *Historical notes on Hoddlesden Village* (no publisher and undated), (in Darwen Library).

Aspin, C., *Lancashire the first industrial society*, (Helmshore Local History Society, 1969).

Aspin, C., *Manchester and the textile districts* (Helmshore Local History Society, 1972).

Aspin, J., *Darwen's ancient highway*, (Aspin, 1990).

Baines, D., *Migration in a mature economy: emigration and internal migration in England and Wales, 1861-1900*, (Cambridge University Press, 1985).

Baines, D., 'Population, migration and regional developments 1860-1939', in R. Floud, & D. McCloskey, (eds.), *The economic history of Britain since 1700:* vol. 2 (2nd Ed, Cambridge University Press, 1994).

Baines, E., *History, directory and gazetteer of the County Palatine of Lancaster*, vol. 2 (William Wales & Co, Liverpool, 1824, reprinted 1968).

Barnwell, P. S. and Giles, G., *English farmsteads 1750-1914*, vol. xiv (Royal Commission on the Historical Monuments of England, 1997).

Beattie, D., *Blackburn – The development of a Lancashire cotton town* (Ryburn, Halifax, 1992).

Beattie, D., *History of Blackburn* (Carnegie, Lancaster, 2007).

Bennett, W., *The history of Burnley from 1850*, Parts 3 & 4 (Burnley Corporation, 1946 – 51).

Benson, J., *The working class in Britain 1850-1939* (Longman, London, 1989).

Berg, M., *The age of manufactures 1700-1820* (2nd Ed, Routledge, London, 1994).

Berg, M., Factories, 'workshops and industrial organisations', in R. Floud, & D. McCloskey (eds.), *The Economic History of Britain Since 1700:* vol. 1 (2nd Ed, Cambridge University Press, 1994).

Best, G., *Mid-Victorian Britain, 1850-70* (Fontana, London, 1979).

Bland's *Encyclopaedia of education* (ed.), E. Blisham (Bland Educational, London, 1969).

Bowker, B., *Lancashire under the hammer* (Hogarth Press, London, 1928).

Boyson, R., *The Ashworth cotton enterprise: The rise and fall of a family firm* (Clarendon Press, Oxford, 1970).

Burnett, J., A *social history of housing 1815-1985* (2nd Ed, Methuen, London, 1986).

Bythell, D., *The handloom weavers* (Cambridge University Press, 1969).

Bythell, D., *The sweated trades* (Batsford, London, 1978).

Catling, H., *The spinning mule* (David Charles, Newton Abbot, 1970).

Chambers, J. D., *Population, economy and society in pre-industrial England* (Oxford University Press, 1972).

Chambers, J. D. and Mingay, G. E., *The Agricultural Revolution 1750-1880* (Batsford, London, 1966, Reprint 1984).

Chapman, S. D., *The history of working-class housing* (David & Charles, Newton Abbott, 1971).

Chapman, S. D., *The cotton industry in the Industrial Revolution* (MacMillan, London, 1972).

Clapham, J. H., *An economic history of modern Britain: free trade and steel 1850-1886* (Cambridge, 1932)

Clapham, J. H., *An Economic History of Modern Britain*, vol. 1 (Cambridge University Press, 1967 reprint of 1926 edition).

Clay, C. G. H., *Economic expansion and social change 1500-1700*, vol. 2 (Cambridge University Press, 1984).

Coppock, J. T., 'Mapping the agricultural returns: A neglected tool of historical geography', in M. Reed (ed.), *Discovering past landscapes* (Croom Helm, London, 1984).

Collier, F., *The family economy of the working classes in the cotton industry 1784-1833* (ed) R. S. Fitton (Manchester University Press, 1964).

Crafts, N. F. R., *British economic growth during the Industrial Revolution* (Clarendon, Oxford, 1985).

Crosby, A., *A history of Lancashire* (Phillimore, Chichester, 1998).

Crosby, A., *Leading the way: A history of Lancashire's roads* (Lancashire County Books, Preston, 1998).

Crosby, A. C. (ed.), *The family records of Benjamin Shaw, mechanic of Dent, Dolphinholme and Preston, 1772-1861* (Sutton, Stroud, 1991).

Daniels, G. W., *The early English cotton industry* (Manchester University Press, 1920).

Deane, P., *The first Industrial Revolution* (Cambridge University Press, 1965).

Deane, P. and Cole, W. A., *British economic growth 1688-1959* (Cambridge University Press, 1962).

Department of Economic Affairs, *The north west-A regional study* (H.M.S.O., London, 1965).

Duckworth, A., *Darwen's Day* (Calderprint, Burnley, 1993).

Eversley, D. E. C. in Wrigley E. A. (ed.), *English historical demography* (Weidenfeld and Nicolson, London, 1965).

Farnie, D. A., *The English cotton industry and the world market, 1815-1896* (Clarendon Press, Oxford, 1979).

Fleischman, R. K., *Conditions of life among the cotton workers of southeast Lancashire 1780-1850* (Garland, London, 1985).

Fowler, A. and Wyke, T., *The remarkable rise and long decline of the cotton factory times* (Carfax, UK, 1998).

Freeman, T. W., Rodgers, H. B. and Kinvig, R. H., *Lancashire, Cheshire and the Isle of Man* (Nelson, London, 1966).

Gaskell, S. M., *Model housing: from the Great Exhibition to the Festival of Britain* (Mansell, London, 1957).

Gauldie, E., *Cruel habitations: A history of working-class housing 1780-1918* (Allen & Unwin, London, 1974).

Gibson, R., *Cotton textile wages US and GB* (Kings Crown Press, New York, 1948).

Gray, E. M., *The weaver's wage* (Manchester Univesity Press, 1937).

Habakkuk, H. J., *Population growth and economic development since 1750* (Leicester University Press, 1974).

Hart, F. J., *The rural landscape* (The John Hopkins University Press, Baltimore, 1998).

Hartley, J. B., *Yates map of Lancashire 1786* (Gardener, Liverpool, 1968).

Hey, D., *Family history and local history in England* (Longman, London, 1987).

Higgs, E., *Making sense of the census: the manuscript returns for England and Wales 1801-1901* (HMSO, London, 1989).

Hogg, D., *A History of Church and Oswaldtwistle 1860-1914*, vol. 2 (Accrington and District Local History Society, 1973).

Hopwood, E. A., *A history of the Lancashire cotton industry and the Amalgamated Weavers Association* (Manchester, 1969).

Hoskins, W. G., *The making of the English landscape* (Penguin Books, Harmondsworth, 1981).

Hoskins, W. G. and Stamp, Dudley L., *The common lands of England and Wales* (Collins, London, 1963).

Howkins, A., *Reshaping rural England: A social history 1850-1925* (Harper Collins, London, 1991).

Hudson, P., *Regions and industries: a perspective on the industrial revolution in Britain* (Cambrdge Univesity Press, 1989).

Hudson, P., *The Industrial Revolution* (Edward Arnold, London, 1992).

Jones, E. L., *The development of English agriculture 1815 – 1873* (Economic History Society, MacMillan, London, 1976).

Joyce, P., *Work, society and politics* (Harvester Press, Brighton, 1980).

Kain, R. J. P. & Oliver, R. R., *The tithe maps of England and Wales* (Cambridge University Press, 1995).

Kearns, G., 'The urban penalty and the population history of England' in Brandstrom, A. and Tedebrand, L. (eds.), *Society, Health and Population During the Demographic Transition* (Stockholm, Sweden,1988).

Kernot, C., *British coal* (Woodhead Publishing Ltd, Cambridge, 1993).

Kerridge, E., *The Agricultural Revolution* (Allen and Unwin, London, 1967).

King, S. & Timmins, G., *Making sense of the Industrial Revolution 1700-1850* (Manchester University Press, 2001).

Lemire, B., *Fashions favourite: The cotton trade and the consumer in Britain 1660-1800* (Oxford University Press, 1991).

Langton, J. & Morris, R. J. (ed.), *Atlas of Industrializing Britain 1780-1914* (Methuen London, 1986).

Laslett, P., *Size and structure of the household in England over three centuries* (Cambridge University Press, 1972).

Levine, D., *Family formation in an age of nascent capitalism* (New York, 1977).

Lawton, R. and Pooley, C., *Britain 1740-1950: An historic geography* (Edward Arnold, London, 1992).

Lawton, R., *The census and social structure*, in R. Lawton (ed.), (Frank Cass, London, 1978).

Lawton, R., 'Rural depopulation in 19th century England', in D. Mills (ed.), *English Rural Communities: The Impact of a Specialized Economy* (McMillan, London, 1973).

Lawton, R., *Regional population trends 1750-1971*, in J. Hobcraft and P. Rees (eds.), *Regional Demographic Development* (Groom Helm, London, 1977).

Lee, C. H., *British regional employment statistics 1841-1971* (Cambridge University Press, London, 1979).

Lee, E. S., 'A theory of migration', in J. A. Jackson (ed.), *Migration*, (Cambridge University Press, 1969).

Marriner, S., *The economic and social development of Merseyside* (Croom Helm, London, 1982).

Marshall, J. D., *Lancashire* (David and Charles, London, 1974).

Marshall, J. D., *The Old Poor Law 1795-1834* (MacMillan, London, 1968).

Marshall, J. D., *Furness and the Industrial Revolution* (Barrow in Furness, 1958).

Marshall, J. D., 'Colonisation as a factor in the planting of towns on north-west England' in H. J. Dyos (ed.), *The study of urban history*, (Edward Arnold, London, 1968).

Mathias, P., *The first industrial nation: An economic history of Britain* (2nd Ed, Methuen, London, 1983).

Mathias, P., 'The Industrial Revolution: Concept and reality' in P. Mathias, and J. A. Davis (ed.), *The first Industrial Revolutions* (Oxford, 1989).

Maxton, J. B., *Regional types of British agriculture* (Allen and Unwin, London, 1936).

Miller, G. C., *Blackburn: The Evolution of a cotton town* (The Blackburn Times, 1951).

Mills, D., *A guide to nineteenth-century census enumerators' books* (Open University Press, 1982).

Mills, D. R., *Lord and peasant in nineteenth-century Britain* (Croom Helm, London, 1980).

Mingay, G. E., *The Agricultural Revolution: changes in agriculture 1650-1880* (Adam and Charles Black, London, 1977).

Mingay, G. E., *Rural life in Victorian England* (Heinemann, London, 1977).

Mingay, G. E., *Rural life In Victorian England* (Sutton, Stroud, 1998).

Mitchell, B. R., *British historical statistics* (Cambridge University Press, 1988).

Mitchell, B. R., and Deane, P. *Abstract of British historical statistics* (Cambridge University Press, 1962).

Mitchison, R., *British population change since 1860* (MacMillan, London, 1977).

Moffit, L., *England on the eve of the Industrial Revolution* (Frank Cass, London, 1963).

Mokyr, J. *The economics of the Industrial Revolution* (Allen and Unwin, London, 1985).

Morrison, P. A., 'Functions and dynamics of the migration process', in A. A. Brown, & E. Neuberger (eds.), *Internal migration: A comparative perspective* (Academic Press, London, 1977).

Mutch, A., *Rural life in south-west Lancashire, 1840-1914* (Centre for North-West Regional Studies, Lancaster, 1988).

Muthesius, S., *The English terraced house* (Yale University Press, London, 1982).

Newton, M. P. & Jeffrey, J. R., *Internal migration* (HMSO, London, 1951).

O'Connor, D. *Barrow Bridge, Bolton, A model industrial community of the nineteenth century* (Bolton Central Library, undated).

O'Connor, D., *Barrow Bridge, Bolton, Dean Mills Estate, A Victorian Achievement* (Bolton Central Library, 1972).

O'Grada, C., 'British agriculture, 1860-1914', in R. Floud, & D. McCloskey (eds.), *The economic history of Britain since 1700*, vol. 2 (2nd Ed, Cambridge University Press, 1994).

Open University, *The changing countryside* (Croom Helm, London, 1985).

Overton, M., *Agricultural Revolution in England: the transformation of the agrarian economy 1500-1850* (Cambridge University Press, 1996).

Parker, M. S. J. & Reid, D. J., *The British Revolution 1750-1970: A social and economic history* (Poole, Blandford, 1972).

Pawson, E., *The early Industrial Revolution: Britain in the eighteenth century* (Batsford, London, 1979).

Pawson, E., *Transport and economy: the turnpike roads of eighteenth century Britain* (Academic Press, London, 1977).

Perkin, H., 'Social history' in H. P. R. Finberg (ed.), *Approaches to history* (Routledge and Kegan Paul, London, 1969).

Perry, P. J., *British farming in the Great Depression, 1870-1914* (David Charles, Newton Abbott, 1974).

Phillips, C. B. and Smith, J. H., *Lancashire and Cheshire from A.D. 1540* (Longman, London, 1994).

Phillips, D. and Williams, A., *Rural Britain – A social geography* (Blackwall, Oxford, 1984).

Pooley, C. and Turnbull, J., *Migration and mobility in Britain since the 18th century* (ULC Press, 1998).

Poplin, D. E., *Communities* (MacMillan, London, 1972).

Postan, M. (ed), *Cambridge economic history of Europe* (1966 edn.).

Reay, B., *Microhistories: Demography, society and culture in rural England, 1800-1930* (Cambridge University Press, 1996).

Redford, A., *Labour migration in England 1800-1850* (2nd Ed, Manchester University Press, 1964).

Report of the Land Utilisation Survey of Britain, Pt. 45 (Lancashire, 1941).

Reynolds, J., *The great paternalist* (Temple Smith, London, 1983).

Roberts, B. K., *Rural settlement in Britain* (Dawson-Archon Books, Folkstone, 1977).

Robson, R., *The cotton industry in Britain* (MacMillan, London, 1957).

Rogers, A., *Approaches to local history* (2nd Ed, Longman, London, 1977).

Rogers, A., *English rural communities* (Rural Development Commission, London, 1945).

Roebuck, J., *The making of modern English society from 1950* (2nd Ed, Routledge & Keagan, London, 1982).

Rose, M. B. (ed.), *The Lancashire cotton industry: a history since 1700* (Lancashire County Books, Preston, 1996).

Rose, M. B., *The Gregs of Quarry Bank Mill* (Cambridge University Press, 1986).

Rosemann, C., *Changing migration patterns within the United States* (Association of American Geographers, Washington D C, 1977).

Rostow, W. W., *The stages of economic growth* (3rd Ed, Cambridge University Press, 1990).

Rothwell, M., *Industrial heritage: A guide to the industrial heritage of Blackburn* Pt. 1: *The textile industry* (Hyndburn Local History Society, 1985). *Industrial heritage: A guide to the industrial heritage of Blackburn* Pt. 2: (Hyndburn Local History Society, 1986); *A guide to the industrial heritage of Darwen including Hoddlesden, Yate and Pickup Bank, Eccleshill and Tockholes* (Bridgestone Press, UK,1992); *A guide to the industrial heritage of Church & Oswaldtwistle including the villages of Belthorn, Knuzden and Stanhill* (Bridgewater Press, 1993).

Salter, W. E. G., *Productivity and technical change* (2nd Ed, Cambridge Univesity Press, 1966).

Sandberg, L. G., *Lancashire in decline* (Ohio State University Press, Columbus, 1974).

Saville, J., *Rural depopulation in England and Wales 1851-1951* (Routledge & Kegan Paul, London, 1957).

Shaw, J. G., *Darwen and its people* (T.H.C.L. Books, Blackburn, 1991).

Short, B., *Land and society in Edwardian Britain* (Cambridge University Press, 1997).

Shoard, M., *The theft of the countryside* (Temple Smith, London, 1981).

Singleton, J., *Lancashire on the scrapheap: The cotton industry 1945-1970* (Oxford University Press, 1991).

Smelser, N. J., *Social change in the Industrial Revolution: An application of theory to the Lancashire cotton industry 1770-1840* (Routledge and Kegan Paul, London, 1960).

Smith, A., *The wealth of nations* (Everymans Library, London, Reprint, 1991).

Smith, W., *An historical introduction to the economic geography of Great Britain* (Bell, London, 1968)

Southgate, G. W., *English economic history* (Dent, London, 1952).

Stephens, W. B., *Sources for English local history* (Reprinted Phillimore, Chichester, 1994).

Styles, J., *Titus Salt and Saltaire: Industry and virtue* (Salts Estates, Bradford, 1990).

Thirsk, J., *The rural economy of England* (Hambledon Press, London, 1984).

Thirsk, J., *England's Agricultural regions and agrarian history, 1500-1750* (MacMillan, Basingstoke, 1987).

Thirsk, J., 'Industries in the countryside', in F. L. Fisher (ed.), *Essays in the economic and social history of Tudor and Stuart England* (Cambridge University Press1961).

Thirsk, J., *The rural economy of England* (Hambledon Press, London, 1984).

Thompson, E. P., *The making of the English working class* (Penguin, London, 1980 Rpt of 1963)

Timmins, G., *The last shift* (Manchester University Press, 1993).

Timmins, G., *Four centuries of Lancashire cotton* (Lancashire County Books, 1996).

Timmins, G., *Made in Lancashire: A history of regional industrialisation* (Manchester University Press, 1998).

Timmins, G., *Handloom weavers' cottages in central Lancashire* (Centre for North-West Regional Studies, University of Lancaster, 1977).

Tillott, P. M., 'Sources of inaccuracy in the 1851 and 1861 Censuses', in E. A. Wrigley (ed.), *Nineteenth century: essays in the use of qualitative methods for the study of social data* (Cambridge University Press, 1972).

Tippet, L. H. C., *A portrait of the Lancashire textile industry* (Oxford University Press, 1969).

Tranter, N. L., *Population and society 1750-1940* (Longman, London & New York, 1985).

Tupling, G. H., *The economic history of Rossendale* (University of Manchester, 1927).

Wadsworth, A. P. & Mann, J. De. Lacy, *The cotton trade and industrial Lancashire 1600-1780* (Manchester University Press, 1965).

Walton, J. K., *Lancashire: a social history 1558-1939* (Manchester University Press, 1987).

White, P. E. & Woods, R. I., *The geographical impact of migration* (Longman, London, 1980).

Winchester, A. J. L. & Crosby, A. G., *England's landscape: The north west* (Collins, London, 2006.

Winstanley, M., 'Agricultural and Industrial Revolutions: reassessing the role of the small farm', in Claus Bjorn (ed.), *The Agricultural Revolution reconsidered* (Landbohistorisk Selskab, Odense, Denmark, 1998).

Wrigley, E. A. & Schofield, R. S., *The population history of England 1541-1871-A reconstruction* (Edward Arnold, London, 1981).

Young, F. A., *Guide to the local administrative units of England*, vol. ii, *Northern England* (Offices of the Royal Historical Society, London, 1991).

B. ARTICLES

Anderton, P., 'Milking the sources: Cheshire dairy farming and the field note-books of the 1910 "Domesday" Survey', *The Local Historian*, 34.1 (Feb 2004), pp. 2-16.

Ashmore, O., 'Low Moor, Clitheroe: a nineteenth-century factory community', *Transactions of the Lancashire and Cheshire Historic Society*. lxxiii and lxxiv (1963-4), pp. 124-52.

Crafts, N. F. R., 'British economic growth 1700-1850: some difficulties of interpretation', *Explorations in Economic History*. No. 24 (1987), pp 245-68. Boyer, G. R. and Hatton, T. J., 'Migration and labour market integration in late nineteenth-century England and Wales', *Economic History Review*. vol. 50, No. 4 (Nov, 1997), pp. 697-734.

Chapman, S. D., 'Workers' housing in the cotton factory Colonies, 1770-1850', *Textile History*. vol. 7 (1976), pp. 112-39.

Crafts, N. F. R. and Ireland, N. J., 'A simulation of the impact of changes in the age at marriage before and during the advent of industrialisation in England', *Population Studies*. 30, 3, (1976), pp. 495-510. Cunningham, H., 'The employment and unemployment of children in England c1680-1851', *Past and Present*. 126 (Feb 1990), pp. 115-50.

Drake, .M., 'Marriage and population growth in Ireland 1750-1845', *EcHR.*, xvi, 1963-4.

Fletcher, T. W., 'Lancashire livestock farming during the Great Depression', *Agricultural History Review*, vol. 9 (1961), pp. 17-42.

Fletcher, T. W., 'The Agrarian Revolution in arable Lancashire', *Transactions of the Lancashire and Cheshire Antiquarian Society.* 72 (1962), pp. 93-122.

French, C., 'Taking up 'the challenge of micro-history': social conditions in Kingston upon Thames in the late nineteenth and early twentieth centuries', *The Local Historian*, 36:1 (February, 2006), pp. 17-28.

Friedlander, D. and Roshier, R. J., 'A study of internal migration in England and Wales', *Population Studies*, 19 (1966), pp. 239-79.

Fussell, G. E. and Compton, M., 'Agricultural adjustments after the Napoleonic Wars', *Economic History*, 3 (1939), pp. 184-204.

Gonner, E. C. K., 'The population of England in the eighteenth century', vol. 86, *Royal Statistical Society Journal*, vol. 76, No. 3 (Feb, 1913), pp. 261-303.

Grigg, D. B., 'The Land Tax Returns', *Agricultural History Review*, vol. 11 (1963), pp. 82-94.

Grigg, D. B., 'E G Ravenstein and the "laws of migration", *Journal of Historical Geography*, 3, 1 (1977), pp. 41-54.

Grigg, D., 'Farm size in England and Wales from early Victorian Times to the present' *Agricultural History Review*, vol. 35 (1987), pp. 179-89.

Habakkuk, H. J., 'The economic history of modern Britain', *Journal of Economic History*, vol. 18, No. 4 (Dec, 1958), pp. 486-501.

Higgs, E., 'Occupational censuses and the agricultural workforce in Victorian England and Wales', *Economic History Review.*, xlviii, 4 (1995), pp. 700-16.

Hills, R. L., 'Hargreaves, Arkwright and Crompton: why three inventors', *Textile History.* 10 (1977), pp. 114-26.

Honeyman, K., 'The poor law, the parish apprentice and the textile industries of the north of England', *Northern History*, xliv: 2 (September 2007), pp. 115-40.

Horn, P., 'Victorian villages from census returns', *The Local Historian*, vol. 15, (1982), pp. 25-32.

Hoyle, R., 'Recent work on the history of Lancashire and Cheshire: The early modern period', *Transactions of the Historic Society of Lancashire and Cheshire*, 1996, vol. 146, Liverpool (1997), pp. 133-47.

Hudson, P., 'Industrialization in Britain: the challenge of micro-history', *Family and Community History*, vol. 2/1 (May, 1999), pp. 5-16.

Jackson, K. C., 'Enterprise in some working-class communities: cotton manufacture in north east Lancashire 1880-1914, *Textile History*, vol. 37, No. 1 (May 2006), pp. 52-81.

Jones, E. L., 'The changing basis of English agricultural prosperity 1853-73', *Agricultural History Review*, 10, (1962), pp. 102-19.

Jones, S. R. H., 'Technology, transaction costs, and the transition to factory production in the British silk industry, 1700-1870', *Journal of Economic History*, vol. xlvii (1987), pp. 102-19.

Kenny, S., 'Sub-regional specialisation in the Lancashire cotton industry 1884 – 1914', *Journal of Historical Geography*, 8 (1982), pp. 41-63.

King, H., 'The agricultural geography of Lancastria', *Journal of the Manchester Geography Society*, vol. 43 (1927-8), pp. 55-73.

King, S., 'Migrants on the margin: mobility, integration and occupations in the west Riding, 1650-1820', *Journal of Historical Geography*, 23, 3 (1997), pp. 284-303.

Lawton, R., 'Population trends in Lancashire and Cheshire from 1801', *Transactions of the Historic Society of Lancashire and Cheshire*, 114 (1962), pp. 189-213.

Lawton, R., 'Population changes in England and Wales in the later nineteenth century: an analysis of trends by registration districts', *Transactions of the Institute of British Geographers*, 44 (1968), pp. 55-74.

Loschky, D. J., 'Urbanisation and England's eighteenth century crude birth and death rate', *Journal European Economic History*, 1 (3) (1972), pp. 697-712.

Marshall, J..D., 'The Lancashire rural labourer in the early nineteenth century', *Transactions of the Lancashire and Cheshire Antiquarian Society*, vol. 71 (1963), pp. 90-128.

Marshall, J. D., 'Industrial colonies and the local historian', *LocalHist* (1993).

Martin, J. M., 'Land ownership and the Land Tax', *Agricultural History Review*, vol. 14 (1966), pp. 96-103.

Mingay, G. E., 'The Land Tax assessments and the small landowner', *Economic History Review*, 2nd Series, 17 (2nd December, 1964), pp. 381-8.

Mokyr, J., 'Has the Industrial Revolution been crowded out? Some reflections on Crafts and Williamson', *Explorations in Economic History*. 24 (1987), pp. 293-319.

Peyton, S. A., 'The village population in the Tudor Lay Subsidy Rolls', *English Historical Review*, 30, (1915), pp. 234-50.

Pollard, S., 'The factory village in the Industrial Revolution', *English Historical Review*, 89 (1964), pp. 513-31.

Razzell, P. E., 'The evaluation of baptisms as a form of birth registration through cross-matching census and parish registration data: a study on methodology', *Population Studies*, 26, (1972), pp. 121-46.

Rew R. H., 'The food production of British farms', *Journal of the Royal Agricultural Society*, vol. 64 (1903), pp. 110-22.

Schwarz, S., 'Economic change in north-east Lancashire, c. 1660-1760', *Transactions of the Historic Society of Lancashire and Cheshire*, vol. 144 (1995), pp. 47-93.

Smith, V., 'The analysis of census-type documents', *Local Population Studies*, vol. 2 (1969), pp. 12-24.

Stedman, J. G., 'The end of history? 3: the changing face of 19th Century Britain', *History Today*, 41:5 (May 1991), pp. 36-40.

Swain, J. T., 'Industry before the Industrial Revolution, north east Lancashire c1550-1640', *Chetham Society*, vol. 32 (Manchester University Press, 1986).

Taylor A. J., 'Concentration and specialisation in the Lancashire cotton industry', *Economic History Review*, 2nd series, 1:2-3 (1949), pp. 114-22.

Taylor, D., 'The English dairy industry 1860-1930', *Economic History review*. 2nd Series, vol. 29, No 4 (1976), pp. 585-601.   Taylor, D., 'Growth and structural change in the English dairy industry, c1860-1930', *Agricultural History Review*, vol. 35, No. 1 (1987), pp. 47-64.

Taylor, R. F., 'A type of handloom-weaving cottage in mid-Lancashire', *Industrial Archaeology*, vol. 3, No. 4 (1966), pp. 251-5.

Tillott, P. M., 'The analysis of census returns', *The Local Historian*, vol. 8, No 1 (1968).

Timmins, G., 'Housing quality in rural textile colonies, c.1800-1850: The Ashworth settlements revisited', *Industrial Archaeology Review*, xxii: 1 (2000), pp. 21-37.

Tranter, N. L., 'Population and social structure in a Bedfordshire parish: the Cardington list of inhabitants 1782', *Population Studies*, 21 (1967), pp. 261-82.

Winstanley, M., 'Industrialization and the small farm: family and household economy in nineteenth-century Lancashire', *Past and Present*. No. 152 (August 1996), pp. 157-95.

Wrightson, K., 'Villages, villagers and village studies', *Historical Journal*, 18 (1975), pp. 632-9.

C. THESES

Counsell, D., 'Population migration and environment: a study of their relationship in Lancashire', unpublished M.Sc. dissertation, University of Salford, 1972-3.

Doherty, J. C., 'Short-distance migration in mid-Victorian Lancashire: Blackburn and Bolton, 1851-71', unpublished Ph.D. thesis, University of Lancaster, 1986.

Fletcher, T. W., 'The economic development of agriculture in east Lancashire', unpublished M.Sc. dissertation, University of Leeds, 1954.

Gaskell, S. M., 'Housing estate development 1840-1918, with special reference to the Pennine towns', unpublished Ph.D. thesis, University of Sheffield, 1974.

Gritt, A. J., 'Aspects of agrarian change in south-west Lancashire c.1650-1850', unpublished Ph.D. thesis, University of Central Lancashire, 2000

Hamilton, S., 'The historical geography of south Rossendale', unpublished M.A. dissertation, University of Manchester, 1974.

Harrison, L., 'Agriculture's role in rural employment: A study of the relationship between agriculture and other rural employment in England and Wales', unpublished Ph.D. thesis, University of Reading, 1992.

Hart, A. J., 'Rural factory settlements in Lancashire c.1780-c.1835', unpublished M.A. dissertation, University of Lancaster, 1993.

Hudson, P. J., 'The transformation of community in a Lancashire mill village, in the nineteenth and twentieth centuries', unpublished M.A. dissertation, University of Lancaster, 1987.

Jackson, B. L., 'The Poor Law in rural Lancashire 1820-50', unpublished Ph.D, thesis, University of Lancaster, 1996.

King, W., 'The economic and demographic development of Rossendale c1650-1795', unpublished Ph. D. thesis, University of Leicester, 1979.

Mutch, A., 'Rural society in Lancashire 1840-1914', unpublished Ph.D. thesis, University of Manchester, 1980.

Smith, L. D. W., 'Textile factory settlements in the early Industrial Revolution', unpublished Ph.D thesis, University of Aston in Birmingham, 1976.

Timmins, J. G., 'The decline of handloom weaving in nineteenth-century Lancashire' unpublished PhD thesis, University of Lancaster, 1990.

Trodd, G. N., 'Political change and the working class in Blackburn and

Burnley 1880-1914', unpublished Ph.D. thesis, University of Lancaster, 1978.

Wallwork, K. L., 'The evolution of an industrial landscape: The Calder Valley, Lancashire from c.1740-1914', unpublished Ph.D. thesis, University of Leicester, 1966.

Wardman, J. S., 'The suburban factory community', unpublished M.A. dissertation, University of Lancaster, 1983.

Index